■ GERMANY'S
LAST MISSION
TO JAPAN

GERMANY'S LAST MISSION TO JAPAN

The Failed Voyage of U-234

Joseph M. Scalia

NAVAL INSTITUTE PRESS
Annapolis, Maryland

Naval Institute Press
291 Wood Road
Annapolis, MD 21402

Library of Congress Cataloging-in-Publication Data
Scalia, Joseph M., 1957–
    Germany's last mission to Japan: the failed voyage of U-234 / Joseph M. Scalia.
        p. cm.
    Includes bibliographical references and index.
    ISBN 1-557-50811-9 (alk. paper)
        1. World War, 1939–1945—Naval operations—Submarine. 2. U 234 (Submarine). 3. Blockade. 4. World War, 1939–1945—Naval operations, German. 5. Germany—Military relations—Japan. 6. Japan—Military relations—Germany. 7. World War, 1939–1945—Transportation. I. Title.

    D781.S43 2000
    940.54'5943 21—dc21   99-043765

Printed in the United States of America on acid-free paper ∞
07 06 05 04 03 02 01   9 8 7 6 5 4 3

For my grandfather, Chief Petty Officer Pasquale Joseph Scalia.
A veteran of the Silent Service of World War II,
he first turned me to the sea.

Contents

Foreword

BLOCKADE-RUNNING with German, Italian, and Japanese merchant vessels and submarines between German- and Japanese-controlled areas during World War II was of great importance to the Axis war effort. From the Japanese, Germany wanted mainly raw materials, especially raw rubber, but also zinc, tungsten, molybdenum, opium, and quinine. The Japanese were interested in operational German weapon systems like aircraft, tanks, torpedoes, and optical and radio location equipment, in addition to drawings and details of German technical advances. As long as the Soviet Union remained neutral, the Trans-Siberian Railroad could be used extensively for the exchange of such materials. The German invasion of Russia closed this route, leaving the sea route around Cape Horn as the only transport connection. With the United States' entry into the war in December 1941, this route changed to a passage around the Cape of Good Hope.

From December 1940 to June 1941, five German merchant vessels departed Japan, with three arriving in western France. By February 1942, nine German and three Italian vessels had made the journey; three of these were sunk en route, with the remainder reaching the occupied French port of Bordeaux. In addition, seven German merchant ships departed Bordeaux and arrived in Japan. During the next navigation period in the winter of 1942–43, conditions were much more difficult because of the Allies' use of MAGIC and ULTRA, which gave the Allies advance information about the movement of merchant vessels. Of fourteen German and one Italian blockade-runners that departed the Far East, four were sunk, four were forced to return to Japan, and seven reached Europe. The final attempt to send surface vessels from Japan failed; of five ships departing Japan, only one reached Europe, with the others being sunk.

The passage of submarines between Europe and Japan was not a new idea in 1943; in 1942 one of the big Japanese submarine cruisers completed a tour from Japan to France and back, only to be lost to a mine in Singapore Harbor. Out of necessity, in the spring of 1943 Japanese and German officials decided to use submarines for transport traffic. Initially, ten Italian submarines at Bordeaux were scheduled to be refitted as transports, but two were lost returning from patrol, with one retained as a combat boat. Of the seven that were reconfigured for the transport mission, three reached Japanese ports, two were sunk, and two never left Bordeaux before Italy's capitulation. In 1943–44 the Japanese sent four submarines to Europe, but only one completed the round trip; two were sunk en route to France, and one was sunk between Singapore and Japan. German and Italian plans to build new submarines solely for the transport mission began too late. Although two Italian boats were completed, they were used in the Mediterranean, and German plans to construct thirty Type XX U-boats were canceled. The only remaining option was to utilize large U-boats previously designated for combat or minelaying operations.

One of these redesignated U-boats was sent to Japan as a gift from Adolf Hitler to his Japanese allies; it reached Japan and was recommissioned into the Japanese navy. A second boat reached Penang to explore the possibilities of the port as a base of operations. In 1943 Germany devised a plan, known as Monsun, which sent a ten-boat group to conduct combat patrols in the Indian Ocean. However, the Monsun plan resulted in disaster; Allied hunter-killer groups destroyed five of the boats in the Atlantic and one in the Indian Ocean, leaving four boats to arrive safely in Penang. Although these boats carried various materials to Penang, their primary task was to attack enemy shipping. A subsequent effort to send Type IXD/2 boats to the Indian Ocean in the transport and combat role failed; most of the boats were sunk en route to the Far East in the Atlantic. Of the eighteen Type IXD/2 boats that departed Penang between 1943 and 1945, six were sunk, six returned to Penang, and six more reached Europe. However, of the six that reached France and Norway, three were lost on their way to Germany, and one surrendered to the British at the end of the war.

Axis problems with blockade-running have been known for a long time. In 1955 Theo Michaux published the article "Rohstoffe aus Ostasien" in the *Wehrwissenschaftliche Rundschau,* which provided many details of the Axis transport effort. In the official British and semiofficial American series on the war at sea, S. W. Roskill and S. E. Morrison discuss the blockade-runners, and in 1981 Martin Bruce published *Axis Blockade Runners of World War II,* which was based on archival research in Germany, London, and Washington. However, the journey of the last U-boat from Germany, *U-234,* has been mentioned only occasionally in the historiography of the blockade-runners, notwithstanding the fact that one of *U-234'*s passengers, Fritz von Sandrart, published his account of the trip, "Japan Fahrt in die Gefangenschaft," in 1955. In the mid-1980s a great interest in *U-234* erupted when it was discovered that the loading list of the boat included, among a great many other items, an entry for "560 kilograms of uranium oxide" for the Japanese army. Questions and speculation arose as to the destination of the uranium oxide as well as the true nature of the material: Was it really radioactive uranium 235, as the two Japanese passengers of *U-234* supposedly wrote on container labels at the cargo's loading, intended for some Japanese nuclear weapon? Was it used by the Americans in the two atomic bombs dropped on Hiroshima and Nagasaki? Despite the lack of definitive information, further speculation arose. In the early 1990s three television networks—Germany's ZDG, Japan's NHK, and the United States' ABC—produced "The Last U-Boat," which gave rise to even greater distortion of the truth. The facts about the journey and the Allied hunt for *U-234* were derived from MAGIC and ULTRA decrypts, and not Norwegian resistance radio operators, as has been alleged in some quarters. In addition, until now no effort has been made to examine the character of the personnel aboard *U-234.*

As historians, we are indebted to Joseph Mark Scalia, who with this book presents the truth about *U-234* and her officers, crew, passengers, and cargo, based on his examination and interpretation of archival materials in Germany, England, Japan, and the United States. By discussing details of the subject with the few remaining living witnesses, as well as with German and Japanese naval historians and experts on nuclear development in both Germany and Japan, he has been able to eliminate practically all of the legends that have arisen from the sensational speculations of journalists and other authors as well as from the recollections of those whose memories have been clouded by the passage of time. The result is a well-researched, impressive examination of the true background of the mission of *U-234*, as well as the tasks and intentions of her passengers. In addition, Mr. Scalia examines the whereabouts of the uranium oxide during the first five months of *U-234*'s surrender, effectively destroying the thesis that it was intended for a Japanese nuclear or radiological weapon or used for the 1945 American atomic bombs. With this book he has provided a valuable service to those searching for the truth among the mysteries of World War II.

DR. JÜRGEN ROHWER
Curator, Library of Contemporary History, Stuttgart, Germany

Preface

IN MAY 1945, weary from years of war, the United States celebrated the defeat of Germany with euphoria tempered by the sobering realization of a task yet unfulfilled in the Pacific. Germany's surrender ended the years of uncertainty and misery endured by America's allies, Britain, France, and the Soviet Union. In the Pacific, however, despite the presence of Allied forces, America assumed the lion's share of the war with Japan.

Charged with the daunting task of formulating a strategy to defeat an enemy who preferred death to capitulation, President Harry S. Truman and his military advisers considered an invasion of the Japanese home islands to be inevitable. Although the prospects for ultimate victory were rated as excellent, the predicted loss of American life was sufficiently high as to promise a Pyrrhic victory at best. Such estimates, which ran as high as one million deaths, were calculated on the assumption that the United States would confront a fanatical enemy employing conventional weapons. However, the various U.S. intelligence agencies could not guarantee that the Japanese would be limited to such weapons.

During the closing months of the war in Europe, the Allies had encountered a variety of new, futuristic weapons developed by the

Germans, such as turbojet-propelled aircraft and the V-1 and V-2 "vengeance" missiles. This military technology appeared too late in the European war to be of any consequence; political intrigue, material and labor shortages, and the effects of Allied bombing had ravaged the Third Reich, and hence delayed the mass deployment of these weapons in Europe. However, intercepted Japanese diplomatic communications revealed that the Japanese were actively seeking to acquire these new weapons and integrate them into their own inventory. American intelligence now confronted a dilemma: whereas the extent of German weapons research and its subsequent practical application was known, the level of Japan's proficiency at producing and employing these weapons remained a mystery. Although the association of the Japanese Bushido warrior with German technological mastery appeared paradoxical, the troubling reality was that Americans had faced both on the field of battle and had yet to develop a definitive defense against either.

The collaboration between Germany and Japan evolved in response to the performance of their respective wartime economies. Waging war in the industrialized era required the mass production of modern weapons; in a modern conflict, a country with a self-sustaining industrial base would have the upper hand. Japan's incursion into China in 1931 and Germany's invasion of Poland in 1939 had demonstrated that both possessed military-industrial bases from which to conduct effective operations. However, whether each could sustain this type of effort through the rigors of an extended war with the Western industrial powers remained to be seen.

Germany's military strategy evolved as a "strategic synthesis," one in which the physical aspects of military operations were designed in proportion to the ability of the economy to support them.[1] Germany's strategic goals were based on the execution of short campaigns with limited objectives; hence, its military was designed to exploit immediate superiority over any potential foe. Because of Germany's successful rearmament program and the apparent weakness of its potential victims, the implementation of this strategy would require no greater degree of commitment of the German economy to military adventurism than had existed in 1939; the allotment of economic resources that had been allowed to the military during the Second Four-Year Plan of 1936 would suffice.[2]

By the summer of 1941 all indications pointed to this "blitzkrieg strategy" as the correct one for the Third Reich. German forces overwhelmed Norway, Denmark, the Low Countries, France, Greece, and the Balkans with a ferocity and efficiency that pronounced the strategy a success. Some of these early successes can, of course, be attributed to Allied miscalculations as to the strength of Germany's economic system; as Paul Kennedy points out, Britain simply assumed that, regardless of the challenge presented by Germany, the Allies "were *in the long run* [original emphasis] financially and industrially the stronger," provided they had time to convert their economies from domestic to wartime priorities.[3] In fact, as long as Germany's material requirements fell within the allowable limits of its strategy, and as long as it was not involved in an extended conflict that would tax its limited resources, the blitzkrieg synthesis proved capable of sustaining Germany's military campaigns. However, these conditions would soon change.

By the spring of 1942, the effectiveness of the blitzkrieg strategy had been severely tested. The Werhmacht's setbacks in Russia at Moscow and Stalingrad, the defeat of the Afrika Korps and the subsequent loss of North Africa, and the initiation of Allied air strikes on Germany proper had strained the Third Reich's economic capacity. Minister of Armaments Albert Speer commented that "until the autumn of 1941 the economic leadership had been basing its policies on short wars. . . . Now the permanent war [is] beginning."[4] Germany now faced a defensive, material-intensive conflict for which the blitzkrieg strategy was not designed.

Realizing that they could not match the Allies armament for armament for long, German planners began the search for yet another synthesis to counteract the Allies' material and industrial superiority. In view of Germany's proficiency in research and development, a record of excellence maintained since the 1920s, German officials decided to embellish armament production with a policy of "qualitative superiority."[5] This strategy was adopted on the basis of dual assumptions: that Allied weapons were inferior because of the "simplification and standardization" of the mass-production process, and that Germany's machine-tool and engineering industries would be able to meet the demand.[6] It was hoped that German advances in areas such as rocketry, turbojet propulsion, submarine and surface vessel design, and nuclear physics could be successfully incorporated into new weapons for which the Allies had no defense.

As it turned out, time constraints, coupled with the fiscal, material, and organizational demands of an advanced research and development program, proved fatal to the qualitative-superiority program. Although German factories were capable of producing new weapons, scientists and technicians labored on shoestring budgets that reflected the lasting constraints of the blitzkrieg strategy, which had allowed little monetary assistance for research programs. In addition, the search for a weapon for which the Allies had no counter was severely hampered by the lack of essential raw materials, and although Germany sought to remedy this predicament with synthetic material production, the substitution of synthetics proved ineffective and costly.[7] The lack of an effective governmental watchdog over the military's wasteful research and development programs resulted in a "bewildering array" of products: at one point Germany had at least 425 different varieties of aircraft under production.[8] By 1945 many German officials agreed with Adolf Hitler that the Reich's survival depended on the deployment of new weapons. However, Germany needed time to mass-produce the "wonder weapons," and consequently relied more and more upon its Japanese allies for such vital raw materials as rubber, tin, wolfram (tungsten), and oil.

Because of the war in China, Japan's economy had been on a war footing for much of the 1930s. Japan typically conducted brief campaigns of conquest designed to capture a precisely defined area that suited its need for a strong material base.[9] Although Japan's target areas were much farther removed than Germany's, the similarities between the two strategies are apparent. However, Japan's economic and material situation was very different from Germany's. In particular, Japan's "Oriental blitzkrieg" strategy continually ran the risk of overextending its meager domestic raw-materials resources. As the war in China raged on, Japan became increasingly dependent on imports of goods such as scrap metal, rubber, and petroleum from the United States. As late as 1936, Japan was importing 66 percent of its oil from the United States.[10]

Japan's plan to develop a system of satellite states that would supply its raw-material needs was based on the assumption that its primary rival in the Pacific, the United States, would remain neutral.[11] However, in 1936 the Japanese cabinet adopted the "Fundamental Principles of National Policy," which outlined an "extension of national influence to the South Seas."[12] It was a move that, for all practical purposes, guaranteed war with the United States. Japanese officials decided that they had sacrificed too much in three conflicts—the Sino-Japanese War (1894–95), the Russo-Japanese War (1904–5), and the ongoing war in China—to accept any compromise that would threaten Japanese hegemony in the Chinese mainland. Therefore, on 5 November 1941 the Imperial Conference decided to strike first at the United States during the following month.[13]

Japan's ability to sustain hostilities against the United States depended on its ability to maintain a material-intensive weapons industry. However, Japanese officials were aware of their limited raw-material base and consequently adopted a strategy to exploit their early advantage in weapons, manpower, and material. A German victory in Europe would permanently weaken the European presence in the Pacific, particularly that of Great Britain, and force the Americans to bear the brunt of the war alone. In addition, Japanese seizure of vital material areas of Indochina and the southern Pacific would deprive the United States of strategic materials.[14] Tokyo assumed that the combination of early Japanese victories in the Pacific and the United States' involvement in a two-front war due to its commitment in the Atlantic would force the Americans to settle for peace.

Indeed, the early performance of the Japanese armed forces seemed to bear this strategy out. Japanese troops became entrenched in the numerous South Pacific island groups while the Imperial Navy prevented the staggering Americans from mounting any effective attempts to dislodge them. Allied victories at Midway in June 1942 and Guadalcanal, which fell to the Americans on 31 December 1942, were turning points in Japan's fortunes in the Pacific; each subsequent retreat pulled Japan further away from the desired limited war.[15] However, the precise point at which Japan began to suffer because of its economy's inability to wage industrial war is not as evident as in the case of Germany, primarily because of the failure of Japanese planners to develop an alternative strategy.[16]

The increased American presence in the Pacific put greater material demands on Japan's weapons industry. In a dramatic reversal of fortunes, America's war industry was evolving into the greatest industrial machine in history, which Japan was forced to engage with increasingly outdated weapons. Japanese industrialists were continuing to produce adequate numbers of armaments, but they lagged desperately behind the Allies in the sophistication of new weapons and technology. By 1944 Japan desperately needed help in deterring improved American aircraft, electronic devices such as radar, and the multiplying numbers of enemy ships and submarines at sea. To achieve equity with the Americans, Japan had but one remaining avenue to which to turn: Germany.

What weapons technology had Germany shared with the Japanese? How proficient were the Japanese in utilizing these new weapons systems? What was Japan's capacity to produce both offensive weapons and countermeasures to American weapons? Most important, how would American soldiers, sailors, and pilots respond when they engaged these new weapons in combat, many of them for the first time? With the specter of an invasion of Japan looming ever larger, America's military hierarchy needed answers, and time was running out.

Answers began to surface on 15 May 1945, off the coast of New-foundland, where the American destroyer USS *Sutton* (DE-771) accepted the surrender of the German submarine *U-234*. This was no ordinary member of Karl Dönitz's dreaded wolf packs. *U-234* carried a unique cargo of contraband and personnel, all destined for Japan. It was the last, and perhaps most ambitious, cooperative effort between the Axis partners, and a windfall of enormous significance to American military intelligence.

Acknowledgments

As with any lengthy research project, the list of those to whom I am indebted is also long. With profound sincerity I express my appreciation, and likewise my apologies, to those who may not be listed in these acknowledgments. Their omission in no way diminishes the value of their contributions.

Because this work originated with a master's thesis, I extend my appreciation to the members of my graduate committee at Louisiana Tech University: Dr. Philip Cook, Dr. Stephen Webre, and Dr. John Bush, chair. An additional debt of gratitude is owed to Mrs. Annette Owen, who provided much-appreciated editorial and formatting assistance, to Ms. Stephanie Robker for her help in examining the overwhelming number of MAGIC decrypts, and to Drs. Glyn Ingram, Abe Attrep, Billy Gilley (professor emeritus), John Daly, and C. Wade Meade for advice and encouragement.

It has been my good fortune to have been assisted by numerous reference and archival experts during the course of my research. Among those to whom I am deeply indebted are Dorothy Jewell and Laura Ogden and their staff at Interlibrary Services at Louisiana Tech; Jim Dolph of the Portsmouth Naval Shipyard Museum; Dr. Richard Winslow III and the staff of the *Portsmouth (N.H.) Herald;* Kathleen Lloyd, archivist at the navy's Operational Archives at the Washington

Navy Yard; Martha Jebb of the Portsmouth (N.H.) Athenaeum; Tom House and Roland Goodbody of Diamond Library, University of New Hampshire; Horst Bredow of the U-Boot Archiv in Germany; and Herr Döringhoff of the Bundesarchiv-Militärarchiv in Freiburg, Germany. To all of these research professionals I extend my sincere appreciation.

Because of its dependence on primary archival sources, this book could not have been written without the help and services of the Textual Reference Branches of the United States National Archives and Record Administration. In addition to the numerous researchers and staff personnel, special appreciation goes to Barry Zerby and John Taylor at College Park, Maryland; Stan Tozeski at the Northeast Regional Branch in Waltham, Massachusetts; and John Celardo and Rich Gelke of the Northeast Regional Branch in New York. The rich value of the National Archives is augmented by the proficiency of these phenomenal people.

I have been fortunate to have become acquainted with several individuals who offered much-appreciated help and advice. Among these, I would like to thank Henry Bonner of the Patuxent River Naval Air Station Museum; Ms. C. L. Householder of the United States Navy Naval Explosive Ordnance Disposal Technology Division; David Kohnen of the Mariner's Museum in Newport News, Virginia; Harry Cooper of Hernando, Florida; Jak Mallman Showell of Kent, England; Charles Backus of Groton, Massachusetts; Frank Jackson of Weymouth, Massachusetts; and Jane Tucker of New York. Additional help came from the men and women of the United States Navy Destroyer Escort Association and the crew members of the USS *Greenfish* and their spouses. Also, many thanks go to Ingo Trautzweitzwer of Hyattsville, Maryland, and Thomas and Gwyn Degner of Baltimore for their help in translation and proofing.

I wish to thank my family: Tammy and Craig Currin, Janet Parr, and my progeny Daniel the Wise and the Unsinkable Mallory Anne for their love, patience, and support. A special note of thanks goes out to Charlene and James L. Evans for their understanding and faith in what I am attempting to accomplish. Of course, I cannot adequately express the appreciation I have for my principal co-conspirator and partner in crime, Marilyn Scalia. She suffered when I suffered, laughed when I laughed, and cursed when I cursed, often longer and louder. "Thank you" does not begin to cover the depths of what I owe her. Much obliged, Spurline.

Possibly the most controversial aspect of *U-234* is her consignment of uranium oxide. The presence and implications of this part of *U-234*'s cargo have launched heated debate that continues to this day. It is my intention to present in the appendix the available evidence and plausible theories in hope that readers will arrive at their own conclusions. I wish to express my appreciation to Geoffry Brooks of Essex, England, Philip Henshall of Cheshire, England, and Sidney Trevethan of Anchorage, Alaska, for their theories and information regarding *U-234*'s uranium cargo. I also wish to express my appreciation to Robert Wilcox of Sherman Oaks, California, for sharing his notes and thoughts on the matter.

In addition to the various theories and conjectures surrounding the uranium issue, I was able to rely on documentary and expert data from professionals in the field of nuclear research in Germany and Japan during World War II. Among these, I wish to thank Dr. Michael Thorwart of the Institute of Physics at the University of Augsburg in Augsburg, Germany; Dr. Helmut Rechenberg of the Max Planck Institute of Physics in Munich; Dr. Carl Friedrich von Weisäcker of Starnberg, Germany; Dr. Kigoshi Kunihiko of Gakushuin University in Tokyo; and Richard Rhodes of Madison, Connecticut. A special note of appreciation is extended to Dr. Jürgen Rohwer for meeting with me on a rainy morning at the Library for Contemporary History in Stuttgart to share his phenomenal insight and knowledge. I thank him for his patience and interest in this project. His help was invaluable in the completion of this book.

Much appreciation is extended to my editor, Mary Yates, for her patience and suffering while editing the original manuscript. The clarity of this book is a reflection of her abilities; any confusion or awkwardness is a reflection of mine. I also extend appreciation to Paul Wilderson and Randy Baldini of the Naval Institute Press in Annapolis for their support of the project and for allowing me an avenue by which to relate the true story of this often misunderstood saga.

I have reserved my final expression of appreciation for a group of remarkable men. These individuals rode *U-234*, in addition to other German submarines, during World War II and emerged survivors of both the war and the hazards of submarine warfare. Therefore, special appreciation is owed Erich Menzel, Heinz Schlicke, and Wolfgang Hirschfeld (*U-234*), Jürgen Oesten (*U-61*, *U-106*, *U-861*), and Thilo Bode (*U-858*). Additional gratitude goes to Capt. Hans-Joachim Krug, Maj. Gen. Goda Yutaka, and Rear Adm. Hirama Yoichi for sharing their vast experience. I have had the honor of corresponding with all of these gentlemen and have developed a sincere admiration and respect for them.

The personnel of *U-234* embarked on an extremely dangerous mission, with limited chances of success. These are proud and honorable men who during the years 1939–45 simply performed their duty, serving their country without any vestige of political dogma. Their courage and devotion, emblematic of all veterans, regardless of nationality, constitute the guiding spirit of this book.

Author's Note

THE STUDY OF HISTORY is a matter of perspective; many times, what seems inconsequential to contemporary society was actually a matter of dire consequence to those directly affected. The story of *U-234* provides an excellent example. While the presence aboard *U-234* of German scientists, technicians, "modern" rocket technology, turbojet aircraft, and nuclear material might seem like an antiquated threat to us at the dawn of the twenty-first century, it provoked deep concern among those charged with sending American soldiers and sailors into harm's way in 1945. It is my hope that while reading this book, the reader will consider the effect *U-234* had upon the thinking of the American military officials who were planning the proposed invasion of Japan.

Japanese names are presented according to the Japanese custom of placing the surname first. German military titles are translated as follows:

Kapitän zur See: captain
Fregattenkapitän: commander (senior to a *Korvettenkapitän*)
General der Flieger: general of the air force
Kapitänleutnant: lieutenant commander
Korvettenkapitän: commander
Leutnant zur See: ensign
Oberfunkmeister: chief radioman
Oberleutnant: first lieutenant
Oberstleutnant: lieutenant colonel

The source materials cited in the notes that pertain to the interrogation of *U-234*'s passengers include two types of transcripts that may warrant explanation: "independent room conversations" and "interroom conversations." An independent room conversation was an interrogation, either a formal question-and-answer session between interrogator and prisoner or an informal conversation taking place after confidence had been established between the two. An interroom conversation was an eavesdropping event, a covert recording of prisoners as they talked among themselves. The prisoners knew full well that they were being overheard. Some didn't care, but most used it as an opportunity to let the Allies know indirectly that they were willing to cooperate.

Part I

Evolution
of the
Last Voyage

■

After all, our real enemies are England and the United States. . . .
The logical thing for Germany to do would be to fall in line
with us. It would serve the interests of us both. . . . If we are
allies, we ought to exchange all possible material assistance,
open up our minds and exchange the frankest of opinions, so
that we can really wage joint warfare.

FOREIGN MINISTER MAMORU SHIGEMITSU

■

After a long wait and much preparation we stand today on the
plank of our own boat, which I have the honor of putting in
your service. Herewith a weapon has been entrusted to us . . .
to lead in the spirit of our immortal German ancestors.

In this hour we want to pledge to live, to work, and to fight
for those who sacrificed their lives and who are now looking
down upon us from eternity and demanding the same ability to
sacrifice. The entire German people expects to be delivered
from the misery of this war by its sailors. That's what we all
want to think of.

We also think of the German men who worked on [the boat]
and made it what it is today. You we thank the most when we
plant into this former dead piece of iron our spirit and our love
and have given it a soul.

We want to consider our boat a living being that needs ten-
der loving care so that [it] will be a home and a friend. If we
treat it so as genuine sailors, it will never abandon us in our
hour of need.

JOHANN HEINRICH FEHLER

1

Genesis: German- Japanese Cooperation

JAPANESE FOREIGN MINISTER Mamoru Shigemitsu's 1943 comment to his German counterpart, Joachim von Ribbentrop, subtly acknowledged a fact of which both men were already aware. Of the Axis powers, Germany was clearly the strongest industrially and economically, resulting in expectations that Germany would extend aid to its Japanese and Italian partners in those developmental areas in which they were deficient. As early as 1937, then-Captain Kojima Hideo, the Japanese naval attaché in Berlin, recognized the necessity of German aid for the Japanese war effort and proposed a protocol for the exchange of tactical and technical information and materials between the Japanese and German navies.[1] However, primarily because of German fears that such an exchange would be one-sided,[2] a definitive cooperative agreement was delayed until 1940.

On 27 September 1940 Germany, Italy, and Japan signed the Tripartite Pact, thereby committing themselves to mutual economic, political, and military support in the establishment of Axis hegemony throughout Europe and Asia. To ensure the solidarity of the alliance, Article 3 of the treaty called upon the allies to recognize each other's spheres of influence within the new order, by directing the signatories to "cooperate [in] their efforts" and to "assist one another . . . when one of the three

Contracting Parties is attacked by a power not involved in the European war or in the Sino-Japanese Conflict." Another thinly veiled reference to the potential involvement of the United States appeared in Article 4. Cognizant of the potential of American industrial prowess, Japan insisted upon a provision that called for military collaboration, resulting in the formation of a Joint Technical Commission that was to assemble "without delay."[3]

The extent of Japanese and German concern over military and technical cooperation was evident throughout the various amendments to the treaty. In a notation marked "Strictly Confidential," the German representative, a General Ott, pledged that Germany would "use her industrial strength and other technical and material resources as far as possible in favor of Japan."[4] In return, Tokyo promised to return Germany's former Pacific possessions then under Japanese mandate.[5] In a supplementary protocol on military aid, the allies agreed to "exchange . . . without delay all useful inventions and devices of war and to supply one another with war equipments, such as aeroplanes, tanks, guns, explosives . . . together with technical skill and men should they be required."[6]

Despite the enthusiasm that surrounded the signing of the Tripartite Pact, the Axis spirit of solidarity soon soured, as both Germany and Japan grew frustrated by a perceived lack of reciprocity. Former Reich war minister General Field Marshal Werner von Blomberg outlined the seriousness of the situation by complaining that "our relations with our ally Japan [are] more grotesque than anything in previous history," and he reminded his colleagues that Japan was "a country to which we have no spiritual bonds except some peculiar SS interpretation of the *Bushido* code of ideology."[7] Furthermore, the Oberkommando der Kriegsmarine (OKM), or German Naval High Command, charged that Japan's offer of anchorages and ports for German auxiliary cruisers in the Far East "in no way justifies the prevailing view of a one-sided assistance on the part of Japan. . . . It is therefore necessary to challenge any such Japanese notions . . . and to emphasize the absolute reciprocity provided for under the Pact." To guard against the assumed inequity, the OKM placed certain sensitive items that might be requested by the Japanese under the discretion of the Naval War Staff, who would subject such items as sonar and radar to strict guidelines. In addition, the staff would determine which new equipment, then under development, would be available for Japanese assessment.[8]

In December 1940 the Japanese, alarmed by Germany's reluctance, dispatched a joint army and navy mission to Berlin to present their material concerns. In early February 1941 this joint committee, headed by

Gen. Yamashita Tomoyuki (the future "Tiger of Malaya") and Adm. Nomura Naokuni, presented a "wish list" of Japanese requests, to which both the Kriegsmarine (German Navy) and German business interests were vehemently opposed; the navy demanded that any material aid afforded Japan must be used directly against the British in Asia, while German businessmen feared that their products would be turned against them by the Japanese in the postwar years.[9] However, the doubts of naval and business leaders were not shared by either the Wehrmacht (German Army) or, more important, Adolf Hitler.

On 5 March 1941 Hitler issued Basic Order Number 24, which addressed the deteriorating relationship between Germany and Japan. The key provision of the order was item number 2, which stated that Japan's military potential must be strengthened "with all means available," particularly in technical matters. Hitler further directed all branches of the German military to comply with Japanese requests in a "comprehensive and generous manner" and stated that "while reciprocity is desirable, it should not stand in the way of negotiations."[10] To accommodate the *Führer*'s wishes, the Military-Economic Section of the Wehrmacht Armaments Office was appointed the responsible agency for the direction of German aid to Japan.[11]

Despite the expressed wishes of Hitler, the OKM sought to stall German compliance with Japanese requests. The OKM pointed out to Ambassador Karl Ritter that since the wish list had been issued before Japan's official entry into the war, it would have to be reviewed and possibly amended in light of the changing logistics of transport. In addition, the OKM argued that Russia would refuse any request to allow traverse of the Trans-Siberian Railroad for the delivery of these items. As a result, no simple route of conveyance existed. It was determined that although there was no "secure means of transporting goods in quantity," it would be possible to transport "a few models with the relevant technical drawings and plans" needed to facilitate Japanese production of German equipment.[12]

Notwithstanding internal resistance to the cooperation provisions of the pact, Germany nevertheless intended to honor the treaty and subsequently began sending blockade-running vessels to the Far East from Bordeaux during the fall of 1941. However, the Japanese were generally disappointed with the cargo. Whereas the original wish list reflected Japan's potential defensive weaknesses in its requests for large-caliber artillery, radar, tanks, submarine and aircraft components and models, and precision instruments and machine parts, the cargo consisted mainly of industrial chemicals and machinery.[13] And however disappointed the Japanese were with the cargo, the Germans were even more disappointed with what they received in return. A top-secret OKM memorandum dated 27 May 1941 concurred: "The Japanese are unable to pluck up the courage to do anything in our interest that involves the slightest risk for them."[14] On 29 December 1941 the chief of the Special Staff for Economic Warfare issued a memorandum to the German Foreign Affairs legation, which stated that "what has been received from the Japanese . . . is very limited. . . . More must be demanded [particularly] the exchange of all war experiences in [Japan's] previous naval, land, and air operations."[15] The Japanese reminded their ally that, in addition to supplies, they had provided refueling and rest stations for German blockade-runners, reciprocal actions that in their opinion placed Germany in Japan's debt. The OKM was not impressed, however, replying that "the material and technical support that Germany has received in the provision of anchorages and supplies" did not represent adequate compliance with the pact.[16]

Although the *Führer* expressed his desire to allow the Japanese to study German munitions factories and research facilities, resistance to handing the Japanese carte-blanche access was substantial.[17] During the spring of 1941, representatives of the Japanese military mission were offered the services of specialists in the "strategic, tactical, and technical spheres" of Germany's military and—thanks to what the Germans called "the maximum degree of openness on our part"—were guests at numerous briefings on the German war experience. In addition, the Japanese were escorted on "extensive visits to the front line as well as military-economic facilities" and given instruction on projects that previously had been highly secret.[18]

The German High Command, while fully intending to comply with Hitler's wishes, also sought to guard Germany's armament secrets. On 3 April the chief of the High Command, Field Marshal Wilhelm Keitel, addressed the order and stated that while admission of Japanese officials to German manufacturing and development facilities must be allowed, every effort would be made to "prevent [the Japanese] from obtaining a deeper insight into German armaments than we minimally have to provide to them. . . . Secret processes which involve advantages for the German economy and technology in the long term must be kept out of consideration."[19]

As the war progressed, Japan's demands on the Reich increased dramatically in disproportion to those Germany made on Japan. Initially the Germans complied, as evidenced by a 19 March 1942 decision to grant a credit of 10 million Reichsmarks to Japan in payment for war materials already delivered. However, by August the Japanese requests were of such magnitude that Ambassador Oshima Hiroshi advised Tokyo that "Japan must take into account Germany's diminished supply reserve of munitions," as well as the fact that certain German companies were switching their production from machinery to munitions, thereby causing the cancellation of Japanese machinery orders.[20]

Despite the shift in Germany's military-industrial priorities, Japanese orders continued to pour in unabated, and Germany, though with trepidation, did its best to accommodate its partner. However, as the conflict on the Russian front began to deplete German war material, Reich officials informed Oshima that Japan must consider changing the nature of its requests to those services and items that Germany could afford to provide. Consequently, on 9 December 1942 Japan and Germany finalized yet another cooperative agreement, this one addressing technical cooperation. The two Axis powers pledged to "exchange certain patents, licenses, and drawings [and to arrange] the sending of engineers . . . and technical experts, and the practical training of technical experts."[21]

Japanese officials had long been taking notice of German developments and subsequently sought patent approval for the Japanese manufacture of armaments and equipment. In September 1942 the Japanese diplomatic mission in Berlin had requested that the Ordnance Branch of the War Ministry in Tokyo seek the patent rights to several new German inventions, including an improved filtering system for air raid shelters, a portable device for evacuating poison gas, an improved valve for diving pressure chambers, and an underwater siren, used by divers "to scare off dangerous fish."[22] Armed with the December protocol, Japanese industrialists now had the promise of technical expertise as well as patent rights and could begin putting German methodology into Japanese production.

By 1943 Japan was requesting increasing amounts of military hardware while requests for goods of an industrial nature had dropped dramatically, an indication that the Pacific war was straining Japan's ability to develop effective weaponry to counter the advances made by the Americans. For example, whereas the Imperial Army had previously sought to acquire a German manufacturing technique to produce cartridge steel for use in large gun barrel linings, by late 1943 this objective had been abandoned in favor of a request for finished goods, such as German artillery pieces. German artillery constituted the bulk of the initial armaments shipped from Germany, the most popular being the

10.5- and 12.8-centimeter antiaircraft guns, the versatile 88-millimeter field piece, and the 75-millimeter antitank gun, in addition to light weapons such as machine guns and automatic rifles. Germany also began to send rudimentary technology to Japan, as evidenced by the Würzburg and Rotterdam radar systems. By the spring of 1944 Germany had widened the scope of its armament shipments, which now included naval innovations such as a 750-ton submarine pressure hull as well as a Tiger tank.[23]

However, the greatest area of Japanese interest was the field of aviation. In 1940 General Yamashita's investigative commission opened negotiations with the Junkers Aircraft Company, ostensibly to formulate an agreement by which Junkers aircraft would be produced in Japan. However, by the spring of 1941 the talks had stalled, resulting in Junkers representatives traveling to Japan to try to revive the moribund discussions. The Tokyo talks were more successful and reached fruition on 20 September 1941 with Junkers agreeing to allow the Manchuria Manufacturing Company to produce Junkers aircraft. Manchuria was no stranger to the German manufacturing processes; by 1940, as part of a previous agreement with Messerschmitt, the company was producing "twenty-five medium bombers and twenty ME 109s per month."[24] To facilitate their own venture with Manchuria, Junkers agreed to send 115 technical personnel and tons of industrial equipment to aid in the setup and debugging of the manufacturing process.

In Berlin, however, the Luftwaffe High Command disapproved of the contract, citing the difficulty of sending the unusually large complement of technicians and industrial equipment to Japan, opting instead to furnish limited "technical knowledge and production experience," which would be considered 10 percent of Germany's total investment. Thus, Germany and Japan established an active trade that focused on the transfer of aircraft and aircraft components to Japan in return for vital raw materials such as wolfram (tungsten) and rubber. Both the Imperial Navy and Army air forces took immediate advantage of the exchange; by late 1944 Japanese officials had requested and received models and designs of some of Germany's most effective aircraft, including the Focke-Wulf (FW) 190 and Messerschmitt (ME) 109 fighters, the ME 110, ME 210, Henschel (HE) 129 and Junkers (JU) 88 attack planes, and the JU 188, FW 200, ME 264, HE 177, and Dornier (DO) 217 bombers.[25]

It is no surprise that upon Germany's development of turbojet aircraft, the Japanese soon requested models and designs to help buttress their waning presence in the skies over the Pacific. In November 1944

Messerschmitt agreed to a contract that would result in the shipment of various Messerschmitt aircraft, including the turbojet ME 262 and rocket-powered ME 163. In addition, Messerschmitt agreed to send the appropriate technicians and engineers to aid Japan in establishing mass production of the new aircraft. These missions would be divided into three shipments: the first would carry the propeller-driven ME 309, 209, and 264, the second the jets ME 163 and 262, and the third the heavy fighter ME 410 and the transport ME 323. In addition to the air-craft, the cargo was scheduled to include a pressure cabin, fire-control computers, Lorenz 7H2 bombsights, a B/3 and FUG 10 airborne radar set, and 25 pounds of bomb fuses.[26]

While the Japanese continued their aggressive pursuit of German innovations and personnel, the Germans' lingering distrust of their ally severely hampered the program's chances of success. German officials were reluctant to allow the trade of copyright and patent rights and would not authorize Japanese procurement of certain German arma-ment projects lest secrecy be compromised. This bottleneck became a major sticking point in German-Japanese relations, and after discus-sions with Ambassador Oshima Hiroshi, Hitler once again stepped in. While his military leaders had severe reservations about granting the Japanese too much access to Germany's armament secrets, Hitler demanded that "in the interests of the joint management of the war," armaments, weaponry, and "practical knowledge" must be afforded the Japanese "on the broadest basis." In addition, Hitler ordered that the Japanese be instructed "through our initiative regarding all weapons and devices which . . . could be used to advantage in the common cause."[27] As a result, in November 1944 the Axis partners initiated negotiations for a secret convention that would address the matters of both patent rights and invention security. By the end of the year the con-vention was ratified and, in addition to inventions, guaranteed security and patent rights for "findings, experiences, manufacturing methods, and manufacturing instructions."[28]

In August 1944 the Japanese mission in Berlin alarmed Tokyo by reveal-ing that upon the assumed defeat of Germany the American victors "intend to transport at least 20,000 German engineers to the United States. . . . This would increase the armament potential of America in a way that could have decided effects on Japan." As a result, Tokyo now specifically requested the transfer of German technicians and engi-neers, ostensibly to prevent their capture by the Allies. In addition, the Japanese requests concentrated on inventions of importance to the war effort, with only a few specialists originally scheduled to accompany the necessary material.[29] On 16 November 1944 Germany agreed to this proposal in principle and began transferring technical information and personnel for the construction of state-of-the-art weaponry, such as aircraft, high-speed submarines, and new antiaircraft systems.[30] By the end of the year Ambassador Karl Ritter had finalized a plan to send twenty-seven German technical specialists to Japan to facilitate the development of V-weapons (rockets) and turbojet aircraft.[31] In concordance with Ritter's efforts, Japanese liaison officers combed Germany for "highly qualified specialists" who could be induced to move to Japan, an effort in which Japan would "not shy back from any expenses."[32]

The way cleared for a resumption of material shipments to Japan, discussions began concerning specific missions. On 25 November 1944 the OKM initialized such a mission by informing the naval attaché in Tokyo, Adm. Paul Wennecker, that to ensure closer collaboration in technical matters German specialists "with most recent experiences" would be sent to Japan to serve as aides at the disposal of the Japanese. The OKM also noted that since the Japanese had bemoaned the lack of a technical staff for Wennecker, immediate steps were being taken to remedy that situation as well. The first appointment was that of Cdr. (Freggatenkapitän) Gerhard Falcke—a prominent naval architect and propulsion engineer who was highly regarded by Admiral Nomura and other members of the Japanese naval attaché mission in Berlin—as Wennecker's technical assistant on naval matters. In addition, Heinz Schlicke, a renowned researcher in radar and electronics, would accompany Falcke to aid the Japanese in his professional capacity and to serve as a technical interpreter.[33]

Because Germany's naval war was limited to submarine and coastal actions, there was no opportunity for Kriegsmarine officers to gain the experience in fleet actions they would need to rebuild the German fleet.[34] Consequently, on 3 December Grand Admiral Karl Dönitz announced that he planned to send a contingent of naval officers to Japan to benefit from the large-scale operations of the Pacific war. Two naval officers, Lt. Cdr. (Kapitänleutnant) Richard Bulla, a naval aviator instructed to study the success of the Japanese naval air force, and 1st Lt. (Oberleutnant) Heinrich Hellendorn, a specialist in shipboard antiaircraft gunnery, were directed to report to Tokyo. Dönitz had initially proposed that Bulla and Hellendorn be assigned as auxiliary officers to the Imperial Japanese Navy and serve under the command of Japanese officers.[35] However, the German Foreign Office opposed the assignment, opting instead for Bulla and Hellendorn to be assembled into an independent technical staff, to avoid "politically undesirable contin-gencies."[36] The Foreign Office explained its objection by pointing out that Japanese naval officers in Germany did not serve under the Kriegsma-rine but rather under the Japanese embassy. Upon further considera-tion, Dönitz agreed and reassigned Bulla and Hellendorn as members of the German naval attaché's technical mission. In addition to Bulla and Hellendorn, Kay Nieschling, a military judge, was assigned to Tokyo to direct German military jurisdiction in Japan as well as to investigate the aftermath of the Sorge spy scandal. Bulla, Hellendorn, Falcke, Schlicke, and Nieschling were scheduled to depart Germany in late January 1945.

On 1 September 1944 Reichsmarschall Hermann Göring appointed Gen. Ulrich Kessler as Luftwaffe military attaché to Tokyo. Kessler, not entirely thrilled at the prospect of serving out the war in Japan, never-theless accepted his mission. He was ordered to form a liaison staff and subsequently requested that "a considerable number of officers" accom-pany him to Asia to form an "Expanded Office of Air Attaché."[37] Although not allowed his "considerable number," Kessler nonetheless was able to acquire the services of antiaircraft specialist Lt. Col. (Oberstleutnant) Fritz von Sandrart and radio and reconnaissance specialist Erich Men-zel, who were to assist the Japanese in preparing adequate defenses for the home islands. In late December the general and his party were informed that they too would be departing Germany in January 1945.

Also scheduled for a January departure were two civilians, August Bringewald and Franz Ruf. Both men were employees of Messerschmitt, Bringewald as an engineer and Ruf as a manufacturing and procure-ment specialist, and they were assigned to "assist and arrange mass production of the ME 163 and ME 262 airplanes."[38] Bringewald, who did not want to go to Japan, had been scheduled for an earlier departure; however, prior to leaving he had a premonition of disaster and subse-quently requested that he be allowed to wait.[39] Although his request for a delay was granted, his wish to remain in Germany was not, and he, along with Ruf, likewise prepared to depart Europe in January 1945.

Because of the difficulty of traveling to Japan from Europe, all of the personnel scheduled to leave Europe were combined into a single mis-sion. German officials, particularly Göring, desired a January 1945 departure and determined that travel by air would be the quickest way. Three Junkers 290 transports were selected for the trip; however, this plan was discarded in deference to Japanese fears that the aircraft might be forced down into Soviet territory and thus jeopardize the fragile Japanese-Russian nonaggression pact.[40] Finally, because the transport of individuals was not space-intensive, the decision was made to send the contingent to Japan via submarine.[41]

The exchange of material between Japan and Germany was the result of a cooperative effort directed through distinct military and diplomatic channels. In 1943 Admiral Dönitz, while developing the command structure for East Asian operations, designated Paul Wennecker, German naval attaché to Japan, as area commander for all German naval activities in the Far East, including the supply exchange program with the Japanese.[42] To help coordinate matters, two members of Wennecker's staff, Commander (Fregattenkapitän) Souchon and Commander (Korvettenkapitän) von Krosigk, were charged with consulting with Japanese military officials to determine which items would be included in the cargo inventory.[43] In addition, the Japanese ambassador in Berlin, Oshima Hiroshi, maintained liaison with the Imperial Army and Navy and forwarded their most urgent requests through diplomatic channels in meetings with German foreign minister Joachim von Ribbentrop and, often, Hitler himself.[44] This information was subsequently relayed to the Kriegsmarine Supply Office in Berlin, where the requests were processed and delegated to the proper procurement authorities, who in turn would direct shipment of the material to the French port of Bordeaux.

By the spring of 1945, even while preoccupied with its futile efforts to stave off impending defeat, Germany nevertheless continued to attempt last-minute shipments of contraband to Japan. In the Pacific, Japanese dependence on German assistance had reached desperate proportions. On 9 April 1945 Vice Adm. Abe Katsuo, Japan's representative to the Tripartite Commission in Berlin, reported to Tokyo that he and his staff, in an effort to "have the Germans contribute to Japan's prosecution of the war directly and indirectly by having them fight on as long as possible," had been trying to convince the Germans that the two countries "have a common destiny not only in this war, but in times to come."[45] On 3 May, after a meeting with German foreign minister von Ribbentrop, Abe assured Tokyo of Germany's commitment to Japan, reporting that von Ribbentrop had "prayed that strenuous efforts might be made to increase . . . cooperation with Japan more and more."[46] However, the Axis partners were once again faced with the dilemma that had plagued the cooperative effort since the beginning of the war: the problem was not so much what to send as how to send it.

In 1940, when Germany and Japan signed the Tripartite Pact, the means of shipping the contraband of cooperation had been the least of their worries. During the first five months of 1941, for example, Germany had received 212,366 metric tons of commodities from Japan via the Trans-Siberian Railroad, while in return Japan received heavy machinery, armor plating, vehicles, and even aircraft.[47] However, the 1941 German invasion of Russia closed this vital artery, forcing Germany to explore other means of transport.[48] The obvious solution seemed to be transport by air.

On 11 December 1941 Germany, Italy, and Japan amended the Tripartite Pact with a "Military Agreement" defining each signatory's military sphere of operation. More important, however, the agreement called for the establishment of transport routes, preferably by air, among the three allies, as well as the restoration of preexisting shipping routes via the Indian Ocean, all of which would facilitate Japanese-German cooperation.[49] However, air transport proved difficult, for the most logical route from Europe to Asia violated Soviet airspace, and alternative routes over India were too lengthy for existing aircraft to undertake. As a result, the bulk of Axis merchant shipping would be conducted by blockade-runners.

The surface vessels on which Germany and Japan were to rely were known as *Yanagi* transports. Between April 1941 and May 1942 the initial *Yanagi* missions, which carried scarce raw materials to Germany and machinery to Japan, resulted in six German vessels escaping the Bay of Biscay, while another twelve arrived in Bordeaux from the Far East. During the early stages of operations the British possession of the Enigma decrypting apparatus did little to deter the *Yanagi*s; by June 1942 only three blockade-runners had been sunk, and one of these mistakenly by a U-boat. Britain's Ministry of Economic Warfare calculated that during the first six months of 1942, Axis blockade-runners had delivered 60,000 to 65,000 tons of rubber, wolfram, and other scarce commodities to Germany; if this figure reached the 100,000-ton plateau, Germany's needs for 1942 would be met. Despite the Admiralty's introduction of increased antishipping measures, the *Yanagi* missions did not suffer substantially.[50]

The *Yanagi* missions declined in late 1942, when British interception of Japanese diplomatic decrypts provided advance information of ship movements. This information, in addition to successful Royal Air Force mining of the Bay of Biscay and the concentration of warships that accompanied the Torch convoys, severely disrupted the blockade-runners' effectiveness. By the end of April 1943 Germany had received only 28,500 tons of rubber, or less than one-third of what had been received the previous year, and Allied surface vessels and submarines had cost Germany over 55,000 tons of scarce resources like tin and tungsten. During the period from September 1942 to April 1943, seventeen merchantmen left French ports for the Far East; of these, three returned to port and four were sunk, with the remaining ten reaching Japan. However, during this period only five departed after December 1942.[51] By November 1943 blockade-running was considered so dangerous that Ambassador Oshima recommended that ships' captains receive decorations *before* they sailed.[52] As a result, the Special Staff for Economic and Commercial Warfare Measures reported to General Field Marshal Keitel that a review of shipping totals for 1943 indicated the "termination of surface blockade running."[53]

In his 31 March 1943 report to Tokyo, Oshima described a conversation with Field Marshal Fritz Erich von Manstein, whom Oshima identified only as "MA."[54] During this conversation von Manstein informed Oshima that "Germany regards it as exceedingly urgent that effective liaison be made between Japan and the Reich . . . as it has recently gotten too hot for blockade-running ships, we think we are going to use submarines," and he indicated that plans were already under way to reconfigure older submarines to perform cargo-carrying missions. Oshima suggested that, in addition to cargo, the two allies might also consider exchanging personnel via submarine, to which von Manstein readily agreed.[55] As a result, Germany planned to send three submarines to Japan in May 1943, to be followed by four more in June.[56]

During prewar planning sessions, Admiral Dönitz had already proposed the deployment of U-boats on transport as well as attack missions. By 1941 the idea of an expanded role for U-boats had begun to intrigue even the *Führer;* in a 13 December meeting Hitler had informed Oshima that Germany desired to establish consistent channels of contact with Japan, and "if nothing more than people are concerned, we expect to accomplish this by use . . . of submarines."[57] However, Kriegsmarine commander-in-chief Grand Admiral Erich Raeder had refused to allocate funding to the development of large cargo-carrying submarines, opting instead to finance construction of more surface vessels, and hence the submarine cargo mission was temporarily shelved as a low priority.

On 30 January 1943 Karl Dönitz succeeded Raeder as the head of the Kriegsmarine, and he promptly resurrected the submarine cargo plan by authorizing the reoutfitting of existing submarines to transfer goods and personnel from Europe to the Far East and back.[58] Japanese possession of strategic Southeast Asian islands, all of which could be used as submarine bases, generated additional interest within the OKM as to the feasibility of U-boat voyages to the Indian Ocean and the transfer of equipment and cargo at sea.[59] For now, the success of Germany's blockade-running program, along with the Kriegsmarine's need for combat submarines in the Battle of the Atlantic, precluded any attempt to initiate regular submarine service to the Far East. However, by the spring of 1943 Germany's blockade-running missions had been severely crippled; of the thirty-four vessels allocated to run the blockade, seven had turned back to Europe because of British pressure, while eleven others had been sunk by Allied hunter-killer groups.[60]

By mid-1944 the Kriegsmarine could no longer guarantee German merchantmen safe passage to the Far East. Shipments between Japan and Germany suffered accordingly, but by no means did they shrink in importance. Indeed, as the war progressed, Japan became increasingly dependent on Germany for aid in the defense of the home islands. Transport had become not simply a matter of convenience to the Japanese but rather one of survival. A method of conveyance would have to be found, and given the scope and size of the requested shipments, the Axis partners had few options.

Because the principal barrier to German surface trade was Allied control of the sea, the Kriegsmarine had little choice but to enlist its U-boats, and by mid-1943 the bulk of trade from both Germany and Japan was being conveyed by submarines departing from German-occupied ports along the French coast.[61] However, German submarines in their current configuration did not lend themselves to the cargo mission. Storage inside a U-boat was at a premium, with only 1 cubic meter (1.3 cubic yards) available for each metric ton of cargo; in general, most freight was bulky, requiring at least 3–4 cubic meters (4–5 cubic yards) per ton. In addition, while every available space on board was utilized for cargo, the submarine had to be packed with buoyancy in mind.[62]

While the availability of U-boats of sufficient size and range was a primary consideration, any decision about which submarines to use would also have to take into account the type of cargo being transferred to the Far East. The Kriegsmarine's initial priority for its submarines was the delivery of its own equipment to German facilities in the Pacific, such as the submarine base at Penang. To provide the necessary room for these items, the OKM proposed that 80 to 100 tons of keel ballast be removed. However, stowing cargo in the keel compartments was no easy matter, because of the requirements of the submarine's balance and trim. Originally, iron tubes filled with mercury, along with bars of lead, both of which were in great demand by the Japanese, were successfully used to fill the keel spaces. However, with the deple tion of German stocks of lead and mercury, other items would have to be found that could both satisfy the Japanese and provide the proper keel ballast for the submarine.[63]

At first the OKM engineers attempted to fill the keel spaces with aluminum, which the Japanese had purchased in great supply, and optical glass. However, because of their light weight, both aluminum and glass could only be stored in the keel in relatively small amounts. To assure the appropriate weight for ballast, large amounts would have to be secured in the keel, leaving insufficient room for heavier items. German engineers next considered using specially machined bar steel, of which the Japanese had purchased and stocked several hundred tons. However, the steel was machined into bars 3–5 meters (9.8–16.4 feet) in length—too long to fit into the keel spaces. As a result, the Special Staff ordered that lateral compartments be built into the keel spaces to accommodate lengthy items. This upgrade was of sufficient success that all transport boats were reconfigured to include the lateral keel compartments; in addition to allowing the shipment of items of excessive length, the compartments could accommodate up to 30 tons of vital contraband such as rubber on the return trip to Europe.[64]

In January 1943 Oshima had informed Hitler that the Japanese were considering the construction of freight-carrying submarines to avoid the dangers of surface transport.[65] Impressed, Hitler now directed the Kriegsmarine to embark on a similar construction program for a fleet of Type XX U-boats with a carrying capacity of 500 tons. Scheduled for completion by mid-1944, twenty such submarines would, according to German estimates, be able to transport up to 20,000 tons of supplies from the Far East annually.[66] However, several factors doomed Hitler's ambitions. Allied antisubmarine countermeasures proved more than a match for the prototype of the new boats, and subsequent modifications were both ineffective and impractical. In addition, the Special Staff of the OKM determined that each cargo U-boat built would mean one less operational boat, and so the new cargo boats were deducted from the operational estimates for 1946.[67] As a result, Dönitz was forced to cancel the building program, and alternative methods, such as the towing of underwater cargo containers and the use of Italian submarines, failed.[68] The Kriegsmarine was forced to search for other options and eventually returned to a program of reconfiguration.

Germany's operational requirements for attack submarines meant that any undersea transfer of material to Japan would have to be handled by those boats that Dönitz could afford to spare from operations in the Atlantic. By 1943, because Germany's fortunes at sea depended heavily on the offensive U-boat campaigns in the Atlantic, only a few U-boat types remained available for cargo duty. The oceangoing Type IXD was originally used for the bulk of the long-range cargo missions, but the growing need for offensive-capable boats in the Atlantic saw increasing numbers of the IXDs leave the cargo mission. As a result, in July 1943 two Type IXD boats were joined by nine IXC boats and one XIV tanker to constitute the "First Monsun Group," or the Far Eastern cargo U-boat group.[69]

The results of the Monsun missions were mixed, at best. In 1944, nineteen U-boats of the Second Monsun Group were dispatched to the Far East, each with storage in both the keel and hull spaces. The keel cargoes consisted of mercury, lead, steel, uncut optical glass, and aluminum; the hull spaces contained blueprints, drawings, and models of weapons and vehicles. By the end of the year eight of the U-boats had reached their destination, six had been lost, and the remaining were still en route. In other words, of the 1,801 tons of goods shipped from Europe, 755 tons actually arrived, 615 tons were lost at sea, and 491 tons were in transit. Of the twelve boats that left the Far East in 1944, three arrived in German-controlled territory, four were lost, and five were forced to return to their points of origination. The total delivery of these boats was 434.7 tons, 390 tons of which was rubber and tin.[70]

Cognizant of the declining numbers of submarines adaptable to the cargo mission, Dönitz decided to utilize the 1,600-ton Type XB minelayer, of which only a few remained.[71] These boats, which had previously performed the dual role of minelaying and refueling, would bear the brunt of Germany's material exchange during the latter stages of the war; by April 1943, nine Type IXD and XB U-boats had been assigned to Far Eastern transport duty, with expectations of two round trips per year.[72] Still, the dearth of submarines concerned Dönitz: operational planning for 1945–46 depended on Far Eastern commerce to maintain material stocks at sufficient levels to defer the further use of the scarce U-boats for the cargo mission.[73]

Even with the dubious results of the submarine cargo mission, the logistics of undersea cross-oceanic commerce were staggering, and it required special talents to coordinate the vital merchant exchange between Germany and Japan. Following the German occupation of France, Germany designated several French ports as points of origin and reception, naming Bordeaux as the headquarters for all of Germany's foreign trade. The organization that controlled Germany's blockade-running and, later, submarine commerce was known as the Marinesonderdienst-Ausland (MSD). While Germany initiated the bulk of its commerce from the Bay of Biscay, Japan designated Kobe as its principal receiving port; indeed, by February 1942 traffic into Kobe was so heavy that the OKM assigned additional traffic-control personnel in the persons of Fritz Ernst Muff and Hans-Joachim Rohreke to assist the Japanese in coordinating it.[74]

Earlier in the war the MSD had directed all of Germany's blockade-running traffic by coordinating the ships and their bills of lading with timely dispatches, all of which had to be organized in step with the fortunes of the war at sea. To ensure success, the MSD maintained liaison with the civilian and military shipping agencies of all of Germany's trading partners, as well as the operational and intelligence arms of the Kriegsmarine. In addition, the MSD provided training for officers who would need experience traveling in foreign seas. During the early days of the war, when German blockade-runners and auxiliary cruisers roamed the southern seas, many officers graduated from the MSD's training school. One of them was a young junior ordnance officer, headed for sea duty aboard the raider *Atlantis*, named Johann Heinrich Fehler; another was an administrative officer named Becker who would one day head the MSD.[75] Nevertheless, the MSD's primary mission remained the direction of outgoing and incoming commerce and the establishment of efficient methods of transport through seas that were becoming increasingly difficult to traverse.

In consideration of the ninety-day trip to Japan, Germany and Japan designated the months of February, May, September, and November as the prime "season" for trade. In order to avoid enemy patrols and facilitate refueling at sea, a distinctive route was designated. A ship leaving from Bordeaux would proceed to longitude 21° west, then turn due south toward the Antarctic. As the vessel approached the tip of Africa, she would alter her course so as to shadow the coastline, proceed around Cape Horn, then continue on to either Kobe or one of five German Far Eastern bases. However, Allied advances in countermeasures, particularly in the field of radar, took a heavy toll on the existing transports, and the Cape Horn route was discontinued in late 1941. The new route, which led U-boats around the Cape of Good Hope, fared only marginally better. By the fall of 1943 the losses of transport U-boats nearly matched those of their surface predecessors; of twelve U-boats that departed Japan for Europe, only four reached Bordeaux.[76]

The success of Germany's submarine service to the Far East was dubious. While the advantage of stealth did allow some U-boats to arrive in Japan when surface ships probably could not have, the overall effort was a case of too little too late. All of the material transported to Japan by all of the U-boats that survived the journey amounted to approximately one-eighth of the cargo that a single blockade-runner could have carried.[77] By the spring of 1945 Germany's attempts to keep Japan fighting were being hampered as much by unreliable means of delivery as by the lack of materials to transport.

During his last weeks in Berlin prior to Germany's surrender, Vice Admiral Abe renewed Japan's requests that Germany send submarines to the Far East both to engage the American navy, which had all but annihilated Japan's own submarine and surface force, and to bring munitions and weaponry to help Japan stave off the anticipated American invasion of the home islands. On 5 April 1945 Abe sought to discuss the matter personally with Hitler but, unable to obtain an audience with him, met instead with Field Marshal Wilhelm Keitel and Foreign Minister Joachim von Ribbentrop, neither of whom could offer a commitment. In a 15 April meeting Dönitz informed Abe that Germany could no longer afford the fuel required to send U-boats to the Far East, and in any case the OKM considered the entire operation "a waste of time."[78] Time was running out for the German Reich and, for that reason, also for the Japanese empire.

Abe returned to Dönitz for one last, desperate attempt to acquire help. Dönitz, who sympathized with his Japanese ally, could offer nothing more than before, once again citing the shortage of fuel. Although the refusal to dispatch more submarines was Germany's final official answer to Tokyo's requests, Dönitz did inform Abe that what little Germany could do had already been initiated: "There are only two or three submarines of the large type which can be sent to Japan," he said. "Of those, one is already on its way."[79] The vessel to which Dönitz was referring was a Type XB former minelaying submarine, which had left Kristiansand, Norway, in March and was identified by the designation *U-234*.

2

The
Last Boat

THE TYPE XB SUBMARINE was born of Germany's desire to use the U-boat's inherent stealth to facilitate the laying of minefields. The effectiveness of mine warfare lay in the large area that the mines covered; the larger the minefield, the greater the chance of success. Consequently, a minelaying submarine had to be large enough to transport numerous mines and substantial enough to operate away from operational ports. Like the submarine itself, the technology for a minelaying boat evolved over time, the cumulative result of trial and error. Like many of Germany's U-boat innovations, the evolution of the Type XB submarine began during the early years of the twentieth century.

At the beginning of World War I, the German Naval Staff assigned their fledgling U-boat corps to a defensive role, as large-scale offensive operations were regarded as "beyond the technical capabilities of our U-boats." German strategists believed that the British navy would attempt to engage the German High Seas Fleet by initiating operations in the coastal areas of the North Sea. Consequently, U-boats were placed in a static position behind a front line of destroyers, whose task was to lure the British warships to the submerged and waiting submarines. The success of this strategy led to the realization that a weapon of such value could not remain devoted solely to coastal defense. By December 1914, technological and tactical improvements had transformed the U-boat into a deadly offensive weapon, the presence of which consistently forced ships of the British fleet to seek refuge.[1]

Despite the success of the U-boat offensive, strategists in both Germany and England realized that, for blockading an enemy as well as erecting a defensive perimeter around fleet anchorages, submerged mines were "the most effective killing weapon."[2] The usefulness of the submarine for this task was not lost on the German Naval High Command.[3] On 29 May 1915 the UC-11 (Schmidt commanding) conducted the first minelaying voyage by a German submarine, laying a field of twelve mines near the English coast. By September, German UC boats had sown 420 mines throughout forty-nine fields in the vicinity of the Thames River estuary.

The potential of the UC and, later, the UE minelayers prompted the Naval High Command to allocate funding to their construction. By the war's end a total of 212 UC and UE submarines had been ordered, with 115 becoming operational. The mining campaign peaked in 1917, when Germans boats sank 532,272 tons of enemy shipping. The total Allied merchant losses due to mines reflected Germany's dedication of resources to the minelaying campaign: by the end of the war in 1918, Germany UC and UE boats had laid over eleven thousand mines throughout 1,360 separate fields, accounting for the loss of 1.2 million gross tons of Allied shipping.[4] Although Germany was forced to forfeit its U-boat fleet by the provisions of the Treaty of Versailles, the success of the minelaying campaign validated the investment of resources in the program and guaranteed that the minelaying submarine would be an integral part of any future German submarine fleet.

After the war German design of submarines and development of submarine technology continued, albeit covertly. In 1922 the Reichsmarine allocated secret funding to a Dutch-based organization known as Ingenieurskantoor voor Scheepsboww (IvS), or the Shipbuilding Engineering Office, in which designers continued to experiment with submarine design.[5] These labors bore fruit in 1932, when German-designed prototypes for oceangoing and coastal vessels were constructed in Spain and Finland, respectively. Encouraged by the success of the secret construction program, the German Naval Staff drew up a proposal for a projected U-boat fleet that included both a 1,000-ton oceangoing minelayer and a 500-ton coastal minelayer.[6] When, on 18 June 1935, England and Germany signed the Anglo-German Naval

Agreement, which allowed Germany to maintain a submarine fleet up to 100 percent of the tonnage of the British fleet,[7] German yards were well on their way to completing twenty-four U-boats of the new German fleet; indeed, only eleven days after the signing, Germany commissioned its first submarine since 1918. However, of the initial complement of U-boats, none was of the minelaying class.

On 28 August 1939, on the eve of war with England, Dönitz submitted a memorandum to Grand Admiral Erich Raeder, in which the U-boat chief stated that "the main weapon for U-boat warfare in the Atlantic is the torpedo-carrying submarine; in the Type VIIb and Type IX we possess boats well suited to our purpose." Dönitz therefore proposed an emergency construction policy that called for the immediate construction of as many U-boats as possible, with special emphasis on the Types VIIB and VIIC, as well as the larger Type IX.[8] Consequently, the devotion of resources to minelayer development became a much less urgent matter, lost in the crisis posed by Germany's declaration of war against England.

That Germany should possess a submarine minelaying capability was never in doubt; Admiral Dönitz considered the submarine ideal for sowing minefields because it could "penetrate unseen into the enemy's coastal waters" and, "without having aroused any suspicion that mines had been laid, . . . slip away again."[9] After the start of hostilities, however, Hitler limited the U-boats' freedom of engagement in an attempt to avoid a confrontation with American shipping. This, plus the relatively small size of his force, caused Dönitz to rate an active U-boat offensive against British shipping, dominated by torpedo and surface attacks, as unlikely to succeed.[10] As a result, he chose to attack the British merchant fleet within Britain's 3-mile territorial limit using submarines armed with TMB and TMC magnetic mines.

The TMB and TMC mines were essentially ground devices reconfigured into anchored nautical mines that could be fired from a conventional torpedo tube. The TMB measured 230 centimeters (90.6 inches) in length, weighed 740 kilograms (1,632) pounds), and carried an explosive charge of 580 kilograms (1,279 pounds). The larger TMC was 338 centimeters (133.1 inches) long, weighed 1,115 kilograms (2,459 pounds), and possessed a 1,000-kilogram (2,205-pound) warhead.[11] The smaller TMB, which was used exclusively from the outbreak of war in 1939 until 1940, was somewhat limited by its operational depth ceiling of 12–15 fathoms (72–90 feet). In 1940 the newer TMC was introduced, which extended the mine's reach down to 20 fathoms (120 feet).[12] Both mines were activated magnetically by the metal hulls of ships passing overhead, and they performed quite well; Dönitz regarded them as "technically thoroughly efficient, and . . . [a] fine achievement [by] the Inspectorate of Mines and Harbour Defences."[13] The effect of TMB and TMC mines was to convert any U-boat with standard torpedo tubes into a minelayer.

Laying mines in enemy waters was a difficult task; however, Dönitz's commanders proved themselves worthy. By 1 March 1940, U-boats had completed thirty-four mining missions along the east, west, and Channel coasts of England. U-boat commanders rated their performance by intercepting their victims' emergency signals, notifying the Naval High Command that the minefields "were taking their toll."[14] Indeed, by 1 March 1940, 115 British merchantmen had been sunk, totaling 394,533 gross tons.[15] Clearly, Dönitz's strategy of a dual role for his attack boats was paying dividends.

Regardless of the reduced priority of a submarine devoted solely to laying mines, work nevertheless continued on the development of such a vessel. In 1937, Kriegsmarine engineers improved upon a design based on the World War I–era UEII class of oceangoing minelayers. Designated Type XA, the boat was a doubled-hulled 2,500-ton ocean cruiser that featured four mine shafts paralleling the port and starboard longitudinal axes, two launching tubes located in the stern, and internal dry storage for additional TMB and TMC mines. The XA also brandished four 53.3-centimeter forward torpedo tubes as well as an array of antiaircraft and surface artillery on its deck and conning tower.[16] However, the XA was built to accommodate TMB and TMC mines and hence lost much valuable storage space.

By 1938 the TMB and TMC mines had been replaced by the Sondermine A (SMA), which was designed exclusively for vertical shaft delivery.[17] Whereas the TMB and TMC were deployed through standard torpedo tubes, the SMA was much larger and required a launching apparatus peculiar to its design. Hence, the storage requirements of the SMA, whose larger size required an individual anchoring system, rendered the internal storage feature of the XA obsolete. As a result, the Type XA was redesigned to accommodate the SMA. The new boat featured increased internal space made possible by the use of exterior, or wet, mine storage. This extra space permitted the addition of a larger diesel power plant for increased surface speed. The new boat was designated Type XB.

On 1 October 1938 the keel for the first Type XB was laid at the Germania Werft in Kiel, and *U-116* (von Schmidt) entered service in 1941. While the XB was originally projected to cost over 7 million reichsmarks, construction costs came in under budget at 6.35 million marks.[18] The Kriegsmarine's largest submarine, the XB displaced 1,763 tons on the surface and 2,177 tons submerged, had a length of 89.80 meters (296.34 feet), measured 9.20 meters (30.36 feet) across the beam, and had accommodations for a complement of five officers and forty-seven crewmen.[19]

Designed as a long-range oceangoing cruiser, the XB held 368 metric tons of fuel and possessed a greater pressure ceiling than its predecessors: it could safely dive to a depth of 120 meters (394 feet), with a safety margin of 0.8 meter (2.5 feet) before hull integrity was compromised.[20] The XB featured an impressive propulsion system. The power plant consisted of two Krupp nine-cylinder 2,100-horsepower diesel engines whose performance could be boosted by a Kapsel-type supercharger. Under normal operation the XB had a range of approximately 18,450 nautical miles at a surface speed of 10 knots and 188 nautical miles at a submerged speed of 2 knots. In addition, the XB featured two 560-horsepower double electric motors powered by corresponding accumulator batteries of 1,960 amperes per hour.

Because the XB was designed to wage war in a passive role, it was not allotted an extensive defensive capability. In addition to its twin stern torpedo tubes, deck armament consisted of one 10.5-centimeter forward cannon with a capacity of two hundred rounds; one 37-millimeter antiaircraft gun, capacity twenty-five hundred rounds, mounted abaft of the conning tower; and one 2-centimeter antiaircraft gun, capacity four thousand rounds, mounted on the aft section of the conning tower.[21]

The XB possessed physical characteristics that were peculiar to its role as a minelayer. The boat was fitted with thirty vertical mine shafts 134.6 centimeters (53 inches) in diameter capable of holding a total of sixty-six mines. Unlike previous U-boats, the outer hull of the Type XB was devoted solely to the storage of mines and had been modified to provide maximum storage capacity. To accomplish this, the forward compartment of the pressure hull was pierced from deck to keel by mine wells.[22] These six bow mine shafts were the XB's most prominent physical feature and were configured symmetrically along the longitudinal axis of the submarine, directly forward of the conning tower. The bow fairing was extended beyond the plane of the weather deck to accommodate three SMAs each, resulting in a conspicuous raised area of the foredeck.

The port and starboard amidships ballast tanks contained three wells, which extended through each half of the four ballast tanks on each side. These twenty-four shafts, as in the XB's prototype, the XA, paralleled the boat's longitudinal axis and held a total of forty-eight mines. The arrangement of the port and starboard mine wells contributed to the unorthodox shape of the pressure hull, which was more rectangular than the oval of previous submarines. Consequently, longitudinal framing was added to help buttress hull continuity throughout the areas where these wells were located.[23]

All of the mine shafts were free-flooding and were open to the sea at the keel while covered at the deck level. Each deck hatch had a relief valve, which was used to help vent air from the shafts when diving. The SMA mines were loaded from the deck and released by a hydraulic releasing gear through the keel openings. This mechanism was located on the exterior of the mine wells, inside the pressure hull for internal access. As a result, any individual shaft could be evacuated from inside the submarine, whether on the surface or submerged, with little or no indication.

The extra weight and storage requirements of the XB's mines presented problems that previous submarines had not encountered. The XB's "box hull" was inherently stable, requiring a loaded ballast rating of 91,835 kilograms (202,496 pounds); however, the additional weight of the mines, although distributed symmetrically throughout the boat, limited reserve buoyancy. To help compensate for this lack of buoyancy, a system of eight mine-compensating and trim tanks was added, distributed fore and aft, port and starboard. In addition, the two torpedo tubes held a volume of 1,740 cubic meters (61,448 cubic feet) each and could be used to help maintain buoyancy in an emergency.[24] In addition, the tanks, with a capacity of 15,100 liters (3,986 gallons) each, could be used for supplementary fresh-water storage if necessary.

The XB did not lend itself to survivability at sea; the boat's size rendered it difficult and clumsy to maneuver both above and beneath the surface. In addition, the XB took an abnormally long time to dive, which, combined with its meager complement of two stern torpedo tubes, severely hindered the boat's ability to defend itself.[25] Consequently, only eight Type XB boats were constructed, with only *U-219* (Burghagen) and *U-234* surviving the war.[26] *U-116* (von Schmidt), *U-117* (Neumann), *U-220* (Barber), and *U-233* (Steen) were all sunk in the North Atlantic, while *U-118* (Czygan) and *U-119* (von Kameke) met their fates in the mid-Atlantic. Tragically, of these boats, only *U-233* listed survivors; the rest sank with all hands.

By 1942 the Type XB had been discontinued because of the growing scarcity of resources and the number of XBs lost in action. In September 1942 construction of the last Type XB commenced at the Germania

Werft. The keel for this last boat, assigned yard number G 664, was laid on building slip 7, where, upon completion, she would be designated *Unterseeboot* number 234.[27]

Command of *U-234* was assigned to a newcomer to the U-boat corps, Lt. Cdr. Johann Heinrich Fehler. Fehler, thirty-four, was born in the Charlottenburg area of Berlin and as a boy longed to become a merchant marine officer. However, Fehler's father, a municipal judge, insisted that Johann complete the compulsory *Volksschule* and *Gymnasium* (primary and secondary school) rather than enter nautical school. Upon graduating in 1929, he was now too old at nineteen to enter nautical school and consequently enlisted in the merchant marine as a deck boy on a sailing vessel in order to gain the necessary experience for a seaman's apprenticeship. After twenty-seven months in the Baltic, Fehler became eligible for his apprenticeship aboard oceangoing freighters, and he departed on a two-year voyage to the Far East aboard a Norddeutscher Lloyd vessel, the 7,600-ton *Havel*.[28]

Upon his return from the Far East, Fehler entered the German merchant marine academy, the Seefahrtschule, earning his mate's certificate. He was completing his training with a three-month course at Radio School when, in November 1933, he joined the National Socialist Party, which was actively recruiting new members throughout Germany. Fehler did not possess any strong political philosophy, and while his reasons for casting his lot with the National Socialists is not known, Wolfgang Hirschfeld, who served under Fehler and knew him well, states that "no deep political conviction lay behind his decision."[29]

In April 1936 Fehler joined the German navy as an officer cadet. He completed his eight-week basic training at Stralsund and proceeded to Kiel for Marine Artillery School. In 1937, after nine months at the Kriegsmarine's War School in Flensburg, Fehler returned to sea, this time aboard the *Schleswig Holstein* on a six-month voyage around Africa. He returned to Germany in 1938 and, after a brief administrative duty in Glückstadt, was assigned as a watch officer with the Sixth Minesweeping Flotilla.[30] In 1939 he was serving aboard his first command, the minesweeper M-145, which sortied out of Wilhelmshaven, when war erupted in Poland.[31] By early 1940 Fehler had been reassigned, this time as the mines and explosive officer for Schiff 16, the legendary auxiliary cruiser *Atlantis*.

The *Atlantis* was one of the most successful German commerce raiders, responsible for the sinking or capture of twenty-two Allied vessels for a total of 145,698 tons.[32] Built in 1937 as the merchantman

Goldenfels, she was outfitted as a warship in 1939 and was the first of the raiders to sortie, leaving the Baltic via the Denmark Straits on 31 March 1940. Under the command of Capt. Bernhard Rogge, the 7,860-ton vessel was outfitted with 15-centimeter deck guns, torpedoes, and magnetic mines, all carefully hidden to preserve the raider's identity as a merchantman. As ordnance officer, Fehler was responsible for maintenance and direction of minelaying and torpedo operations as well as demolition and scuttling of captured vessels.

Of the *Atlantis*'s twenty-two victims, two stand as noteworthy. During the spring of 1941 Rogge sighted and sunk the Egyptian steamer *Zam Zam,* which he mistook for a British troop transport. Although the *Zam Zam* was laden with British contraband of lubricating oil and steel, she also carried over two hundred civilians. Upon realizing his mistake, Rogge was able to rescue all survivors and transferred them to the German supply ship *Dresden* for passage to France. However, in Berlin, Kriegsmarine authorities worried about the effect on world opinion, and the use of the event by the British propaganda ministry, should the *Dresden* be attacked and sunk en route to France. Although the *Dresden* ultimately arrived unscathed in France with all of the *Zam Zam*'s survivors, considerable damage had been done: one of the survivors, the editor of *Fortune* magazine, wrote a blistering account of his ordeal, and another, a *Life* photographer, took a clandestine photograph of the *Atlantis.* Both the article and photograph, which were published in *Life,* would later result in dangerous consequences for the *Atlantis.*[33]

Of more immediate value to the Axis war effort was the capture of the British merchantman *Automedon.* Rogge sighted and captured the *Automedon* on 11 November 1940 en route to Singapore. While searching the vessel, the *Atlantis*'s boarding party discovered the British war cabinet minutes of 15 August 1940, which were addressed to the commander-in-chief, Far East, Air Chief Marshall Brooke-Popham. These minutes discussed Britain's political relations with Japan and included an assessment of the defenses of Singapore, which determined that Hong Kong, French Indochina, Malaya, and the Dutch East Indies were virtually indefensible. On 12 December, German officials passed this information along to their Japanese allies, who subsequently presented Rogge with a ceremonial samurai sword, an honor extended to only two other Germans: Hermann Göring and Erwin Rommel.[34]

During his service on the *Atlantis* Fehler actually gained command of an enemy vessel. On 16 February 1941 the *Atlantis* seized the tanker *Ketty Brövig* off the coast of East Africa. Rogge determined that the prize should accompany the *Atlantis* to his scheduled rendezvous in the

Indian Ocean with the pocket battleship *Admiral Scheer,* to aid in refueling the warship.[35] Rogge charged Fehler with command of the *Brövig,* which accomplished her mission by accommodating the *Scheer.* However, after the fueling mission the *Brövig* was attacked and sunk from under Fehler in the Indian Ocean.[36]

Before returning home the *Atlantis* logged 622 consecutive days at sea, covering over 102,000 nautical miles.[37] She was homeward bound when, on 22 November 1941, she stopped in the South Atlantic for repairs to her engine and to refuel the submarine *U-126* (Bauer). While engaged with the refueling, her lookouts sighted the heavy cruiser HMS *Devonshire,* which was closing rapidly. *U-126* immediately disengaged from fueling and dove to position herself for a torpedo attack. Meanwhile, Rogge informed the *Devonshire* that his vessel was merely a merchantman, and not a belligerent. The ruse almost worked, but then the cruiser launched her scout aircraft, which, with the aid of the *Life* magazine photograph, identified the *Atlantis* as a warship. The *Devonshire* opened fire at 10 miles, and upon assessing the *Atlantis*'s situation as untenable, Rogge ordered his command abandoned.

Because the *Devonshire* pulled away and did not attempt a rescue, *U-126* was able to save the survivors, which included Johann Fehler. Arranged in groups of three, the *Atlantis*'s survivors were ferried first by *U-126,* then by other submarines of a nearby wolf pack. Upon learning of the episode, Dönitz sent more submarines to aid in the rescue, and the survivors of the *Atlantis* arrived home unharmed. Because of the valor of the crew, Rogge received the Knight's Cross from Hitler at a reception for the crew in Berlin. The notoriety gained by the *Atlantis* saga would forever influence Fehler's career, affording him opportunities that might not have been available otherwise.

However, such opportunities would have to wait. Soon after his return to Germany, Fehler, who was impressed by his rescue by U-boat, requested transfer to the U-boat corps, with the ultimate goal of a combat command. However, his request was denied, as was a subsequent request for command of a surface ship. Instead, in March 1942 Fehler was assigned a one-year tour of duty to the Kriegsmarine's War School in Mürwik as an instructor. The static duty of instruction ran contrary to Fehler's restless nature; this period of, as he put it, "having to pour wisdom into the wooden heads of other people's children" was "not one in which an active thirty-one year old could feel very happy."[38] Fehler soon made himself a nuisance to his superiors with his continual badgering for a combat command, and despite counseling by his colleagues, including his former commander Rogge, to remain patient, he could not be reconciled to his fate at Mürwik. However, his persistence paid off, and in early 1943 he received a posting to the U-boat fleet.

Fehler attended the various training facilities for prospective U-boat commanders at Pillau, Flensburg, Travemünde, and Neustadt. He soon completed his chief officer training and by September had completed his captain's course, thereby qualifying for command.[39] However, by the fall of 1943 the U-boat offensive against Britain had been substantially weakened by effective new Allied countermeasures. leaving Dönitz with a surplus of personnel for the available submarines. In short, Fehler was called on once again to be patient. By March 1944 his wait was over, albeit not to his complete satisfaction. Rather than the combat vessel he desired, he was directed to report to Kiel to observe the construction of his new command: a Type XB minelayer, hull number *U-234.*

"She was big . . . by far the largest U-boat I had ever seen." Though "fascinated" at the first sight of his new command, Fehler nonetheless requested that he be considered for another boat. The *U-234* was a minelaying submarine whose sister boats were currently being used as *Milchkuhs,* or fuel tankers. This was a far cry from the offensive role Fehler had envisioned, but his protests fell on deaf ears.[40] Any postponement of his *U-234* command would result in a return to the waiting list, or even another shore assignment. Weighing his options, Fehler conceded that with command of *U-234,* at least he could return to sea duty.

Although *U-234* was completed on schedule in late 1943, her construction was not without incident. In September 1942 *U-234*'s keel was laid down at the Germania Werft in Kiel and construction began on the 1,650-ton vessel. However, by November, Allied bombers had begun to raid the Kiel submarine yards, and despite substantial defenses, the Germania Werft was not invulnerable. On 14 May 1943 the American Eighth Air Force dropped an estimated 250 tons of explosives on the Germania yards, severely damaging a 30-foot section of *U-234*'s foreship area.[41] Despite the delay that resulted from the need to replace the damaged area, *U-234* was launched on 23 December 1943 and was commissioned into the Fourth U-Boat Flotilla on 3 March 1944.

In early 1944 Fehler reported to the Germania Werft yard in Kiel to observe the final outfitting of his boat, as well as to select and train his crew.[42] Although *U-234*'s construction proceeded without any substantial further incidents, Fehler found it difficult to muster an experienced crew. Two factors hampered crew selection. First, an experienced submarine crew was valuable to its commander, as the familiarity bred between crew and captain gave both a feeling of reassurance. Veteran

U-boat commander and Knight's Cross holder Jürgen Oesten explained that "as the staff situation was very tight, [a commander] tried to get the people back whom [he] knew from previous boats. For their part, the crew members tried to get back to commanders whom they knew and trusted. . . . To regain qualified and experienced men one had to use all tricks possible, as this was sort of a life insurance for both parties concerned."[43] As a new commander, Fehler had no previous crew to call on nor any reputation to use as an enticement, and consequently there was no reason for an experienced crewman to cast his lot with *U-234*.

A second inhibiting factor was the toll that the U-boat campaign had taken on the U-boat crews. In his memoirs, Dönitz stated that of 863 operational boats, 630 were lost at sea, for a staggering 73 percent mortality rate.[44] Consequently, by 1944 there simply were not that many experienced crewmen from which to choose; they either were dead or had already been assigned to other boats. As a result, Fehler had to settle for recent graduates of the various submarine training schools. The majority of his crew were as new to the submarine corps as he was; 70 percent of the crew were nineteen years old, and the youngest was only seventeen.[45]

Fehler was more fortunate, however, with his noncommissioned officers (NCOs). All of *U-234*'s NCOs were U-boat veterans, with at least fifteen operational missions behind them. While Fehler was reassured that this experience would be priceless once *U-234* put to sea, the NCOs were skeptical about their new commander. Chief Radioman (Oberfunkmeister) Wolfgang Hirschfeld stated that although he liked Fehler's "buoyant optimism and warm personality . . . I was doubtful whether he would keep us alive very long once we hit the Atlantic."[46] Fehler would have to earn his men's confidence over time, and under the rigors of submarine warfare. Unknown to Hirschfeld and the others, their wait would not be as long as they might have liked.

U-234's lengthy series of sea trials began directly after her commissioning in March 1944, but they were marked by continual delays and repairs. Upon completion of her initial two-week trial at Kiel, she returned to the Germania Werft to have her malfunctioning oil pressure system rebuilt. She departed Kiel and after a brief port of call at Warnemünde arrived at the Baltic island of Bornholm on 27 April for seven days of subsurface sound testing.

Although the scheduled sound tests were normally brief, Fehler was forced to remain at Bornholm for a week waiting for German minesweepers to clear the Baltic of British mines. By 1944 British aircraft had littered the northern approaches to the Baltic Sea, where the Kriegsmarine concentrated its U-boat training, to such an extent that Germany's "U-boat nursery" was no longer safe. Indeed, of all the Allied aerial mining operations, the mining of the Baltic was considered the principal concern for the U-Boat Command.[47] *U-234*'s stay at Bornholm would not be the last time her trials would be postponed by minesweeping operations.

Upon the eventual completion of the sound tests, Fehler directed his boat to Swinemünde for a series of antiaircraft trials; however, on 7 May, *U-234* experienced problems with her electric air compressor and bilge pumps and reported to the repair yards at Danzig.[48] On 25 May, Fehler returned *U-234* to sea for the continuation of her trials, this time heading to Hela for working-up exercises.

The exercises at Hela were designed to expose the young crew and commander to simulated emergencies and to rate the crew's competence in working under pressure. On 20 June, Fehler guided *U-234* westward for a practice emergency dive in 180 feet of water. As the dive alarms sounded throughout the boat, *U-234* dove at an unusually steep angle, her bow eventually boring into the soft mud of the sea bed. Fehler surveyed the situation through the periscope and calmly informed Chief Engineer and Diving Officer Horst Ernst that while *U-234*'s bow was embedded in the mud, her stern remained above the surface. Fehler's veterans were appalled. Quartermaster Paul Rische complained, "We've been training for four weeks, and all the Chief has learned to do so far is this. . . . He's a typical learner." Fehler might have saved face if no one on shore had witnessed the fiasco, but it was not to be: the training command on shore had seen the mishap and dispatched several launches to *U-234*, all of which inquired whether Fehler had any survivors. Ernst was finally able to trim the boat horizontally, although it was of little relief to the crew; Hirschfeld remembered that "the only comfort we drew was from the continued presence of the launch slowly circling above us."[49] Fortunately *U-234* experienced no further emergencies and was able to complete her surface and underwater minelaying trials.

Upon completion of the minelaying trials, Fehler was forced once again to Danzig and the Holm Werft repair slips. *U-234* was beset by a litany of problems, primary among them being a malfunctioning electric propulsion system and problems with her radio communications and radar. After these repairs Fehler sailed to Pillau for eight days of tactical exercises, upon completion of which he made for Libau for torpedo trials. After Libau he was forced yet again to the repair yards, this time because of continuing trouble with the boat's electronic surveillance and communications equipment.

Fehler's continuing troubles with *U-234*'s shipboard electronics were a cause for alarm. Concerned about the frequency of radio, radar, and transmitter breakdowns, Chief Radioman Hirschfeld inquired as to the existence of more reliable systems, particularly radar. Most U-boats in 1944 were equipped with the clumsy "Cross of Biscay" radar-observation device, which was so detested among skippers that some refused to sortie with it aboard. One such captain, former *U-581* skipper Lt. Cdr. Wilhelm Wissman, informed Hirschfeld that the Luftwaffe possessed the Hohentwiel radar system, which would enable a submarine to track surface targets. Aware of the danger of conducting extended underwater operations with an inferior surface radar, Hirschfeld approached Fehler with a request to procure a Hohentwiel set, which Fehler eventually did. The significance of the ship-borne Hohentwiel cannot be overstated. Hirschfeld claimed, "It was to save our lives."[50]

By late summer, *U-234*'s trials and training period had been completed. Fehler's boat was cleared for duty as seaworthy, and all of her systems were pronounced functional; however, the numerous trips to the repair yards had instilled a general lack of confidence among the crew. There were more repairs to come, however, including a major physical reconfiguration and the installation of one of the great technological innovations of World War II.

On 30 August *U-234* returned to her home port of Kiel and was transferred to the Fifth U-Flotilla, where Fehler received orders to return his boat to the Germania Werft. Here he was informed that Allied success in destroying German supply submarines required a change of plans. Eight new cargo submarines would be canceled in favor of reconfiguring the existing Type XBs to fill the supply mission.[51] *U-234* would now undergo refitting from a minelayer to a cargo submarine, with the implication that her unnamed mission would likely be that of a supply vessel.

On 23 March 1944 the Germania Werft completed *U-234*'s final overhauling, conversion, and loading. Cargo containers were designed to fit inside the six forward vertical mine shafts, each secured by the mine-releasing mechanism. One important change to *U-234*'s configuration was the removal of the lateral shafts to create four cargo spaces, which were outfitted with eight horizontal cargo tubes.[52] Designers also added four horizontal containers topside, evacuated the outer keel duct to accommodate cargo, and welded two 20- by 4-foot steel cylinders to each side of the conning tower.[53] On 25 March 1944, accompanied by the Type IX *U-516* (Wiebe), *U-234* departed Kiel. Wiebe's *U-516* had been reconfigured as a cargo carrier, complete with increased storage and one of the most important submarine developments of the war, the new breathing mast, the *Schnorchel*.

In 1944 the Kriegsmarine began equipping its U-boats with an apparatus that would allow a submarine to travel submerged on her diesel engines, thereby recharging and saving her batteries. This device was a Dutch prewar invention—a design the British Admiralty had turned down in 1940—which the Germans named *Schnorchel*. The *Schnorchel* was a breathing tube, which, like the periscope, would extend above the surface while the boat was submerged, simultaneously acting as an air intake and an exhaust outlet to allow the internal combustion diesel engines to operate without surfacing. As a result, a *Schnorchel*-equipped submarine could remain submerged indefinitely and was extremely difficult to detect with radar.

Although the *Schnorchel* was a formidable enhancement to an already-lethal weapon, it was not without serious drawbacks. To keep water from flooding the air pipe, the *Schnorchel* had a check valve, which would close when seawater rushed over the exposed breathing mast. Although the valve prevented water from flooding the engine, it also blocked the flow of outside air and caused the diesel engine to draw air from the interior of the submarine. When kept to a minimum, this caused no immediate problems, for the valve would soon reopen and allow fresh air to reach the engine. But prolonged periods of the diesel drawing on the submarine's internal air supply could sicken, even suffocate, the crew. In addition, if the clutch system of the *Schnorchel* jammed, the carbon monoxide exhaust would be expelled into the submarine, increasing the danger of poisoning.

U-234's crew got an inkling of the danger of the new device during trials in late March 1944. While the boat was running on diesel engines with the *Schnorchel*, her conning tower cut beneath the surface; the check valve engaged, shutting off the engine's air supply and thus causing the diesel to suck air from the interior of the boat. After about five minutes the continuous suction caused a partial vacuum, which Hirschfeld said "was particularly unpleasant on the ear drums and rapidly became intolerable." As the discomfort worsened, all of the engineers in the engine room passed out except for Warrant Officer Wilhelm Winkelmann, who struggled with and finally disconnected the diesel engines. When the boat surfaced and the air intake opened, "a storm-wind swept through the boat."[54]

In December 1944 Fehler was summoned to Berlin, where Marinesonderdienst-Ausland director Becker notified him and his officers that their destination would be Japan. Taking supplies to Japan by submarine was considered tantamount to suicide, previous attempts having resulted in an estimated loss of up to 75 percent of the valuable boats and crews.[55] But whatever the perils of submarine cargo traffic, and however reluctant the U-boat leadership may have been to undertake it, it was the only recourse left to the Germans for conducting trade with Japan.

Because of space limitations and the uncertainty of underwater transport, the shipments sent to Japan via U-boat could not be sizable.[56] The Japanese army liaison to Germany, Maj. Gen. Okamoto Seigo, had already recognized this dilemma and more than a year earlier had dispatched a message to Tokyo that proposed a solution: "[Because] it is extremely hazardous to ship big samples . . . the only thing left for us is to exchange technical experts."[57] Consequently, Fehler learned that in addition to *U-234*'s material cargo he would also be carrying twenty-six passengers on the already overcrowded submarine. To make room for the passengers, he would be forced to leave behind eighteen of his crew—an arrangement that he successfully fought. Fehler argued that the number of passengers was excessive and subsequently had the number reduced to twelve.[58]

U-234's German passengers included the new air attaché to Tokyo, General of the Air Force (General der Flieger) Ulrich Kessler, his staff, a scientist, and two civilian technicians. Kessler's staff consisted of two military advisers, 1st Lt. Erich Menzel and Lt. Col. Fritz von Sandrart; Gerhard Falcke, a naval engineer; Heinrich Hellendorn, a naval artillery specialist; Richard Bulla, a naval aviator; and naval judge Kay Nieschling. The technical contingent consisted of electronics expert Heinz Schlicke and Messerschmitt aircraft technicians August Bringewald and Franz Ruf. In addition, two Japanese passengers were listed on the roster: Lt. Cdr. Tomonaga Hideo of the Japanese Imperial Navy and Lt. Shoji Genzo of the Air Force. All of the passengers boarded *U-234* in Kiel, with the exception of Kessler, Nieschling, and the Japanese, who boarded in Norway at Kristiansand.

Although there was little that Fehler could do about the overcrowding of his boat, he did attempt to make the best of the situation by dismissing his first watch officer, 1st Lt. Albert Klingenberg, with whom Fehler had a tenuous working relationship. Rather than bring a new first officer aboard, Fehler elected to save the spot on the roster for one of his crew and on 1 April appointed passenger Richard Bulla, a trusted friend with whom Fehler had served aboard the *Atlantis,* as his first officer.[59]

At the December meeting the Marinesonderdienst-Ausland also determined the cargo destined for Japan and sent a Lieutenant Commander Longbein to Kristiansand to supervise the loading of *U-234* in the absence of MSD director Becker.[60] Fehler, characteristically distrustful of the naval bureaucracy, enlisted the aid of a merchant marine veteran, one Captain Übel, who, as the former commander of the supply ship *Münsterland,* had met *U-234*'s skipper in the Indian Ocean when Übel supplied the *Atlantis* and other commerce raiders.

U-234 was loaded with an estimated 300 tons of cargo as well as sufficient fuel and supplies for a six- to nine-month trip. The cargo included an estimated 8 tons of documents and technical drawings, 1 ton of diplomatic and personal mail, and approximately 210 tons of war material.[61] The weapons and technology that made up the bulk of the cargo foreshadowed the future of warfare, as many of the devices intended for Japan had yet to be encountered at the front on a large enough scale for adequate countermeasures to have been developed. Many of Germany's latest armaments and developments were packed into *U-234*'s cargo spaces, ranging from a high-altitude pressure chamber for pilots, numerous explosives and ammunition, and prototypes and working models of new radar and ranging equipment, to antitank and armor weapons such as the Panzerfaust antitank launcher, small rockets, and even a Messerschmitt 262 jet fighter, which was stored in sections in amidship mine container 30549 X.[62]

U-234 also carried supplies and ammunition intended for Germany's Indian Ocean submarine bases at Batavia and Penang as well as clothing, medicine, tools, and dry stores. Because regular communication between Germany and Japan was no longer viable, all dispatches deemed too sensitive for radio traffic were now sent via courier; hence *U-234* carried one ton of mail, for the various attachés and diplomats as well as for civilians based in Japan. At the other end of the cargo spectrum were personal items ranging from Hellendorn's paint set and Kessler's hunting rifles to cognac, card and board games, and "mouth organs."[63]

Perhaps the most notable cargo item, and certainly the most intriguing, was uranium oxide, identified on the cargo manifest as item ST 1270/1-10. Packed in ten containers weighing 560 kilograms (1,235 pounds) in all, the ore was addressed to the "Jap [*sic*] Army" and was, according to Hirschfeld, "highly radioactive." Hirschfeld recalled witnessing Shoji and Tomonaga write "U235" in Japanese characters on ten cubical containers measuring about 9 inches square, "possibly steel and lead . . . and enormously heavy." These packages were loaded into the vertical mine shafts by a detachment under the supervision of ensign (Leutnant zur See) Karl Pfaff and Boatswain Peter Schölch.[64]

When Hirschfeld asked Tomonaga about the contents of the mysterious packages, the Japanese officer allegedly told him that the containers had originally been intended for the submarine *U-235*, a boat no longer assigned to travel to Japan. Doubting the truth of this explanation, Hirschfeld asked about it at the Fifth Flotilla Office and was told that *U-235* was actually a small Type VII training vessel, which was scheduled for training in the Baltic only.[65] Realizing that he had been misled, Hirschfeld reported his concern to Fehler, who instructed his chief radioman to refrain from discussing the subject with the Japanese.[66] To Hirschfeld, the secrecy surrounding the Japanese and their cargo lent an air of urgency to *U-234*'s mission. (*U-234*'s uranium consignment will be discussed in greater detail in the appendix.)

Another indication of the importance of *U-234*'s cargo occurred when the commander of the Fifth Flotilla, Führer der U-boote (FdU) West Capt. Hans Rösing, arranged an elaborate reception for Tomonaga and Shoji, which doubled as a farewell ceremony for the officers and crew of *U-234*. The ceremony was held at Kristiansand and included the Japanese ambassador to Germany, Oshima Hiroshi, as well as the Japanese naval attaché, Rear Adm. Kojima Hideo, and officials of the Ausland commission. The reception was intended to reaffirm the solidarity between Germany and Japan, and speeches mentioned "war to the death" and the Axis partners' "indissoluble comradeship." To the cynical Fehler, to whom Japan's disenchantment with its failing ally was obvious, the political trappings of the ceremony were a farce. "We got on nicely together," he wrote, "comradely at least in our mutual determination to preserve illusions."[67] In a "festive and religious ceremony," Oshima demonstrated his faith in "the man responsible for [Tomonaga and Shoji's] safety" by charging Fehler with the custody of Tomonaga's three-hundred-year-old samurai sword.[68]

With the political preliminaries out of the way, Rösing next arranged a final reception, to be held at the pier at which *U-234* was docked. The reception, which the disgusted Fehler described as "such incredible bull," featured a martial band playing patriotic anthems, countless political and military dignitaries, a "deputation of young *Helfs* [maidens] to wave the boys good-bye," flowers for Fehler, and a "quayside valediction" to the crew and officers.[69] Finally, on the afternoon of 25 March, Fehler prepared to depart from Kiel.

Although Fehler was keenly aware of the importance of crew morale to his mission's success, he nevertheless refused to conceal from his subordinates any matter that might concern them. Such was the case with the deteriorating German resistance to the advancing Red Army. Hirschfeld recalled that, while at Memel during *U-234*'s trials, the townspeople "knew that the Soviets had reached nearby Mitau," and upon the inevitable occupation of Memel, they "feared for the women and girls." Upon asking Fehler whether he thought the German army could repel the invaders, Fehler remarked that "it was a long way from Stalingrad to Mitau. . . . Now we have a European war on two fronts. Do you want me to spell it out?"[70]

Fehler likewise did not conceal from his crew his assessment of the military situation in Germany. On 25 March 1945, as *U-234* slipped out of the yards at Kiel, he informed his crew of their destination and announced his personal conviction that they would never reach Japan.[71] Addressing the rumors of Germany's imminent collapse, Fehler acknowledged the deterioration of the German war effort but vowed, "No matter how this war turns out, I promise to do everything I can to bring you safely back."[72] Although many of the crew appreciated their commander's candor, some believed that his assessment of their chances was merely a statement of the obvious, given *U-234*'s operational history. An air of nervous anticipation, pessimism, and uncertainty permeated the bloated submarine as she crept north to Norway.

The trip to Kristiansand from Kiel was fraught with hazards and was regarded as the most treacherous leg of the entire journey. Fehler would be guiding his fully laden boat north through waters that were infested with the mines of both Allied and German origin, and over which the Allies enjoyed uncompromised air supremacy. In addition, in 1945 numerous antisubmarine aircraft prowled the approaches to northern Germany, especially in the treacherously shallow Kattegat narrows between Norway and Denmark, where a submarine could not seek refuge in the deep.

Fehler departed from Kiel on the afternoon of 25 March and, at sea at 1006, dispatched a message to the Fifth Flotilla Command confirming his rendezvous with *U-516* (Petran) and an escort ship, which would guide him to Horten and Larvik.[73] However, in view of the increasing Allied antisubmarine aircraft in the Baltic, Fehler determined that the escort might attract Allied aircraft. Consequently, he radioed Kiel and informed the Fifth Flotilla Command that, at 1520, he had released his escort at 57°00' N, 11°00' E, and was continuing north with *U-516* to Horten.[74] On 27 March *U-516*'s Petran radioed Kiel that he and *U-234* had entered Horten at 1625.

In another harbinger of her fortunes, *U-234* once more skirted catastrophe during further *Schnorchel* trials at Horten. On 31 March, while running at *Schnorchel* depth, *U-234* collided with Type XIIC *U-1301* (Lenkheit), which was also conducting *Schnorchel* trials. Lieutenant Commander Lenkheit's boat rammed *U-234* directly abaft of the conning tower on the port side. The resulting gash, 24 feet square, caused severe damage to fuel tank 7, which subsequently spilled approximately 30 tons of fuel oil into the fjord. Upon arriving at Kristiansand for repairs, Fehler was notified that there were no repair slips available, and that the nearest repair facilities were in Bergen, a full three days' journey in dangerous waters. Fehler radioed in reply that he could effect his own repairs and was ordered to the south entrance of Kristiansand to begin work.[75] He was able to acquire a section of steel plating and by flooding the forward ballast tanks caused *U-234* to lower her bow sufficiently to allow the damaged section of her stern to clear the surface. After a week's work, *U-234*'s crew had succeeded in removing and replacing the damaged hull plates.

Fehler prepared once more to proceed with his journey. On 5 April *U-234* departed Horten for Larvik, where she met *U-2326* (Jobst) and soon departed for Kristiansand. Later that day Fehler relayed a message to the commander of submarine operations, the commanding admiral of U-boats, the sea defense commandant of the Oslo Fjord, and the port captain of Kristiansand Harbor, informing them of his intention to arrive at Kristiansand at 0700 on 6 April. In addition, he relayed the position of two enemy drift mines, which he had encountered in Areas of Operation (Grid Squares) 4124 and 4125 (58°57' N, 10°12' E, and 58°57' N, 10°24' E).[76]

U-234's time in Europe was rapidly coming to an end. On 12 April the commander of submarine operations radioed Rösing in Kristiansand with a request for *U-234*'s fuel status and orders that Fehler was not to depart until especially ordered. The following day Rösing received a message from Berlin instructing him to advise Fehler that he was to "leave for war cruise as originally ordered."[77]

Fehler and *U-234* departed Kristiansand under the cover of darkness on 15 April. To maintain secrecy, Fehler had masked his actual departure date by dispatching numerous requests for the delivery of stores, complete with fake dates and times at which *U-234* would need them. He also dispatched to naval officials detailed planning records of work parties and shore leave and subsequently notified the harbormaster—falsely—that he intended to depart on 16 April. In a message to the U-Boat Command in Kiel, the Fifth Flotilla duly reported *U-234* and her escort as departing at 2200 on 16 April.[78] This was exactly what Fehler had intended. By 1945, sea-borne radio communication security could not be guaranteed; Fehler knew that the enemy was likely to intercept any communiqué regarding his departure (and in fact they did). By feeding false information to Kiel, and subsequently Berlin, the Fifth Flotilla had unwittingly provided Fehler with a full day's head start. His long wait finally over, an apprehensive Fehler and his nervous crew and passengers turned their attention to the volatile Atlantic and prepared for the initial leg of their journey to the equator.

Tokyo was anxiously expecting news of Fehler's departure from Europe, with good reason: the initial attempt to send German armaments to Japan had resulted in disaster. On 9 February 1945 *U-864* (Wolfram), the first of three attempts to reach Japan by submarine, was sunk by HMS *Venture* off Norway, with all hands lost. The cargo of *U-864* was similar to that of *U-234;* indeed, both Kessler and Messerschmitt engineer Bringewald had been tentatively scheduled to depart on *U-864.* Kessler, however, had duties in Berlin that prevented him from leaving in February, while Bringewald had a premonition of disaster and refused to board the ill-fated boat.[79] With one-third of their acquisitions at the bottom of the Baltic, Japanese officials were justifiably concerned about the status of Fehler's mission, and on 19 April, in an effort to assure that the second mission had not been canceled, they requested the name of *U-234*'s commander.[80]

Attempts by the Germans and Japanese to track Fehler's progress were complicated by the uncertainty of their diplomatic code security. Accordingly, in a 15 April message from the chief inspector in Kiel to the chief of military preparations in Berlin, Fehler and *U-234* were first referred to by the code name Anton 1.[81] However, this ruse did not deter Allied code-breakers, who had been monitoring German-Japanese diplomatic dispatches since the breaking of the German Enigma and Japanese Diplomatic codes; in fact, *U-234*'s mission security had been violated long before her departure for Japan.

Prior to his departure, both in Kiel and Kristiansand, British propaganda radio broadcasts addressed Fehler nightly, facetiously greeting him and his crew and making certain that the *U-234*'s skipper knew that the British were very much aware of his mission. That mission security could be breached came as no surprise. Fritz von Sandrart recalled that the Norwegian docks were full of suspected spies,[82] and Fehler suspected that someone in either the Naval High Command or the Ausland commission was feeding the British the particulars of his mission. Nevertheless, the voyage to Japan was to continue, and Fehler guided *U-234* south, making way for the gap between Iceland and the Faeroe Islands.

U-234 departed Kristiansand in misty, rainy weather, initially with the company of an escort vessel. *U-234* trailed her escort, making 16 knots, until she reached Lindesnes, where Fehler signaled that the escort was no longer required. Shortly before midnight Fehler relieved the bridge watch and gave the order to clear the conning tower in preparation to dive. Von Sandrart recalled his apprehension as he took "one last drag on the cigar . . . a last deep breath, and the cover closed. Would it ever be opened again?"[83] Fehler secured the hatch, and *U-234* submerged, trimming at periscope depth. Hirschfeld echoed the general sentiment when he wondered aloud whether he would ever again see the light of day.[84]

Fehler's orders were to make the month-long voyage to the equator submerged on batteries, utilizing the *Schnorchel* when necessary. Prolonged underwater travel was a daunting mental and physical task for even veteran U-boat personnel. To save electricity, only a minimum of lighting was allowed while submerged, usually only a small emergency light. No allowance was made for internal electric heating, and subsequently the temperature on board soon dropped to that of the surrounding water, which in the northern latitudes of the North Atlantic can approach zero degrees Celsius. The chill was aggravated by the condensation that constantly dripped from the bulkheads. It was a wet, numbing environment that became increasingly inhospitable.[85]

In addition to the physical discomfort, the crew and passengers of *U-234* were exposed to the psychological stress of war as well as crippling periods of monotony. Oxygen was always at a premium on board a submarine, particularly one traveling submerged for extended periods of time. To conserve oxygen, anyone who was not on duty was consigned to his bunk and ordered to keep any physical activity to an absolute minimum. Because of the submarine's vulnerability to echo-sounding, noises inside *U-234* had to be muffled or eliminated. Conversation was discouraged, and any speech above a relative whisper could result in disciplinary action. Von Sandrart recalled, "If you are in the dark for hours in the silence of a narrow bunk, you can't shake the impression of being in a ghost ship."[86] Whether on duty or off, tempers grew short and nerves became frayed.

During the first days of the mission *U-234* skirted disaster on two occasions. The first instance occurred off the coast of Bergen, when she encountered a large aircraft. Anticipating a depth-charge attack, Fehler dove to 300 feet, where his hydrophones picked up three telltale splashes, but no explosions. Chief Radioman Hirschfeld notified Fehler of a new British antisubmarine countermeasure known as sonar buoys, which used three underwater microphones to locate an enemy submarine by triangulation. Fehler's only hope of avoiding detection was to descend further and attempt to locate a distinct layer of colder water; the changing density from warm to cooler water would refract the sonar beams. Fehler's tactic was successful; *U-234* dove to her maximum operating depth of 550 feet and encountered no depth-charge attack.[87]

Upon breaking away from the relative safety of the Norwegian coast, *U-234* had a second brush with disaster. The boat suddenly became sluggish and difficult both to steer and to maintain trim; her bilge had filled with seawater. A troubleshooting detail discovered that the culprit was a soggy bag of potatoes. The potatoes had been stored near the mine shafts and in the high humidity had become swollen. They had burst their waterlogged containers, fallen out, and clogged the bilge drain pumps. The end result was a failure to hold the *Schnorchel* at a proper depth, which rendered it ineffective when submerged beneath the rough seas, flooding the interior of the boat with diesel fumes. To add to the misery, a fire broke out in the engine room, filling the boat with a noxious smoke that, on top of the diesel fumes, caused several crew members to pass out.

By this time it was not just hard to breathe but hard to see; in some areas of the submarine, smoke had reduced visibility to less than a yard. Because Fehler's orders required *U-234* to remain submerged during this phase of the journey, he could not surface to evacuate the contaminated air. Acting upon an idea from Warrant Officer Winkelmann, the crew disconnected the *Schnorchel* from the diesel engines, which delivered surface air to the bow and stern compartments as the diesels drew their air from the contaminated atmosphere of the boat's interior.[88]

Winkelmann's idea helped the situation, but it did not eliminate the danger posed by the fumes and smoke. Fehler realized that he could not continue under these conditions, and after passing through the Iceland–Faeroe Islands straits, he surfaced for the first time in two weeks to rid his boat of the contaminants. The conning tower watch was greeted by the fury of the raging North Atlantic, whose cold waters poured through the open hatch into the already damp interior. Members of the watch chained themselves to the railing to keep from being swept away as a repair party struggled to remove the spoiled potatoes from the bow keel room and throw them overboard, thus freeing the bilge pumps. After an exhausting effort, the bilge was cleared, and *U-234* could once again operate under normal conditions.

On 2 May, at 60°21' N, 17°19' W, *U-234* was lurching through the violent seas of a North Atlantic spring storm when the emergency dive alarm shattered the relative quiet of the boat. The con watch, struggling to see through the blinding squall, had spotted a surface vessel in close proximity to *U-234*, bearing down on her position. Fehler ordered all ballast tanks blown in a crash dive, and as the submarine plunged into the icy depths, she barely missed having her conning tower sucked into the wake of the surface vessel's screws. Because the watch could not positively identify the vessel as a belligerent, Fehler took no chances and sent *U-234* plunging to a safe depth of 100 feet. After a suitable wait he concluded, from the absence of enemy depth charges, that either the vessel had not detected *U-234* or was not an enemy warship.[89] In any case, *U-234* returned to her regular cruising depth of 80 feet and continued her voyage south.

Fehler's orders called for him to proceed submerged through the North Atlantic by way of the Iceland-Faeroes strait. However, Hirschfeld soon discovered that the preset course would guide the submarine through a shallow area known as the Rosengarten, which U-boats were advised to avoid at all costs.[90] The Rosengarten was actually a shoal extending from Iceland south to the Shetland Islands, which had posed both advantages and disadvantages for German submariners. During the early years of the war, submarine commanders would take advantage of the 150-foot depth of the Rosengarten by resting their boats on its soft sand bottom during particularly stormy periods at sea. However, as the war progressed and the Allies tightened their control of the northern Atlantic, the Rosengarten became infamous as an area into which returning Allied aircraft would drop their remaining bombs, perhaps in hope that an errant U-boat skipper would be using the area to rest his boat before entering the North Sea.[91] Because the Iceland-Faeroes passage was a favorite of U-boats sortieing from Norway, Allied antisubmarine forces kept the Rosengarten under close observation, and many U-boat skippers chose to avoid the area by returning to Norway via the ice border of eastern Greenland and western Denmark.[92]

Hirschfeld warned Fehler that they were rapidly approaching this area, but Fehler, distrustful of electronic navigation, dismissed Hirschfeld's concerns. To convince Fehler of his instruments' reliability, Hirschfeld used a primitive form of sonar known as an echo sounder, and its subsequent indication of changing depth persuaded Fehler to alter his course, proceeding on the surface until he cleared the Rosengarten, then heading south into the Atlantic. This change in course would soon prove significant.

On 4 May, with *U-234* at 59°65' N, 19°24' W, Hirschfeld informed Fehler that he had received a signal ordering all U-boats at sea to cease fire, and for attack boats to return to Norway. Because *U-234* was not an attack boat, Fehler disregarded the order and proceeded on his mission. Hirschfeld next received word to tune to a special frequency for "a message of the utmost importance."[93] However, the chief radioman discovered that *U-234* had been given incorrect frequency tables, and he therefore could not identify the special frequency. Early on 8 May, Radioman Second Class Werner Bachmann finally succeeded in locating the designated frequency, and *U-234* received the following:

> All U/B's including East Asia U/B's and Fehler (234) are to cease warlike activities immediately. Begin return cruise unobserved. Absolute secrecy is to be maintained. . . . On return cruise avoid all possibilities for attack by A/S groups.
> ComSubs West[94]

Later on the evening of 8 May, Hirschfeld picked up a message addressed to Fehler and broadcast in the Japanese cipher. In an eyes-only message, the FdU in Bergen, Rösing, ordered Fehler either to continue to Japan or return to Bergen.[95] When Hirschfeld relayed the message to Fehler, the skipper stated that he was definitely not going back; instead, he ordered *U-234* south at full speed. Later that evening, however, the Reuters news agency reported that the Togo government of Japan had severed all relations with Germany, and as a consequence all German citizens in Japan were being arrested.[96] Amid the confusion and secrecy surrounding *U-234*'s mission, the lone area of consistency had been Japanese solidarity, however self-interested. Now, that surety had been cast to the wind, and Fehler found himself facing a command dilemma of exactly what to do next.

3

The
Problem
of Surrender

ON 10 MAY 1945 Fehler received the Allied order for all U-boats to proceed to specified ports to surrender. However, *U-234*'s unique mission rendered her capitulation a matter of consequence beyond normal parameters. During the planning stages of the mission, the possibility of Germany's capitulation had not been ignored; Fehler had taken the matter into consideration while still in Kiel.

In February, during a courtesy visit, General Kessler and Fehler discussed the possibility of Germany's surrender while *U-234* was at sea. They agreed that the men of *U-234* "possibly were among the very few Germans who, after the foreseeable defeat of their country, might be able to take their fate into their own hands." Moreover, *U-234* was laden with fuel, food, and provisions for a lengthy voyage; a diversion from internment to a neutral country was a viable option. Assessing the impending postwar situation in Europe, Fehler concluded that "East and West most certainly would start quarreling over the German carcass, the outcome of [which] quarrel we might be able to outstay."[1] Faced with the reality of surrender, Fehler determined that time was on his side and decided to postpone an immediate decision, pending a meeting with his officers to enlist their opinions.

Fehler convened a meeting of *U-234*'s officers and passengers in the officer's wardroom to inform everyone of the capitulation as well as to entertain opinions as to which course to pursue. A lengthy discussion ensued, but Fehler decided that the ideas put forward were not well thought out. He therefore dismissed the meeting and informed the participants that they would reconvene in twenty-four hours, after they had had time to consider the options and could make informed decisions.

During the next meeting a consensus was reached, albeit regarding only where not to go and what not to do. Because of the number of U-boats at sea, the Allies had divided the North Atlantic into control grids and assigned each grid a capitulation port; *U-234*'s designated point of surrender was Halifax, Nova Scotia. However, her position was on the dividing line between the areas designated for surrender to American and British authorities, a fact that prompted considerable discussion as to which course to follow.[2]

Richard Bulla and Karl Pfaff suggested sailing to an island in the South Pacific, while Wolfgang Hirschfeld felt that the best course was to obey Rösing's order and either return to Bergen or continue to Japan. Kay Nieschling and *U-234*'s doctor, Franz Walter, were united in their desire for immediate surrender to the Americans.[3] Other suggestions included surrender to Britain or Canada or asylum in a neutral country such as Ireland or Spain.

General Kessler apparently wanted to sail to either Argentina or Uruguay, where his oldest son resided, and trade the submarine and "whatever other personal property items the others had," presumably for their freedom.[4] In addition, Kessler pointed out that von Sandrart had resided in Argentina for eighteen years; between his acquaintances and Kessler's son, there would be ample sources of asylum.[5] Fehler later testified that although Argentina had declared war on Germany and therefore might not be so friendly, it probably would have been possible to carry out the general's proposal.[6] However, although the *U-234* cargo included "things that might have been scientifically interesting to the Argentineans," Fehler pointed out that "they could not have used them."[7]

Still undecided as to what to do, Fehler once more gathered his officers, as well as General Kessler, to discuss the alternatives. He listened to "all kinds of strange and childish plans" and weighed the fact that they "had 480 cubic meters of oil and supplies for five months, [which was] awfully tempting." Fehler finally decided that he "owed it to [the] crew to at least get them home alive." Given the Allied announcement that renegade submarines would be sunk on sight if they did not comply with the surrender order, he thus decided to surrender rather than seek asylum.[8]

Fehler's decision did not go unchallenged. General Kessler continued to besiege him with ideas for avoiding surrender, plans that the skipper thought were "totally insane [and] would have failed anyway." Fehler considered the Argentina proposal for quite a while; however, a wireless message from Grand Admiral Dönitz pleaded with U-boat commanders to comply with the surrender order, and in the process save the lives of one hundred thousand Germans in the eastern part of the country who would otherwise be imperiled by the onrushing Red Army. Fehler later confessed to fellow prisoner Thilo Bode that this order from Dönitz persuaded him to comply; otherwise he would not have surrendered but would have opted instead to "go ashore somewhere with the crew."[9]

Fehler and his officers reached the consensus that they should avoid the British and Canadians, who might turn the crew and officers over to the French, and take their chances with the Americans.[10] This decision, however, presented yet another dilemma: two passengers on board U-234 were Japanese nationals, citizens of a country that remained at war with the United States.

Lt. Cdr. Tomonaga Hideo was a naval aviator, military observer, and submarine specialist who had traveled extensively throughout Germany. Lt. Shoji Genzo, also an aircraft specialist, had formerly served as the naval attaché at several Japanese embassies throughout Europe and had reportedly been last stationed in Italy and Sweden.[11] Both officers were considered honorable men who embodied the samurai spirit; it was because of their reputations that they had been selected to escort U-234's precious cargo, already paid for by the Japanese government, to Japan. With this in mind, Fehler wondered how the pair would react to his surrender decision, and what actions, if any, they would take to ensure the success of their mission.

Tomonaga Hideo had received his military and technical training in Tokyo. As a student in ship construction at the Imperial University of Tokyo, he was tabbed by the Imperial Japanese Navy to become a construction technician. Upon receiving his commission in 1932, Tomonaga further honed his shipbuilding skills at a naval artillery school, becoming proficient in the area of submarine construction. The young lieutenant gained fame with his invention of a submarine buoyancy compensator, which automatically held a submerged boat to negative buoyancy and thus made the once-difficult task of trimming a submarine at depth easier for the crew. This invention caught the attention of the German navy, which requested Tomonaga's services, and consequently in 1943 he was ordered to Europe aboard the Japanese submarine I-29.[12]

In Germany, Tomonaga was admired and respected for his proficiency in submarine matters. Japanese naval attaché Kojima once commented that Tomonaga "was always treated specially by the German Navy and his requests to visit sites were always granted unconditionally." Tomonaga was an expert at combining the theoretical technical aspects of submarines with actual combat data, and he was instrumental in obtaining and transmitting to Japan detailed data on Germany's new high-speed submarines. Tomonaga admired German construction methods and cooperated closely with German engineers in the design and construction of U-boat prototypes, including the equipping of the new Type IXC/40 *U-501* (Förster), which at that time was considered the outstanding German U-boat.[13] The Germans admired Tomonaga's expertise; his superiors in Japan considered him indispensable.

By 1945 the Japanese navy had suffered the loss of two of its primary submarine designers, Commander Nemot and Captain Arima—ironically, aboard German submarines.[14] In response to the worsening war situation, the Japanese Naval Ministry ordered Kojima to send Tomonaga back to Japan. Kojima, who had been instrumental in effecting Kessler's transfer to Japan, considered the submarine the safest way to return Tomonaga to Japan; hence, in January 1945 Tomonaga received his official recall to return, departing in March from Kiel aboard *U-234*.[15]

Shoji Genzo's early career mirrored Tomonaga's. Shoji attended the Imperial University in Tokyo, majoring in aeronautics, and upon graduation in 1929 was selected by the Japanese navy as a weapons officer. After his basic indoctrination Shoji was transferred to the naval arsenal at Hiro, where he helped in the development of the Nakajima Type 95 and Type 91 seaplanes. Recognized for his proficiency in aeronautical technology, he was later promoted to a position in the Naval Institute for Aeronautical Technology.[16]

In March 1938, as part of Japan's increasing attempts to form an alliance with the European Axis, Shoji was transferred to Italy as a representative of Japanese weapons systems. In Italy he formed close working relationships with several contacts who supplied him with technical information, which he in turn transferred to Japan. In addition, Shoji became involved in Italian research into the development of turboprop aircraft engines, and he was successful in sending detailed drawings of the prototypes to Japan.[17]

Shoji's devotion to his work was legendary. During the summer of 1944 he worked tirelessly to obtain the drawings and technical information for the Italian Caproni rocket engine, as well as the successful Italian midget submarines. Vice Admiral Abe noted that during this time Shoji offered valuable suggestions for improvements to the projects, and whether his ideas were acknowledged, pilfered by rival designers, or ignored, he worked diligently, "forgetting food and sleep . . . and finally succeeded in obtaining manufacturing plans for them."[18]

In August 1944 Shoji was transferred to Berlin, where he was to wait until his scheduled recall to Japan aboard the first available submarine. While in Berlin, Shoji assisted the Japanese inspector, investigating the methods of volume production of Henschel aircraft and Messerschmitt rocket planes. In December he once again moved, this time to the office of the Japanese attaché in Sweden, Vice Admiral Abe. While in Sweden, Shoji assisted the Japanese mission by obtaining technical intelligence until February 1945, at which time he left for Berlin to receive his orders to return to Japan.[19]

In February 1945 both Tomonaga and Shoji were awaiting final arrangements for their return voyage when they received orders to leave Sweden and report to Berlin. The order was urgent, reflecting Kojima's desire to rush the pair onto *U-234*, whose passenger list had already been revised in response to the protests of its commander, Fehler. In addition, the importance of *U-234*'s cargo to the Japanese war effort made an escort not only desirable but necessary. Tomonaga and Shoji stayed but for a brief time in Berlin, mainly receiving instruction and descriptions of *U-234*'s cargo and mission. In addition to accompanying the boat and her cargo to Tokyo, the officers were charged with delivering secret diplomatic and military correspondence. Once fully briefed, they traveled to the Lehrte train station to await their transport to Kiel. While waiting, Tomonaga gave his escort, Nagamori Yoshio, his wife's address and asked his friend to contact her to ease her worry. Tomonaga also confided to Nagamori that the Japanese fleet doctor, a Dr. Kobayashi, had given Shoji and himself sleeping tablets, to be used in "a worst-case scenario."[20]

Fehler recognized the problem that the surrender order presented for his Japanese passengers, and he kept news of the surrender from the pair for several days while he decided how best to approach them. After his initial meeting with his own officers concerning *U-234*'s situation, Fehler met with Tomonaga and Shoji, for whom the consequences of surrender were far greater than for the Germans aboard. Fehler explained the recent political and diplomatic estrangement between Germany and Japan, expressed his personal reservations about continuing on to Tokyo, and frankly revealed to the Japanese officers that he did not know exactly what to do.[21] Shoji responded by giving his own personal assurance that the crew of *U-234* would not be imprisoned once in Japan.[22] Fehler, however, had little faith in the Japanese government and requested that Tomonaga and Shoji consider themselves internees and remain in their quarters.

In retrospect Fehler's decision to imprison the Japanese passengers under these stressful circumstances may appear cruel, but as usual, *U-234*'s skipper was acting from caution and foresight. Fehler knew that *U-234*'s valuable cargo had already been bought and paid for by the Japanese government,[23] and that the submarine herself would be turned over to the Japanese as a gift upon their arrival. Consequently, Japanese officials considered *U-234* and her cargo possessions of the Japanese empire, which reserved the right to determine *U-234*'s fate. This factor took on added significance in light of Tomonaga's expertise as a submarine engineer; the brilliant Japanese officer would have little trouble scuttling the submarine, if necessary, to prevent the cargo from falling into enemy hands. Although both Japanese officers had assured Fehler that no harm would come to either his boat or his crew, Fehler decided to gamble on the side of caution, as the situation aboard *U-234* was explosive enough without the Japanese moving about under suspicion.

For his part, Fehler promised Tomonaga and Shoji that he would do everything in his power to prevent their capture by the Americans.[24] Although Fehler was struck by their composure, he nonetheless attempted to console them by citing the surrender of Japanese military attaché Oshima in Berlin as an example of capitulation without disgrace. However, Kessler pointed out that no Japanese officer of the samurai class could accept surrender before death, and it was his belief that Tomonaga and Shoji would try to prevent the boat's surrender by any means. They could easily escape from their confinement if they so pleased; drowsy from the effects of foul air and dim light, the guards assigned to watch them tended to doze off. As a result, it was agreed that Fritz von Sandrart, who shared a space adjacent to the pair and had become quite friendly with them, should speak privately with them to express the concerns of the Germans.

Von Sandrart wasted no time with formalities and quickly revealed his concerns to Tomonaga and Shoji. They appreciated his honesty and reciprocated by admitting that they had entertained plans to scuttle the submarine, destroying the boat and everything aboard her. However,

Tomonaga explained that the comradeship and goodwill shown to them by the German officers and crew had deeply affected them; Shoji was particularly touched by the extreme concern the Germans had shown for the safety of their families. Consequently, neither Tomonaga nor Shoji could bring himself to destroy the boat and her inhabitants. Von Sandrart was impressed by this demonstration of "astounding human greatness."[25] Once again the pair gave their word that no harm would befall *U-234* through their agency, and this time Fehler relieved their guard.

On the evening of 13 May, Tomonaga and Shoji moved about the submarine and distributed watches and clocks, which they had bought for their families in Switzerland, to the crew in appreciation for the Germans' kindness and comradeship.[26] After visiting with the crew for a time, they returned to their cabin for the night. Later, Nieschling reported to Fehler that there was something wrong with the Japanese passengers; they were breathing in a labored manner and couldn't be wakened. Tomonaga and Shoji, evidently having determined that their situation was indeed a worst-case scenario, had ingested a lethal amount of Luminal, the drug given to them by the Japanese fleet doctor prior to their departure from Germany. Fehler instructed his medical officer to make every attempt to revive them; however, two hours had elapsed since the ingestion of the drug, and its effects were now irreversible.[27] A letter in an envelope, addressed to Fehler and attached to the pillow on Tomonaga's bunk, explained that the pair had become worried upon hearing the increased revolutions of *U-234*'s screws, which they had interpreted as a sign that Fehler was expediting his search for a port of surrender. Obviously they had lost faith in Fehler's promise to land them at a neutral site, although Fehler later claimed that he had intended to deliver the pair, had they lived, to Spain or the Canary Islands.[28]

In their suicide letter Tomonaga and Shoji explained their decision to die by informing Fehler that "as soldiers of the Emperor we are not permitted to fall alive into enemy hands. . . . We feel that a concern for our future may be embarrassing to you in the decisions that you have to make."[29] They expressed their appreciation for the crew's hospitality and told Fehler of their regrets that "because of fate . . . it [is necessary] for us to separate ourselves from you and your boat." They asked of Fehler, "Let us die quietly. Bury our corpses in the high seas. . . . Inform Japan as soon as possible [that] Commander Genzo Shoji [and] Commander Hideo Tomonaga committed suicide on . . . May 1945 on board *U-234*."[30] Also included was a personal request that Fehler inform Tomonaga's and Shoji's relatives in Japan that "we are dead, but have not disgraced ourselves in dying."[31]

Fehler now had no choice but to dispose of the bodies. On the night of 14 May the bodies of Hideo Tomonaga and Genzo Shoji, along with their secret papers and Tomonaga's samurai sword, were wrapped in a canvas hammock, sewn up, and buried with full military honors at sea.[32]

The deaths of Tomonaga and Shoji did not fade from the memories of those who knew them. Fehler was haunted for years by guilt over his failure to accommodate one of their last wishes. Despite their request that he notify their families of their deaths, Fehler could not risk breaking radio silence, and therefore did not notify Japan or Germany regarding his Japanese passengers' fate. He later regretted this omission and confided, "I could have sent a wireless."[33] The postwar naval attaché to Japan, Capt. Hans Joachim Krug, wrote, "My soul keeps hurting that [Fehler] knew so little about the Japanese soul and [the] deeply troubling struggle of conscience of [Tomonaga and Shoji]. . . . He could have put the two Japanese officers on a rubber raft off the coast of a neutral country . . . before he surrendered to the Allied forces."[34]

After the war General Kessler recalled the two Japanese officers for Admiral Kojima, stating that "Tomonaga and Shoji were excellent naval officers and gained the trust of the commander and all crew members."[35] Today, at the U-Boat Memorial in Kiel, Germany, two wooden plaques honor the memory of Tomonaga Hideo and Shoji Genzo. The markers, which give the date of the Japanese officers' deaths as 13 May 1945, are attached to a U-boat ensign mast, adorned with the ancient Germanic rune for life.

The deaths of Tomonaga and Shoji were a personal tragedy for Fehler, who genuinely liked the pair. Nevertheless, he was now relieved of the problem of preventing their capture by the Americans and dealing with their possible opposition to his decision to surrender. He could now redirect his attention to the business of formally surrendering his command.

As in other events of World War II, intelligence played an important, albeit somewhat unappreciated, role in the fate of *U-234*. Not only were the Allies aware of Fehler's presence at sea, they also had a good idea of the contents and passengers aboard the submarine. In late January in Kiel, Bulla and Fehler had listened as Allied propagandists announced, "You have a long trip ahead of you . . . and so have General Kassler [*sic*] and the rest of your passengers."[36] In addition, upon the Kriegsmarine's postponement of *U-234*'s departure until 28 February, the Soldatensender Calais, an Allied propaganda transmitter, publicly informed Fehler of the change scarcely hours after he had received the order. While von Sandrart recalled that the loading docks at Kiel and Kristiansand were rife with intrigue and crawling with suspected spies, Fehler suspected the Naval High Command of harboring a traitor. However, Allied knowledge of *U-234*'s mission came primarily not from spies and traitors but from official German and Japanese sources.

By 1945 the Allies had become adept at decrypting Japanese and German diplomatic and naval radio traffic. As a result, Allied codebreakers knew as early as 13 January that Kessler planned to travel to Japan by air via the northern route over Siberia.[37] However, the flight was contingent on the approval of the Japanese, who preferred that Kessler travel by sea via a southern route to avoid damaging relations with the Soviets.[38] By the end of the month Kessler, who preferred air travel, had acquiesced to conveyance by submarine, although Allied intelligence did not yet know by which boat he and his entourage would be traveling.[39]

The presence of Ulrich Kessler was not the only aspect of *U-234* that was of interest to the Allies. On 26 February the German chief inspector in Berlin cabled his counterpart in the Bureau of Military Preparations that the manufacturing-rights negotiations between Japan and Germany had been completed. The immediate result of this agreement was the allocation of manufacturing rights for Japanese production of the BMW 109-003A power unit, the Jumo 004 turbojet engine, the Schneider Panzerfaust and ammunition, and, most important, the Messerschmitt 163 and 262 jet aircraft. To facilitate prompt shipment of the Messerschmitt prototypes, the shipment of lot numbers 12719-1 (ME 163) and 12719-2 (ME 262) would be divided into three parcels, with each proceeding to Japan via submarine.[40]

By early spring, Kessler's means of transportation was known, as well as the likely carrier for the Messerschmitt aircraft. On 8 March, Allied intelligence intercepted a message from the commander of submarines in Berlin to the Naval Attaché's Office in Tokyo stating that two submarines would soon be en route to Japan, *U-234* (Fehler) and *U-876* (Bahn), departing Germany in March and April, respectively.[41] Eventually the details of Kessler's departure also became clear. A 23 April diplomatic intercept acknowledged that Kessler was "proceeding to Japan by submarine," though Allied intelligence had no information regarding the departure of either *U-234* or *U-876* from Kiel. However, on 3 May, Allied intelligence decoded a 14 April German Admiralty message, which disclosed that Kessler, along with "two members of his party . . . one an expert in aerial defense [and] the other in radar and radio-controlled weapons," had left Europe in late March aboard *U-234*. Furthermore, the decrypt revealed that, in addition to Kessler and the two experts, "five German naval officers . . . two German civilian engineers . . . and two Japanese naval officers" were also aboard.[42] As a result, by 13 May both the Americans and the Canadians knew full well the implications of *U-234*'s capture.

Fehler was determined that if he had to surrender, it would be to the Americans. However, the Allies had designated distinct zones of surrender for U-boats at sea, and *U-234*'s present location placed Fehler in the British zone near the dividing line between the British and American sectors. He needed time to maneuver south and west to the American sector, which was located within an area designated by coordinates 43°30' N, 70°00' W, and 38°20' N, 74°25' W.[43] In addition, Fehler remained suspicious of Allied directives for U-boats to surrender, especially since no word had been received from the Kriegsmarine or any German authority.[44] However, time was running out for *U-234;* a week after the general surrender was announced, the Allies released a message to all U-boats: "Whoever does not capitulate now will be treated as a pirate and put on trial."[45] Although no specific Allied country claimed responsibility for the message, Hirschfeld deduced, from the operator's key mannerisms, that it was of British origin. Reaffirming his desire to steer clear of the British and Canadians, Fehler decided to attempt to buy time by engaging his pursuers in a seagoing game of cat and mouse.

Previously, on 13 May, Fehler had ordered Hirschfeld to release a signal to the Allied monitoring station at Halifax, stating simply, "Halifax: Here is *U-234*."[46] The Canadians responded by requesting *U-234*'s position and then, once that had been established, providing a course for the boat to steer for Nova Scotia. In addition, Fehler received instructions to report his speed and course at regular intervals. However, while Fehler had no intention of surrendering to the Canadians, he did intend to satisfy the Halifax station, albeit marginally, by sending falsified position and speed figures. As a result, while Halifax believed that *U-234* was sailing due west to Nova Scotia, Fehler was actually proceeding full speed on a southwesterly bearing that would allow the submarine to enter the American sector.

Fehler's attempt to reach the American zone of surrender resembled a game of hide and seek. On 14 May, confused by the position discrepancies resulting from Fehler's falsified speed and course bearings, the frustrated Canadians now ordered Fehler to report his position hourly rather than daily.[47] He ignored this request, leaving the Canadians to spend the afternoon frantically calling for *U-234*. Fehler finally decided to satisfy Halifax's curiosity and allowed Hirschfeld to acknowledge their signals. However, when Hirschfeld attempted to respond, he discovered that his heretofore clear transmission was being purposely disrupted by an unknown source.[48] Halifax radioed that it was being jammed and ordered *U-234* to change to another frequency. Pursuant to the request, Hirschfeld had Petty Officer Bachmann adjust his wireless to the new frequency, only to have the new signal interrupted as well. Obviously the interference was deliberate, and when Fehler was notified of the problem, he ordered the set shut down, stating, "That's our reason for not reporting in."[49]

The interruption of *U-234*'s signal, coupled with rough seas, bought Fehler the time he needed and allowed him to turn his attention to the problem of how to contact any American ships that might be in the area. Hirschfeld soon relieved his commander of this burden: the chief radioman discovered the origin of the mysterious interference through a strong, clear signal from a source that identified itself as an American warship, the USS *Sutton*.[50]

For the USS *Sutton* (DE-771), antisubmarine warfare (ASW) patrol had been a matter of numbing monotony, with months spent combing the icy depths of the North Atlantic with acoustic devices in hopes of locating an enemy submarine that had ventured too close to North America. To many, ASW duty seemed a waste of time; however, on 14 May the boredom was shattered as ASW squadrons bustled into activity at the announcement of Germany's surrender. Cautious officials of the First Naval District in Boston realized that any U-boats then at sea could either obey Grand Admiral Dönitz's order to surrender or continue their hopeless undersea war as rogues. Either way, the U.S. Navy would be equipped to handle the situation: the Atlantic Fleet had suffered extreme embarrassment during the early months of American involvement in World War II, as German submarines operated with impunity along America's Eastern Seaboard, and naval officials in Boston were determined that they would not be caught unprepared again. Consequently, squadrons of newly commissioned destroyer escorts were plying the waters of the North Atlantic, uncertain whether their war with Germany was actually over. At the center of this whirlwind of confusion was the USS *Sutton*.

Named after Ens. Shelton B. Sutton, who perished when the heavy cruiser USS *Juneau* was sunk at Guadalcanal in 1942, the *Sutton* was one of the relatively new vessels designed with the requirements of antisubmarine warfare in mind. Her keel was laid on 23 August 1943 at the Tampa Shipbuilding Yards in Tampa, Florida, and work was completed by 6 August 1944. After outfitting and initial trials, the *Sutton* was commissioned on 22 December 1944 and placed under the command of Lt. Thomas W. Nazro.

On 12 January 1945 the *Sutton* sailed to her initial area of operations near Bermuda; however, this assignment was more the result of the requirement that she complete her shakedown cruise than of any pressing need to combat German submarines in the area. After brief stops at the Boston Navy Yard for repairs and Casco Bay, Maine, for ASW training, the *Sutton* was assigned to Escort Division 79, Task Group 22.13, and arrived at her home base of Argentia, Newfoundland, on 1 March. She conducted antisubmarine patrols in the Newfoundland area until the end of March and then returned to Casco Bay, where she joined the North-South ASW Barrier Patrol.[51]

While there had been a noticeable decrease in U-boat activity near the North American Atlantic coast, it had not completely disappeared; as many as nine submarines had been sunk in the Eastern Sea Frontier during April and May 1945.[52] To effect coverage of the area, American and Canadian naval forces combined to patrol the Atlantic coast, and upon Germany's surrender, both sought to claim the U-boats as war prizes. Because there had been a number of German surrender requests received by naval officials, both navies expected ample opportunity to capture and escort the prizes back to Argentia. By 11 May, Task Group 22.13 had employed nine American and Royal Canadian vessels in search of German submarines: the USS *Pillsbury* (DE-133), *Pope* (DE-134), *Otter* (DE-210), *Varian* (DE-798), *Vance* (DE-387), and *Neal A. Scott* (DE-769) and HMCS *Buckingham* and *Incharron*, in addition to the *Sutton*.[53]

On 9 May the *Sutton* and *Neal A. Scott* were relieved from patrol duty to intercept *U-1228* (Marienfeld), which had indicated her desire to surrender. The next day, en route to the designated rendezvous point, the *Sutton* and *Scott* unexpectedly encountered *U-858* (Bode) at 42°00' N, 53°08' W, and subsequently accepted her surrender; this was the first German submarine surrender to Allied forces subsequent to Germany's capitulation. After turning *U-858* over to the *Pillsbury* and *Pope*, the *Scott* and *Sutton* resumed the hunt for *U-1228*, which they eventually located several hundred miles off Newfoundland at 47°45' N, 44°45' W.[54] The two escorts accompanied *U-1228* to Casco Bay, where Nazro held the German boat under his guns as the *Scott*'s boarding party secured the vessel.[55]

On 12 May, at 1245, Nazro received CINCLANT (commander-in-chief, Atlantic) Order 121322, which instructed the *Sutton* to proceed to 50°00'

N, 30°00' W, and intercept *U-234*, which was proceeding on course 260 at 8 knots, presumably for Bay Bulls, Newfoundland.[56] By 1702 the *Sutton* had departed Casco Bay and was racing to those coordinates through heavy seas along the northern route. Although Nazro had been ordered to expedite his departure, he had to exercise caution, as the northern route was quite hazardous; indeed, at 1919 Nazro ordered his gunner's mates to open fire on an iceberg looming off the *Sutton*'s starboard bow. The *Sutton* expended four .50-caliber and twenty-three 40-millimeter rounds until the obstruction was obliterated.[57] Although Nazro encountered no other icebergs large enough to require gunfire to dissipate, reports of fog, squalls, and heavy seas accompanied the *Sutton* as she made her way through the North Atlantic.

The *Sutton* was not alone. On 12 May the First Naval District in Boston notified the assistant commandant for operations that, regarding *U-234*, "several vessels, both Canadian and American, are now presumed to be racing to take this prize."[58] Upon receipt of *U-234*'s last PCS (position-course-speed) report, Canadian authorities dispatched two ships, HMCS *Waskesieu* and *Lauxon*, to intercept the submarine prior to notifying CINCLANT of the message. In response, in addition to releasing the *Sutton* from her duty with the *Scott* with instructions to intercept *U-234*, CINCLANT also alerted the weather ships USS *Milledgeville* and *Forsythe*, which were already "presumed to have been racing the Canadian ships to make the interception." On 14 May, Halifax received another contact with *U-234* and, assuming that the contact was exclusive, sought to guarantee Canadian interception of the submarine by dispatching two additional Canadian escort vessels.[59] However, these were Fehler's bogus position reports, and they succeeded in directing the Canadians yet further away from their quarry. In all, as many as seven vessels were searching the North Atlantic for *U-234*.

Nazro recognized that the race for *U-234* was now an international matter, with dangerous potential should the convergence of several ships of different countries upon a single target get out of hand. Aware that Fehler was in contact with Halifax, Nazro ordered the Canadian radio traffic jammed while the *Sutton*'s navigator used the interference to locate *U-234* and determine her course. Once *U-234*'s bearings were established, Nazro dashed any hopes his Canadian counterparts might have harbored for capturing *U-234* by ordering the Germans to ignore any instruction from Halifax and proceed along a southwesterly course to the Gulf of Maine.[60]

The Canadians, who had maintained close proximity to the *Sutton*, were now confused by the sudden static in a heretofore clear signal and could only steer to the original position that *U-234* had reported to Halifax. During the afternoon the *Sutton* intercepted a communication between the two Canadian ships that revealed that the Canadians were undecided as to which course to follow, and that "a state of chaos reign[ed] at the Admiralty."[61] Continuing due east to a position Fehler had long since abandoned, the *Waskesieu* and *Lauxon* eventually had to admit that they had missed their target. Nazro, heading southwest to *U-234*'s actual position, radioed that when last heard from the Canadians were disappearing on an easterly course bearing 075°. Satisfied that his competitors were searching for a ghost vessel, Nazro turned his attention to the task at hand, adjusting the *Sutton*'s bearing to an intercept course and proceeding at flank speed.[62]

At 2024 the *Sutton*'s radar officer reported a contact at 18,000 yards, and at 2141 the contact was at last intercepted and identified as *U-234*.[63] The *Sutton* closed on the submarine, but in view of the late hour, Nazro decided to escort his captive for the remainder of the night. At 0800 on 15 May, Nazro assembled and addressed the *Sutton*'s prize crew, reminding his men, "This is the enemy so don't stand for any fooling around. . . . On the other hand, don't forget that they have surrendered to us. Good luck."[64] Meanwhile, as the prize crew deployed to *U-234* in whaleboats, the German crew of *U-234* began to jettison those items they considered too valuable to fall into American hands. Hirschfeld disposed of *U-234*'s secret documents and *Kriegstagebuch* (war diary) by stuffing them into a garbage bag, which he hid in the diesel compartment, while Heinz Schlicke joined Fehler on *U-234*'s bridge and tossed several rolls of microfilm overboard.[65] Fehler, although ordered not to do so, also jettisoned his acoustic torpedoes and sent them to the bottom.[66]

At 0823, Lt. (jg) Franklin Gates, commanding officer of *Sutton*'s boarding party, boarded *U-234* and presented Fehler with a letter outlining the procedure whereby the German commander was to surrender his boat. Subsequently, at 1100, at 47°07' N, 42°25' W, World War II finally ended for *U-234* as Johann Heinrich Fehler formally surrendered his submarine to the USS *Sutton*.[67] Gates recalled that as Fehler accepted the provisions of the surrender order, "there were tears in his eyes when he saw the Stars and Stripes flying from the periscope of his ship."[68] Gates and his crew worked quickly, and by 1052 all thirty-seven prisoners of war had left the submarine.[69]

With most of the German crew dispatched as POWs to the *Sutton*, Gates and his crew began to prepare the submarine for the journey to Portsmouth, New Hampshire. Fehler had been ordered to leave a German skeleton crew to operate the submarine, and Bulla remained as the ranking German officer. Gates ordered Bulla to prepare to make way, and as the diesels came to life, Gates posted his watches. Those members of the party who were not engaged in watch duty were dispatched throughout the submarine to jettison small arms and ammunition.

At 1640, while performing an ammunition check, the *Sutton*'s Radioman Third Class Monroe E. Konnemann was accidentally shot in the right buttock by discharged small-arms fire. Konnemann's injury was more serious than originally anticipated, and *U-234*'s medical officer, Dr. Franz Walter, offered to conduct a preliminary examination. Upon completing his examination, Walter informed Gates that Konnemann's abdomen was perforated and would require surgery. At 1750 the medical officer from the USS *Forsythe*, which had recently arrived to assist the *Sutton*, boarded *U-234* to help stabilize Konnemann, and he concurred with Walter's diagnosis. The next day, at 1835, as Konnemann was transferred to the *Forsythe* to undergo surgery, Bulla cynically remarked, "These Americans, when they can't shoot at us, they shoot at each other."[70] Konnemann died two weeks later.

On 15 May the *Sutton* radioed her 1130 position as 46°32' N, 45°20' W, and announced her intention to rendezvous with the Coast Guard surrender unit off Portsmouth around 1600 on the nineteenth. On 17 May the *Sutton* was joined by the *Muir* (DE-770) and *Carter* (DE-112) at 44°00' N, 55°00' W, and the three ships escorted *U-234* to Buoy Baker off Portsmouth Harbor. At 0700 on the nineteenth, the American entourage and *U-234* passed the Coast Guard station on the Isles of Shoals, due east of Portsmouth, where the *Sutton, Muir,* and *Carter* turned the submarine over to the surrender group, which was headed by the Coast Guard cutter *Argo.*[71]

On 3 May 1945 Lt. J. H. Taylor of the First Naval District in Boston notified the district's watch officers that the Eastern Sea Frontier had been designated the responsible agency for the surrender of German submarines. In accordance with the resulting plan of action, the U.S. Coast Guard assigned the cutter *Argo* to standby status in Portland, Maine, to accept all surrendering submarines for delivery to American ports. The *Argo* was instructed to deliver all captured enemy personnel to the Portsmouth Navy Yard, while the boats themselves were to be beached "in the vicinity of Scarboro, Maine."[72]

At 0851 on 19 May, Cdr. Alexander W. Moffat, the officer in tactical command (OTC) aboard the *Argo*, formally accepted *U-234* from the *Sutton* off the Isles of Shoals, which lie 10 miles from Portsmouth. Moffat's involvement signaled the importance of *U-234*. He was not the commanding officer of the *Argo;* during the surrender of the previous three U-boats, the commanding officer of the *Argo*, Lt. Charles E. Winslow, USCG, had acted as OTC. This time, however, Winslow had been asked to relinquish the limelight. On 12 May, Capt. Victor D. Herbster, assistant operational commandant of the First Naval District, had notified Winslow that he was being relieved of OTC duty in favor of Moffat. "You are not being replaced for any lack of confidence . . . in your ability to handle the situation," Herbster told Winslow; however, he explained, Moffat had experience handling "complications affecting publicity and red tape" and was being allowed to supervise the surrender of *U-234* because "the publicity angle of this . . . seems to be full of dynamite."[73]

Winslow's relief signaled that enemy personnel and machinery were not the only important aspects of *U-234*'s surrender; there were also political and publicity considerations. Because the war in Europe had ended, many naval personnel believed that their war was also over; any last chance of wartime advancement must be seized now. For the naval personnel of the First Naval District, *U-234* was the ideal vehicle for fame: no military organization during the war had garnered such notoriety as Dönitz's U-boats, and the individual who brought these sea wolves to justice would be hailed as a conquering hero. In the rush to claim a place in the *U-234* publicity campaign, Lt. Charles Winslow was cast aside, usurped by the chain of command.

The *Argo* continued to escort the submarine and shortly stood out of the entrance to Portsmouth Harbor, entering the harbor gate at 0918. By 0923, *U-234* was moored at a harbor buoy, her long voyage from Europe and war over at last.[74]

4

Portsmouth

As the *Argo*, with Johann Fehler and his crew and passengers secured in her hold, traversed the strait between the Isles of Shoals and Portsmouth, anticipation of *U-234*'s coming disrupted established arrival procedure for enemy submarines. In early May, anticipating the U-boat procession that would likely ensue upon Germany's surrender, the First Naval District in Boston, under the direction of the Office of the Chief of Naval Operations in Washington, began preparations to accommodate the legion of military, intelligence, and media personnel who would undoubtedly descend upon Portsmouth. The navy's arrangements for receiving the surrendered submarines proceeded according to plan for the initial group of U-boats. By 15 May, *U-805*, *U-873*, and *U-1228* had been escorted to Portsmouth by the *Argo*. However, on 19 May the last and largest of the U-boats would arrive, and in view of the intelligence potential of *U-234*'s cargo and personnel, standard arrangements for nonessential access, by both civilian and military personnel, would have to be reevaluated.

Throughout the war, Allied media played a major part in molding a national abhorrence of Germany. Since 1 September 1939, Americans had been inundated with tales of the brutal efficiency of the German military. A combination of fear and loathing of the German soldier, sailor, and airman had come to permeate the American consciousness. The nation's media now sought to exploit this attitude by embarking on a crusade to bring the German juggernaut to its knees through the power of the press. One of the enduring symbols of Germany's military proficiency was the U-boat corps. Predictably, as the U-boats began to capitulate in the spring of 1945, the fourth estate demanded, and was afforded, a front-row seat, particularly at the Portsmouth Navy Yard.

On 5 May, Capt. Victor D. Herbster, assistant commandant of the Northern Group, Eastern Sea Frontier, issued contingency orders, notifying the First Naval District that the Portsmouth Navy Yard would assume responsibility for carrying out "the plan and procedure for the acceptance of German submarines at Portsmouth."[1] In addition, Herbster directed that once the submarines were released from the custody of U.S. Navy destroyer escorts, the USCG *Argo* would assume military control of the surrendered submarines, detain the enemy officers and crew, and escort them to Portsmouth. Addressing the problem of media coverage, Herbster ordered that an auxiliary vessel be designated "for the purpose of affording facilities to the press to observe . . . surrender."[2] By 11 May, Herbster's orders had become operational, and Rear Adm. Felix Gygax, commandant of the First Naval District, advised Rear Adm. Thomas Winters, commandant of the Portsmouth Navy Yard, of the procedure whereby the navy was to accommodate and cooperate with the press.

That the Navy Department was aware of the public-relations value of the surrendered U-boats was evident in the provisions provided the press. On 11 May the commander of the Eastern Sea Frontier released a confidential cable to Gygax that quoted the secretary of the navy as desiring that "representative radio, press, and photo[graphic] agencies be permitted aboard naval vessels assigned rendezvous [with] surrendering enemy units."[3] Gygax subsequently informed Winters that Portsmouth was expected to provide "adequate facilities to permit [the] press coverage of the . . . historical events which may occur in this district." To ensure effective and expeditious liaison with the press, Lt. John Burke and Lt. Sargent Collier of the district Public Relations Office were to report to Portsmouth on 14 May to facilitate cooperation with the print and photographic media. Furthermore, Winters was to designate a "convenient space," complete with desks, chairs, and typewriters, to serve as a press room. This facility would also contain a sufficient number of telephones, from which media representatives were to be allowed to make both local and long-distance calls. Finally, Gygax requested that "arrangements be made to have small craft available to take the press . . . to the point where the surrendering submarines may anchor or moor, in ample time to cover the actual arrivals."[4] Meanwhile, aboard the *Argo,* commanding officer Lt. Charles Winslow was advised that "press representatives will be transferred at entrance [of harbor] to eighty-three footer . . . to follow submarine into harbor."[5]

The press responded to the navy's accommodations by flooding the navy yard with reporters. The base newspaper, the *Portsmouth Periscope,* reported that the arrival of the U-boats had brought forth "the largest congregation of newspapermen since . . . 1941," a throng of "two score newspaper and radiomen who [had] gathered to witness the first formal surrender of U-boats in New England waters."[6] To keep the numbers manageable, Lieutenants Burke and Collier were authorized to clear and segregate certain members of the press who would be allowed to venture to sea and witness the surrenders. Once this group was selected, they boarded the navy tug *Dekanisora,* under the command of Lt. Eldridge Linberry, and were ferried to the area where the *Argo* had assumed responsibility for the submarines.

The press enjoyed unprecedented access to a surrendering enemy; however, limits were imposed. In order to ensure simultaneous release of surrender stories, communication with shore facilities from the *Argo* was prohibited by media, naval, and Coast Guard personnel.[7] In addition, any photographs taken of the submarines from either naval ships or aircraft would have to be submitted to the public-relations officer for approval; to guarantee compliance with this standard, no member of the press was allowed aboard any naval aircraft that might encounter an enemy submarine.[8] However, once ashore at Portsmouth, newsmen enjoyed access to the new prisoners of war, although most of the Germans declined to talk.[9] Overall, the press arrangement served its purpose, resulting in favorable publicity for all agencies involved; however, the era of good feeling between naval officials and the press was soon to end, as *U-234* neared Portsmouth.

From information derived from the interception of German and Japanese messages, by 13 May, Office of Naval Intelligence (ONI) officials had ascertained that the nature of *U-234*'s cargo and passengers was too sensitive to risk disclosure by the media. Consequently, the commander of Task Group 2.1 was directed that although the press might interview the prisoners of all other surrendered submarines, they were not to be allowed access to the prisoners from *U-234* for interviews or photographs.[10] In addition, the results of the *Sutton*'s initial search of *U-234* had revealed that the submarine did indeed possess "a valuable cargo of plans and war materials."[11] On 15 May, Adm. Jonas B. Ingram, commander-in-chief of the Atlantic Fleet, aware that the free access of the press to prisoners at Portsmouth would compromise security, ordered that the prisoners of *U-234* be kept incommunicado until released to the custody of the Navy Department in Washington, D.C.[12]

The navy's decision to designate *U-234*'s surrender as classified was understandable. However, the lure of positive publicity proved too great to ignore. As a result, on 16 May, Secretary James V. Forrestal, along with Ingram, held a "now it can be told" news conference in Washington that all but destroyed the chances of keeping *U-234* shrouded in secrecy. During the news conference Ingram clearly played to the press, relating, in a "colorful recital," the story of the boat's "weird capture." Prompted by Forrestal, Ingram revealed that aboard *U-234*, which was "presumably heading for Japan," U.S. naval personnel had discovered "three major-generals of the Luftwaffe and the bodies of two dead Japanese," as well as "charts and huge piles of aviation equipment."[13]

Ingram's statements reflected a penchant for sensationalism rather than fact. Ingram called the Type XB *U-234* "the latest type [of submarine] developed by the Germans," completely ignoring the new Walter boats, the existence of which had been known to U.S. intelligence authorities for some time. Ingram's assertion that the *Sutton*'s prize crew had discovered three German generals and the bodies of two dead Japanese aboard the submarine was blatantly false: on 14 May, *Sutton* commander Nazro had notified the headquarters of the Eastern Sea Frontier, and subsequently CINCLANT, of the precise identities and ranks of *U-234*'s military contingent, as well as the fate of the Japanese passengers, whose "bodies had been disposed of prior to capture."[14] It is inconceivable that Forrestal, as secretary of the navy, and Ingram, as CINCLANT, would not have known the truth of the passengers' identities and fates; their "sensational disclosures" can only be attributed to a desire to garner publicity.[15]

Ingram's disclosure of the presence of high-ranking German officials aboard *U-234* seemed to validate existing rumors that Germany might be using its U-boats to evacuate fugitive government officials from the ruined Reich. American officials had some basis for this assumption; a 22 April 1945 Japanese diplomatic intercept revealed that Japanese minister to Switzerland Kase believed that "Hitler and other high-ranking Nazi leaders will try to escape at the last moment by [fleeing] to Japan."[16] The first notice of suspicion appeared on 17 May, when the *Boston Post* reported that "word . . . that the rich prize of prisoners was en route [to Japan] set off a hunt for disguised Nazi party chieftains" aboard the *U-873* (Steinhoff) and *U-805* (Bernadelli), which were already berthed at Portsmouth.[17] When subsequent evaluations of the captured crews of *U-873* and *U-805*, as well as *U-1228*, produced no evidence of fleeing party officials, the focus turned to *U-234*. According to an 18 May *Boston Post* headline, Ingram had ordered an extensive search initiated "in belief that Hitler and Himmler [were] now on the way to Japan." Ingram revealed that American intelligence officials had determined that the surrendered submarines at Portsmouth were "acting under definite orders" to divert American attention away from an additional Type XB submarine, which would be ferrying Hitler and Himmler to Japan.

Ingram's news conference, as well as reports that some personnel aboard *U-234* would be escorted to Washington upon arrival, gave rise to speculation as to the identity of *U-234*'s passengers. Most news agencies now dismissed Ingram's earlier assessments and assumed *U-234* to be carrying passengers "more important than [mere] generals of the air force as was first announced by the Navy."[18] As a result, *U-234*'s passengers were now rumored to include individuals ranging from Hitler himself to deposed German foreign minister Joachim von Ribbentrop, Reich Minister Martin Bormann, and ss chief Heinrich Himmler. Naval officials, however, refused to confirm or deny any such rumors, prompting the *Boston Herald* to diffuse the speculation somewhat by announcing that "reports this afternoon that Hitler might have been aboard . . . were given no credence in advances available tonight."[19] Still, the idea of escape by the masterminds of the Third Reich was impossible to dispel completely; while *U-234* herself might not have housed the fugitives, her mission was now interpreted as "a last effort to outfox the huge naval dragnet" that was supposedly searching for the phantom escape submarine.[20]

The media frenzy that erupted after Ingram's news conference had an immediate impact on the public-relations arrangements at Portsmouth. Whereas previous U-boat surrenders had been covered extensively by the press corps, at 1630 on 17 May, Lt. Cdr. Allan Keller, acting public-relations officer for the Eastern Sea Frontier in New York, contacted the First Naval District in Boston with the news that "Washington has put the lid back on the *U-234* . . . The decision was made by someone high up in the Navy Department." Anticipating the furor that would result from a press quarantine of *U-234*, Keller advised

Boston that he had vehemently argued the decision as "ridiculous in light of Ingram's publicity"; however, Washington's decision stood firm. As a result, Boston was instructed that "all press arrangements you have made . . . in Portsmouth are off." To relieve Eastern Sea Frontier commander Vice Adm. H. F. Leary and Portsmouth commanding officer Winters of the task of facing the irate media, "Washington will announce the ban."[21] However, Cdr. N. R. Collier, director of public relations at the First Naval District, sensed an impending publicity disaster and attempted to dissuade Washington from so severe a ban.

At 1700 Collier telephoned CINCLANT headquarters in Washington, speaking to Capt. George W. Campbell, deputy director of public relations for the Navy Department. Pleading his case, Collier explained that "elaborate arrangements had been made to run phone and radio lines," and that regardless of the press ban, the photographic media could easily photograph U-234's arrival from the nearby shore. Collier succeeded in persuading Campbell to advise CINCLANT that the press-ban decision should be modified "in [the] interest of good public press relations." Campbell phoned back at 1730 and informed Collier that CINCLANT had agreed to modify the press ban,[22] and on 18 May, Portsmouth received authorization to allow the media to cover the arrival of U-234 from small craft as they had with previous submarines. However, CINCLANT ordered that "no press interviews with the prisoners will be permitted" and "no press representatives will be permitted to go aboard the U-boat."[23]

During an 18 May phone conversation Captain Herbster, deputy commander of the Northern Group, discussed the confusion created by Ingram's comments with a Commodore Kurtz. Herbster told Kurtz, "The situation has gotten so now that I'm going up there [to Portsmouth] myself this afternoon and take over." Kurtz observed that "the trouble was that [Ingram's] interview made a hot story out if it. . . . As soon as he spilled all that stuff, it made [U-234] the hottest one of the bunch." Herbster's reply echoed what many officials must have been wondering: "I don't know—what the hell's [Ingram] playing for?" The problem now was that although the prisoners aboard the *Argo* could be effectively shielded from reporters and photographers, the skeleton crew still aboard U-234 who would be guiding the submarine into Portsmouth could not. Herbster's solution was to remove the skeleton crew from the sub onto a navy tug, ordering the tug skipper to prevent anybody from getting interviews with them. Kurtz's comment reflected the depth of Washington's concern: "There will be hell to pay if anyone gets talking to them." Once the German prisoners were at Portsmouth,

Herbster planned to guarantee security by "arrang[ing] such a line of guards that [the prisoners] are taken from the ship right smack into the bus and out."[24] As a result, although no reporter would be allowed to interview the U-234 crew, the entire media entourage would be present dockside to witness the prisoners' official arrival in the New World.

The treatment that the crew and passengers of U-234 received from the Americans proved unpredictable, often varying to the extreme. The officers and crew of the Sutton had maintained a strict but professional relationship with their captives, and by the end of their journey, captives and captors appeared to be on somewhat friendly terms.[25] However, after leaving the Sutton and boarding the Argo, the reception the Germans met with was less than cordial, and periodically violent.[26] On 19 May, the officers and crew of U-234 finally touching land as the Argo docked at Portsmouth on a pier uncharacteristically crowded with press correspondents, Fehler realized that he and his men were to be the subject of intense public scrutiny. Sensing the opportunity for notoriety in what can only be described as a carnival atmosphere, Argo commander Winslow stood at the top of the gangplank, heaping disdain upon the Germans as they disembarked. As Fehler prepared to leave the Argo, he confronted Winslow about the unprofessional, even cruel treatment his crew had received at the hands of Argo personnel; in contrast to the respect afforded them aboard the Sutton, he complained, once transferred to the Argo his officers and men had been treated like animals. Winslow, aware that reporters were hanging on every word that passed between the two commanders, responded by berating Fehler and his crew as "Nazi gangsters," then loudly ordering him to "get off my ship!"[27] Winslow's line became a standard tag among the covering newspapers, and in some the Argo commander was afforded hero status. For his part, Fehler was beginning to have regrets. He told Hirschfeld that he now believed it was a mistake to have surrendered to the Americans, a conviction he held for the remainder of his life.[28]

The potential intelligence value of U-234's passengers was not lost on the ONI personnel at Portsmouth, who had previously pondered whether Portsmouth was indeed the appropriate place to interrogate such valuable assets. On 15 May, Lt. (jg) M. T. Brunner alerted senior ONI officials in Washington of the confidential nature of the documents and passengers on the submarine and warned, "[It is] doubtful [that U-234's] personnel should be sent here."[29] However, subsequent directives instructed security personnel at Portsmouth to continue keeping the prisoners incommunicado for the time being.[30] So when *U-234* arrived at Portsmouth on 19 May, officials of the U.S. War Department and the ONI were waiting.

On 19 May *U-234*'s crew and passengers officially became U.S. prisoners of war, as Lt. Cdr. John Ives signed the acknowledgment of their transfer from the *Argo* to the custody of the Portsmouth Navy Yard.[31] As the prisoners left the *Argo,* they sensed the wrath of a public inflamed by four years of propaganda regarding the German role in World War II. Hirschfeld recalled that he and his compatriots were subjected to the abuse of "a hate-filled mob" flanking the "narrow avenue" that led to the prison buses. Thoroughly doused with spit and verbal abuse, Hirschfeld told Bulla that he, like Fehler, now harbored doubts as to the wisdom of surrendering to the Americans; Bulla concurred that "it would have been better to have given ourselves up to the Canadians."[32]

Once ashore, Hirschfeld and his colleagues were interned at the Portsmouth Naval Prison, where they were subjected to physical abuse by the prison staff, which, as Hirschfeld recalled, consisted of "naturalized Poles armed with wooden cudgels." Aboard the *Sutton* many of *U-234*'s personnel had been warned by U.S. naval officers about the army guards they would encounter at Portsmouth—"a gang of thieves" who would rob them of all they possessed. Hirschfeld recalled that he had been "astonished" to hear a U.S. officer speak of a sister service in such a manner; it was only later that he came to appreciate the warning. Once inside the prison, the prisoners were stripped of all personal effects, most of which they would never see again. Of all the personal belongings that Hirschfeld voluntarily surrendered to prison officials, only his pay book and telegraphist service book were ever returned.[33]

Large-scale looting of *U-234* and her crew was evident in Portsmouth, and it constituted a major problem for ONI officials. Official naval policy regarding the pilfering of enemy possessions had been outlined in a CNO (chief of naval operations) directive in 1942, which stated that any items not deemed personal or of intelligence value would be returned to the commanding officer of the particular station, for such distribution as he desired. The CNO directive further defined as allowable "souvenirs" any nonpersonal items such as pocket knives, flashlights, loose keys, or cigarettes, as long as they had no definite personal value to the prisoner.[34] Typically, prisoners and their baggage were searched inside their cells by U.S. Marine guards in the presence of several officers and prison medical personnel, all of whom supposedly guaranteed that no nonessential items were removed from personal baggage. But although looting was officially discouraged, the *U-234* prisoners had practically all their items of value taken from them; when watches or rings were removed by enlisted guards, the supervising officers would relieve the guards of their booty, only to retain them themselves as souvenirs.[35] Fehler vehemently protested the looting of his crew and submarine, reminding ONI officials that he himself had so far acted in good faith: "All he had to do was pull a lever and every one of his mineshafts would have been emptied of its contents." While concerned investigators took up Fehler's case with base authorities, the interrogators had the hydraulic valves aboard *U-234* chained to prevent any attempt to follow through on Fehler's threat.

The looting was at its worst at the prison. On 19 May, because of the large amount of personal luggage aboard *U-234,* all of the baggage was stacked in the lobby of the prison, where it remained from 1600 to 1800 until examined by Lieutenants Buckner and DeCourcy, two ONI investigating officers. According to them, the luggage, particularly General Kessler's, contained very little of intelligence value. However, a studio photograph of Kessler later surfaced in the possession of one of the guards who had been on duty in the lobby during the two-hour interim, and it was obvious that the photograph could have come only from Kessler's luggage; hence, the German luggage must have been ransacked. ONI interpreter Jack Alberti deplored the situation and observed, "This action has had a most detrimental effect on interrogation of the crew and jeopardizes their willingness to cooperate."[36]

Aware that the luggage had been ransacked and faced with the possibility that items of value might never be recovered, ONI officials mustered the enlisted men and officers of the prison guard detachment and promised them that they could retain possession of any items not deemed necessary for intelligence purposes. The ONI's Lieutenant Commander Hatten would assume final authority over the souvenirs, confiscating the German contraband and determining the intelligence or personal status of each item. However, ONI interrogators realized that the guards' compliance with their directive to return the German items was unlikely without a guarantee of clemency. Therefore, an arrangement was effected and approved by Admiral Winters whereby no disciplinary action would be taken against anyone who came forward and returned his souvenirs now.[37] As a result, numerous items were uncovered, including shirts, pants, war decorations (including Kessler's Knight's Cross to the Iron Cross), binoculars, surgical equipment, ceremonial daggers, jewelry, and miscellaneous other items. However, approximately 1,200 Swiss francs and 1,200 Norwegian kroner had disappeared from Kessler's possession, never to be recovered.

After initial ONI interrogations at Portsmouth, senior ONI officials determined that *U-234*'s officers and passengers were too valuable to remain at a medium-security facility and subsequently requested that they be transferred to an interrogation facility. As a result, the Office of the Commander-in-Chief issued Secret Order 151942 to Vice Admiral Leary, commanding officer of the Eastern Sea Frontier, which directed that all of *U-234*'s personnel be transferred to Washington.[38] The transfer of captured personnel to Washington was not in itself unusual; previous POWs had been taken to Boston, then driven by car to Washington. However, *U-234*'s passengers were deemed top priority and were removed to the naval air station at Sanford, Maine, where air transport for those prisoners considered most valuable would be arranged.[39]

Those members of *U-234*'s crew not detained for intelligence questioning began their journey to repatriation in the Charles Street Jail in Boston. Fehler and his officers joined the crew of *U-873* there, amid squalid conditions; Fehler remembered his cell as being "terribly dirty." Throughout the night he heard "much screaming [and] the sound of beating and later moaning," which he later learned came from *U-873*'s commanding officer, Lt. Cdr. Fritz Steinhoff. Steinhoff had gained notoriety as a National Socialist "true believer" and had previously been the commanding officer of *U-511*, which participated in the first successful attempt to launch anti-aircraft missiles from a submarine.[40] At Portsmouth, Steinhoff had conveyed the image of the recalcitrant German, which did little to dispose his American guards to give him decent treatment. Consequently, he was "treated badly at his hearing and on the way to Boston [where] he was abused in his cell." In desperation, Steinhoff eventually broke the lens of his sunglasses and opened up several veins, dying hours later at a Boston hospital. Although *U-873*'s doctor, Dr. Brehme, had called for an immediate blood transfusion to save Steinhoff's life, he was alarmed by the lackadaisical attitude of the American medical personnel, who he thought showed "no interest in keeping [Steinhoff] alive" and delayed the delivery of plasma for two and a half hours. Although they were interned in Boston for only two days, the sounds and sights of the Charles Street Jail did little to reassure Fehler that his decision to come to America had been the correct one; he later recalled that he "was especially bitter about the treatment by the Americans because we gave such special care to the prisoners on the *Atlantis*."[41]

According to U.S. military procedures for handling the influx of enemy aliens, all of *U-234*'s personnel were to be housed at Fort George G. Meade in Maryland before being dispersed to American POW camps. However, after intelligence evaluations, the ONI determined that General Kessler and his staff, civilians Bringewald and Ruf, and *U-234* officers Fehler, Bulla, and Pfaff should be transferred to the joint Army-Navy interrogation facility at Fort Hunt, Virginia. After a brief interrogation there, Fehler and his officers would be assigned to various POW camps to await repatriation, which they assumed would be soon. However, American repatriation policy adhered to the provisions of the Geneva Convention, which stated that repatriation of prisoners should be effected "with the least possible delay after the conclusion of peace."[42] However, peace would not come to the United States until September, so *U-234*'s officers and men languished in captivity.

After their brief stay at Meade, the remainder of *U-234*'s crew were allocated to various enemy alien internment facilities throughout the country, their destinations based on the receiving facility's need for labor as well as on its political affiliation. The Provost Marshal General's Office maintained control over the 348,108 German prisoners of war in the United States and, in view of the alarming regularity with which hard-core National Socialists summarily executed their more democratic comrades in prison, divided American internment facilities into two categories: those housing fervent National Socialists, and those housing less ardent followers of Adolf Hitler.[43] Among *U-234*'s crew, all were considered somewhat radical adherents to National Socialism, except for Siegfried Schramm, Gerhard Wilian, Adolf Mania, and Waldemar Putzas.[44] Each group was sent to the appropriate facility until their repatriation in 1946.

The ONI's MAGIC information—intelligence derived from deciphered Japanese diplomatic communications—had been confirmed by Nazro's on-site assessment of *U-234*'s cargo, prompting officials at Portsmouth to shroud *U-234* in secrecy. On the morning of 20 May, naval personnel at Portsmouth awoke to find the dry-dock area surrounded by a 6-foot green canvas curtain, access to which was now restricted to ONI personnel and U.S. Marine guard detachments. However, any attempt to maintain complete secrecy was futile; *U-234*'s conning tower protruded above the canvas shield, giving away her identity.

Because the majority of American officials at Portsmouth had no idea of the full significance of the cargo, technicians exercised caution as they began unloading it. ONI officials were not certain that the cargo hatches were free of booby traps. Although *U-234*'s crew had forgone their earlier opportunity for sabotage, not scuttling or otherwise damaging *U-234* while still at sea, many of the crew had remained aboard *U-234* while she was docked in Portsmouth, for lack of space in the base prison.[45] Consequently, the potential for sabotage, though small, did exist, and Captain Herbster concluded, "You can't tell about them."[46] As a result, members of *U-234*'s crew were enlisted to help in the physical examination and dissection of the submarine. Portsmouth officials put Peter Schölch, *U-234*'s chief boatswain, in charge of the unloading detail, reasoning that if there were any hidden charges on board, the German sailors would reveal their location before being blown up.[47]

Dock personnel risked overlooking some of the cargo because of the enormous size of the submarine and the complexity of the packing. In this matter the Germans showed a genuine desire to cooperate. Erich Menzel provided ONI investigators with the shipboard location of his personal and military property, which was stored, along with that of Kessler and von Sandrart, in two of the aft mine shafts amidships. This discovery indicated the extent to which the Germans had used even the most minute spaces aboard *U-234* for storage—valuable information in itself. In addition, Menzel's revelation gave ONI officials an inkling of what they might expect to find in the holds; among Menzel's possessions alone were rolls of "secret films and other documents," all pertaining to Menzel's mission.[48]

Upon examining the preliminary intelligence evaluations of *U-234*'s cargo, the Navy Department assumed responsibility for its immediate unloading and disposition. On 23 May, Portsmouth was directed to dispatch all of *U-234*'s documents to Washington and, as soon as the threat of sabotage had been removed by explosives disposal experts, to remove the cargo to a secure storage facility, sending an inventory list to the CNO. After examining the inventory, the CNO's office would direct disposition, as well as "control access to . . . all cargo due to vital importance to Pacific War."[49] Because some of the cargo consisted of weapons systems with which U.S. authorities were not familiar, Portsmouth officials sought to designate an officer to direct the unloading of the suspect items.

The ONI did not have to search long. During his 27 May interrogation, Second Watch Officer Lt. (jg) Karl Pfaff disclosed that he had been in charge of the cargo and had personally supervised the loading of the mine tubes. In addition, Pfaff had prepared the cargo manifest and thus was familiar with the particular type of cargo that was packed into each shaft. For his part, Pfaff desperately wanted to cooperate, leaving his interrogators with the impression that he was "available and willing to aid unloading . . . if desired."[50] As a show of good faith, Pfaff advised that the long cargo containers be handled and stored horizontally, the shorter ones vertically.

Pfaff was aware of much more than the location of the cargo. For example, he revealed that the unique character of the most mysterious item in the cargo, the uranium oxide, was evident even in its packaging requirements.[51] The ONI's concern was thus heightened; in 1945 few military personnel even knew of the existence of uranium oxide, and those who did know were intimidated by it, unsure what the physical properties of the ore might be. Accordingly, the ONI offered Pfaff a personal inducement for his cooperation in unloading and identifying the cargo, to which the young German quickly agreed.[52]

According to Pfaff, the uranium oxide was encased in gold-lined containers, which, left unopened, could be handled "like crude TNT." Under Pfaff's direction, the designated containers were carefully removed from their receptacles by a yard crane, placed in an isolated area of the dock, and secured for shipping. To determine which containers housed the ore, a number of scientists arrived to examine the vessels with Geiger counters; however, all of the containers were contaminated with traces of radiation, with the result that the exact location could not be determined.[53] Pfaff lent a further ominous air to the proceedings by warning that the uranium oxide containers "should not be opened, as [the] substance will become sensitive and dangerous," a declaration that prompted Portsmouth to contact the Navy Department and ask whether the containers in question should be opened in Portsmouth or shipped to Washington; in either case, Portsmouth said, "Pfaff should be available [when] the containers are opened."[54]

The contents of the mine tubes explained the presence of General Kessler and the various civilian technicians on board the submarine. Cdr. Alexander Moffat, who supervised this phase of *U-234*'s unloading, reported that the mine casings contained drawings and prints for "the production of some of Germany's most effective weapons, including the V-1 and V-2 rockets, as well as a disassembled Messerschmitt (ME) 262 jet fighter."[55] The submarine's cargo manifest elaborated on Moffat's observations, with entries for documents and prints for a Junkers trimotor aircraft and the ME 163 jet fighter, aircraft gauges and instruments, a high-altitude pilot's chamber, various electronic and radio devices, and ordnance such as a new proximity fuse for arming missiles and the Panzerfaust antitank grenade.[56] As the search progressed into the internal parts of the boat, the opening of the hull revealed that approximately $5 million worth of mercury and lead, desperately needed in Japan for the production of alloys, was stored in the bilge spaces, serving as ballast.[57]

However, the items of the most immediate interest were the aircraft and aviation technology aboard *U-234*. When navy working parties inventoried the contents of the containers consigned to Messerschmitt aviation engineer August Bringewald and technician Franz Ruf, they discovered a Messerschmitt 262 twin-engine turbojet fighter-bomber (eleven crates), an ME 163 single-engine rocket-propelled interceptor (two crates), and an ME 309 single-engine high-performance fighter (two crates), all complete with a set of airfoil development drawings. In addition to the aircraft, investigators also found a disassembled high-altitude pressure cabin for the proposed Henschel 130 stratospheric aircraft (one crate); complete turbojet power plants for the Italian Isotta Fraschini, BMW 109-003, and Junkers (JU) 109-003 jet engines (three crates); and plans and drawings for the ME 209 high-speed interceptor as well as the ME 210 and JU 88 twin-engine attack aircraft (total four crates).[58] Messerschmitt designers had included a cross-reference table that converted Messerschmitt drawing numbers to standard German army nomenclature, as well as all necessary production jigs and tools to aid in the construction of the machinery.[59] In one of the few packages belonging to Shoji that had not been buried with him at sea investigators discovered blue books and manuals for the ME 163 and an envelope containing blueprints for the ME 262, as well as photographs of ME 109 components and assorted parts for various Focke-Wulf aircraft.[60] Clearly, *U-234*'s cargo of German aeronautical marvels would be invaluable to the future of American aviation.

Having been unpacked and inventoried, the bulk of *U-234*'s aviation cargo was eventually sent to the U.S. Army Air Force (AAF) testing facility at Wright Field in Dayton, Ohio. Although naval officials immediately sent the ME 262 and 163 to the AAF, they balked at surrendering the remainder of their war prizes to a rival service and withheld the remaining accessories until naval air authorities could exploit them. Repeated requests from Wright did little to elicit the navy's cooperation and were eventually redirected to the War Department's chief of the Captured Personnel and Material Branch, Col. Russell H. Sweet. Sweet subsequently informed the director of naval intelligence that the AAF's intelligence section had expressed "extreme interest concerning documents and material making up [the] cargo of *U-234*." As a result, the War Department presented Capt. John Riheldaffer of the ONI a list of items to be sent to Wright without further delay. In addition to various plans, drawings, and documents, amounting to approximately 6,615 pounds of paper, the navy was directed to send the Henschel pressure cabin, 3 tons of aircraft injection pumps, an automatic-pilot mechanism, airborne fire-control computers, three Lorenz 7H2 bombsights, a B/3 and FUG airborne and early-warning radar, and 25 pounds of bomb fuses. As expected, ONI officials vigorously protested this order. However, they were somewhat comforted by Sweet's directive that they could retain all originals in the case of multiple copies of documents, and that in the case of duplicate machinery they were expected to ship only half of the total to the AAF.[61]

Because of naval interest in German innovations in the field of jet and rocket propulsion, Capt. Gerald Phelan of the navy's Technical Intelligence Center determined that the ONI should exercise some control over the dispersal of *U-234*'s cargo. Specifically, he determined that the ONI would "assume responsibility for the custody, screening, and distribution of all . . . material taken from the *U-234*. . . . No material of any sort is to be transferred to any other activity without the express written permission [of the ONI]." Phelan acknowledged that because of an arrangement with the AAF, some designated material would be transferred to Wright Field, but he withheld all plans and prints pertaining to the ME 163 interceptor. Aware that he would be called on this violation of Sweet's directive, Phelan directed that the ME 163 data be transferred to the naval air testing station at Patuxent River, Maryland, where officials would later determine which copies would be forwarded to Wright.[62] Indeed, the controversy surrounding the custodianship of *U-234*'s aeronautical cargo sometimes bordered on the ridiculous; however, it served as yet another catalyst in an increasingly serious and potentially damaging rivalry between the U.S. Navy and Air Force.

Navy officials at Portsmouth responsible for unloading *U-234* were also concerned about the hazards of clearing the submarine of her dangerous cargo. Menzel eased these fears somewhat, indicating that Fehler and Pfaff knew the most about cargo storage and would be of "great assistance" both in identifying the various items and in unloading them safely. This information was of great reassurance to ONI investigators; their constant fear of sabotage due to booby traps was compounded by concern about the inherent hazards of the cargo. Menzel had warned them, for example, about a container belonging to Dr. Heinz Schlicke that contained infrared proximity fuses, which "must be handled with the utmost care as they may explode."[63] Schlicke was enlisted to assist in the unloading of these fuses; later he was placed in the custody of Lts. (jg) H. E. Morgan and F. M. Abbott and Ens. F. L. Granger and escorted to the Bureau of Ordnance to "secure certain infra-red proximity switches [that were] important to BUORD."[64]

While the ONI interrogators had little trouble getting cooperation from the Germans, they did experience some difficulty with U.S. naval personnel at Portsmouth. Interrogator Jack Alberti cited problems with enlisted personnel aboard *U-234*, complaining that "at various times . . . US Navy ratings were found asleep in the bunks while on duty in *U-234*." A closer examination of the culprits revealed that most of them were inebriated, and further investigations enabled Alberti to report that "there has been a certain amount of drinking by USN personnel aboard *U-873* and *U-1228*, but nowhere near the extent that it took place on *U-234*." As to where the sailors had gained access to alcohol in such a security-intensive environment, Fehler provided the answer: *U-234* had originally carried approximately nine hundred bottles of liquor, only part of which, a subsequent inventory revealed, "has been located to this date and removed from the ship."[65]

Investigators sent to evaluate the equipment aboard *U-234* discovered "a strong prejudice" against acting "on any guidance or suggestions emanating from the Germans" who were retained aboard the submarine as advisers. On the evening of 19 May *U-234*'s chief engineer, Lt. Cdr. Horst Ernst, revealed the presence of five unexploded torpedo triggers to an officer of the working party on duty, who ignored the warning. The next morning Ernst repeated the warning to the ONI's Lieutenant Commander Knerr, who proceeded to search for the duty mine-disposal officer, without whom Knerr could not remove the exploders. After a full day of failing to locate the mine-disposal officer, and becoming concerned about the stability of the loose explosives, Knerr requested permission to remove the triggers by enlisting the aid of *U-234*'s chief torpedoman; however, permission was denied. Finally, on 21 May a frustrated Knerr violated the chain of command by contacting Admiral Winters, who ordered the immediate removal of the exploders with the aid of whoever was available.[66]

American distrust of German advice also impeded the attempt to remove the individual containers from the mine shafts. Because of the massive amount of material destined for Japan, *U-234*'s cargo spaces were filled to beyond capacity; each of the forward mine shafts, designed to carry 4 tons of cargo, actually held 7 tons, and the port and starboard shafts carried 4 instead of the designated 2.5 tons. To facilitate access to these spaces, Ernst recommended defueling the submarine, which would elevate the boat and sufficiently expose the heretofore submerged manual access lugs, allowing working parties to remove the containers individually. Ernst warned that it was crucial to locate and handle these lugs accurately, for a man groping blindly for them while they were submerged might instead trip the exterior release trigger, which would fire all the containers out the bottom of the submarine and into Portsmouth Harbor. However, the dock supervisor, one Captain Dudley, stated "very emphatically" that he did not see any need to defuel the submarine and did not intend to do so. Furthermore, Dudley stated that his personal examination of the shafts revealed no reason why they could not be removed, and in the event that access to the manual lugs was required, he would "use a man outfitted with a diving helmet."[67] However, a frustrated ONI officer sidestepped Dudley's objections and on 28 May notified the yard planning officer that because of the prior removal of an estimated 60 tons of cargo and 60 tons of water ballast, in addition to the projected removal of 400 tons of fuel, unloading personnel would require data concerning the draft, trim, and stability characteristics of the Type XB submarine.[68] It is obvious, as Hirschfeld observed, that U.S. naval dockside personnel at Portsmouth had become victims of their own anti-German propaganda, ignoring German advice that would have been beneficial to the continuing American war effort.

Upon completion of her unloading, *U-234* remained isolated in dry dock as naval personnel disassembled her. On 23 May, Washington granted permission for Portsmouth officials to "cannibalize the German subs at Portsmouth of technical devices to install on one [American] sub for trials."[69] Lee A. White, who worked on the docks at Portsmouth, recalled that *U-234* "was the first German submarine they did that to."[70] American naval engineers spent the next two years dismantling the boat, recording every technical detail. One of the most valuable of *U-234*'s technical features involved her *Schnorchel.*

Because of the *Schnorchel*'s ability to allow a submarine to travel submerged on diesel engines, thus saving the boat's silent electric motors for evading an enemy search, American naval engineers were anxious to apply the German *Schnorchel* to American submarines. However, there were enough structural differences between American submarines and German U-boats that detailed drawings would be necessary for the "design of similar equipment for US subs."[71] Again, Pfaff stepped forward to help. While at Fort Meade, Pfaff had not only written a detailed physical and operational description of the device but also provided interrogators with captioned drawings of *U-234*'s *Schnorchel,* which was regarded as representative of the latest in German design. As a result, after naval working parties removed the apparatus, naval engineers required only a translation of Pfaff's document to install *U-234*'s *Schnorchel* into its new position atop an American submarine.[72]

By June 1945 continued Japanese resistance had prompted American war planners to begin developing a plan for the invasion of the Japanese home islands; consequently, any potential advance in Japanese weapons technology was a cause for major concern. As a result, American interrogators examined the contents of *U-234* carefully, and their interrogation focused on what *U-234*'s officers and passengers knew about Japanese procurement of Germany's jet fighters, such as the ME 262 and ME 163; Japanese intentions in regard to the V-2 rocket; Japanese radio, countermeasures, and antiaircraft research; and, of course, the uranium oxide. *U-234*'s cargo, both mechanical and human, assumed new importance as investigators sought to uncover the current status of Japanese weapons production and to learn how *U-234*'s mission might enhance it. The documents, drawings, ordnance, and weapons alone were alarming enough, but the presence on board the boat of personnel with specialized technical expertise raised the disturbing possibility that Japan's capacity to utilize such technology might have progressed from a potential threat to an operational one.

Part II

The
New World

My U-boat men! Six years of war lie behind us. You have fought like lions. A crushing material superiority has forced us into a narrow area. A continuation of our fight from the remaining base is no longer possible. Unbeaten and unblemished, you lay down your arms after a heroic fight without parallel. We remember in deep respect our fallen comrades. . . . Preserve your U-boat spirit, with which you have fought courageously . . . throughout the years for the good of the Fatherland. . . . Long live Germany!

GRAND ADMIRAL KARL DÖNITZ

5

The General

THE MILITARY, TECHNICAL, AND DIPLOMATIC missions of *U-234* were commanded by General of the Air Force Ulrich Kessler, who was traveling to Tokyo to assume the dual responsibilities of German air attaché to Japan and Luftwaffe liaison command.[1] Kessler was no stranger to the Allies; intelligence estimates evaluated his prominence in German military and diplomatic circles as substantial, therefore necessitating surveillance of his activities. In April 1945 Allied intelligence intercepted a Japanese diplomatic dispatch that revealed that Kessler was en route to Japan aboard a submarine, although initial summaries failed to disclose aboard which U-boat he was traveling.[2] As a result, when *U-234* surrendered, Kessler's presence among the passengers was not entirely unexpected.

Ulrich Kessler was a native of East Prussia, born in 1894 in the port city of Danzig. He excelled in primary and secondary school despite his frequent movement from one locale to another. During Kessler's years as a student, he attended elementary school in Zoppot, Saalfeld, East Prussia and Thorn, *Humanistisches Gymnasium* (high school) in Thorn, and Prinz Heinrich Gymnasium in Berlin, graduating in 1913. However, university would have to wait, as dark clouds were forming over the political boundaries of Europe.

Like most German youths, Kessler joined the military when World War I erupted in 1914. Oddly enough, General Kessler of the Luftwaffe began his military career in the Imperial German Navy, training in Norwegian waters aboard the SMS *Hertha*. In the spring of 1914, upon completion of cadet training, he began instruction in radio communications and was named chief of the German navy's radio intercept station at Neumünster. In November, Kessler received his first sea duty aboard the armored cruiser SMS *Friedrich Karl* and was pulled from the Baltic Sea when that vessel was sunk in early 1915. He was subsequently assigned to the SMS *Wittlesbach* and later the cruiser *Lübeck*, aboard which he was wounded in January 1916. After this second brush with death at sea, Kessler returned to shore duty for the duration of the war.[5]

Kessler spent the final years of the war familiarizing himself with naval aviation. During the summer of 1916 he began basic seaplane training and by December had qualified as an observer and pilot in the Second Seaplane Squadron, gaining combat experience in the skies over the North Sea and Flanders. In 1917 Kessler assumed command of the Second Navy Giant Seaplane Squadron, a post he held until the end of the war. Upon the advent of peace, Kessler was discharged from the navy and decided to resume his studies.

In November 1918 Kessler entered the University of Berlin, where he studied political science and law. A month later, like many of his wartime colleagues, he joined the anticommunist Freikorps, serving as an officer of the Lütwitz Battalion. In 1923 he resigned from the Freikorps and joined the Reichsmarine, where he was attached briefly to the command of the Navy Station, North Sea. Also in 1923 Kessler first attracted attention as a military theorist with the publication of two articles, "Is the Organization of the Air Force as a Third Independent Branch Justified?" and "Army Leadership of the Entente during the World War." By the end of August, Kessler had returned to active duty with a two-year tour as an officer on a torpedo boat of the North Sea's Second Flotilla. In 1925, having completed his torpedo-boat duty, he was named adjutant aboard the cruiser *Hamburg*, and in February he embarked on a two-year world cruise, visiting such ports of call as Panama, Los Angeles, San Francisco, Hawaii, and Manila.[4]

Upon his return to Germany in 1927, Kessler was appointed department head for the Navy Air Fleet Arm and subsequently attended the German Naval Academy at Mürwik. Later, in 1931, as a member of the Fleet Staff, he was assigned administrative duty aboard the battleship *Hessen*, which would be his last duty aboard ship. In 1932, in consideration of his background in political science and military strategy, Kessler was dispatched as one of Germany's representatives to the World Disarmament Conference in Geneva. While at Geneva, Kessler, who was growing apprehensive about the emergence of militant political factions within Germany, was introduced to Secretary of State Henry Stimson, to whom he expressed his concerns. Stimson reportedly told Kessler, "If you are ever in any trouble, just let me know. I'll do my very best to help you."[5] It was a promise that Kessler would never forget.

In 1933 Kessler was assigned to the Operational Department of the fledgling Luftwaffe Air Ministry; to assume this position he resigned his navy commission as a *Kapitänleutnant* (lieutenant commander) and assumed a Luftwaffe rank of *Oberstleutnant* (lieutenant colonel). In the fall of 1934 he assumed command of the Aircraft Armament School at Warnemünde, followed by a liaison assignment at the Wehrmacht Academy. Between 1936 and 1938 Kessler served as commander of the First Naval Coastal Flight Command on the island of Sylt and later as chief of staff of the Fourth Air Corps at Westphalia. Kessler's appointment to Westphalia was temporary, and when the corps was disbanded in the summer of 1938, he was returned to the Air Ministry to begin training as Germany's new air attaché to England.[6] It was here that Kessler first ran afoul of the *Reichsmarschall*, the Luftwaffe's own Hermann Göring.

In September 1938 Kessler was summoned to Munich to meet with Göring. In regard to the controversy involving Germany and Czechoslovakia, Kessler had previously expressed the opinion that if Germany forced annexation of the Sudetenland, England would most likely intervene militarily, an opinion that had infuriated the *Reichsmarschall*. In order to obtain reassurance from Kessler that he actually held no such notion, Göring steered the conversation so as to convince Kessler that he had been named chief of the General Air Staff, a role in which Kessler would have to profess total confidence in a German victory over England. When pressed by Göring to say whether he still believed that England could win a war with Germany, Kessler forever incurred the *Reichsmarschall*'s wrath by answering, "A war with England will always be a long war [and] should be prepared for spiritually and materially long beforehand so as to achieve a knockout blow by the first, initial attack. Germany can not go on saying one day that a war with England is entirely out of the question and then the next day start a war for which she would be unprepared."[7] Upon hearing this answer, Göring replied, "Very well; then I can not use you," and disbanded the meeting. On 10 October, Kessler was notified that the *Reichsmarschall* had relieved him of his assignment as air attaché, because Germany could not use an individual in London "who had a feeling of inferiority toward the English."

Despite their disagreements, Göring promoted Kessler to major general and reassigned him as wing commander of Bombardment Wing 1, a post that propelled Kessler into history as the commander of the Junkers 87 (Stuka) squadrons that initiated the invasion of Poland in 1939. In early 1940 Kessler arrived in Berlin as chief of staff of the First Air Fleet and by April had been appointed chief of staff of the Tenth Air Corps, which he directed during the Norwegian campaign. In March 1944, after serving as the Luftwaffe's chief of staff in Berlin and commanding Luftwaffe divisions in Norway and France, Kessler was relieved of his operational command and reassigned to Berlin, where he was attached to the Air Force Command Group for training as air attaché and head of an air force liaison staff to Tokyo. On 15 April 1945, Kessler boarded *U-234* at Kristiansand, Norway, and departed on the journey to Japan that would abruptly end with his seizure by the U.S. Navy.[8]

Although preliminary interrogations of Kessler confirmed his knowledge of several areas of Allied concern, he did not initially express a willingness to cooperate with his captors. However, during the 22 May interrogation Kessler experienced a change of heart and initiated a discussion regarding the possibility of cooperation with the ONI. Consequently, the ONI proceeded to interrogate him on matters concerning German technology and strategy, the utilization of such technology and strategy by the Japanese, and German technicians and "other experts" employed by the Japanese.[9]

American naval intelligence officials were determined to press Kessler for as much information as possible on the state of Germany's U-boat capability. While the Wehrmacht and the Luftwaffe had been virtually destroyed by the time of Germany's capitulation, Dönitz's submarine corps, rejuvenated by the potential of the revolutionary electric U-boats, remained a considerable threat. As a result, the export of German submarine technology to Japan constituted an immediate threat to the U.S. Navy. A major area of concern was Germany's alleged development of submarine ballistic-missile technology.[10] Reports of the submerged launching of missiles prompted the ONI to question Kessler regarding the rumor of U-boats, stationed in Norway, that were able to launch a V-2 rocket while submerged.[11] Kessler denied knowledge of this rumor and said that he doubted the existence of such a submarine. He pointed out that he had recently spent two months in Norway awaiting passage to Tokyo, and because he had been constantly in the company of U-boat officers, he believed he would have heard of such a weapon.[12] Kessler speculated that such rumors had probably been sparked by the presence of the new Type XXI and XXIII submarines in Norwegian waters. These state-of-the-art submarines were capable of firing both the conventional and the new acoustic torpedoes from considerable depths, delivering their payloads with improved accuracy.[13]

Throughout the war German submarine commanders had confounded Allied naval intelligence by avoiding enemy harbors that were protected by extensive underwater minefields. Allied naval strategists attributed this success to one of two possibilities: either German skippers had prior knowledge of the location and depth of the minefields, or German scientists had developed some sort of new hydrophonic sensing technology. However, Kessler dispelled these assumptions, revealing that U-boat commanders utilized neither intelligence nor technology. Because Allied minefields were laid at depths of between 50 and 200 meters (164 and 656 feet), any submarine attempting an approach under the field was susceptible to implosion due to the extreme pressures of depth. Therefore, German U-boat skippers avoided depths in excess of 200 meters and so could not enter enemy harbors.[14]

Although Kessler's explanation eased the concerns of civil and military officials charged with the defense of America's West Coast harbors against the threat of Japanese submarines, it did not address one matter of curiosity that had plagued naval officials since the beginning of the war. Throughout 1942 German U-boats had preyed on Allied shipping off the Atlantic and Gulf coasts of the United States with apparent impunity.[15] Owing to this success, American officials could never comprehend why Germany did not attempt to close the strategically important Panama Canal. Kessler stated that he "was positive that no attempt had been made to enter the [canal]." However, in 1943 Kessler and Dönitz had in fact submitted a report that proposed an air raid on the Gatun Locks. Although the report was delivered to Hitler, nothing else was heard of it. Later, when Kessler approached Dönitz about the possibility of a submarine attack on the canal, the admiral replied that although an attack might succeed, the U-boat would be unable to turn around in the narrow locks, making escape impossible. Kessler considered this explanation curious because German attack submarines had both bow and stern torpedo tubes.[16] Dönitz, however, refused to discuss the matter further, and as a consequence the Panama Canal remained open for the duration of the war. Although this revelation of indecision within Germany's high military command intrigued ONI investigators, there remained more urgent concerns for Kessler to address.

By the spring of 1945 the United States, Japan, and Germany all considered an Allied invasion of the Japanese home islands to be a foregone conclusion.[17] As a consequence, Japan decided to dedicate all available weapons and supplies to its own defense, even at the risk of abandoning some of its Pacific possessions to do so.[18] The ONI considered it a safe assumption that the weaponry aboard *U-234*, particularly the turbojet and V-weapon technology and components, would be deployed to defend Japan. Consequently, the most vital information derived from Kessler dealt with what he knew best: the particulars of offensive and defensive air warfare.

Kessler revealed that since April 1944 the Japanese had received information regarding all German armament either currently in use or in the latter stages of development.[19] As far as aircraft were concerned, the Japanese had shown interest in the German jet fighters, the ME 262 and ME 163.[20] Although the Japanese had not yet received information regarding the ME 262, plans for the ME 163 had reached Japan late in 1943, and initial test flights had been completed by December 1944.[21] As if this information were not alarming enough, Kessler also revealed that the December tests had been conducted with a powered production aircraft rather than a prototype glider.[22]

The ONI feared that Japanese competency in turbojet technology could destroy any hope of a quick ending to the war by successfully countering the American B-29 bombing raids that were then plaguing Japan. Although the Japanese had experimented with jet-propelled aircraft, their efforts had proven ineffective, suggesting a failure of Japanese turbojet research. As a result, by the spring of 1945 American intelligence analysts were confident that the Japanese had not test-flown an operational jet fighter, much less developed one for production.[23] While this confidence was shaken by the discovery of the ME 262 on board *U-234*, it was practically destroyed by Kessler's revelations regarding the extent of Japan's jet aircraft program.

Curiously, the ominous specter of Japanese ME 163 jet fighters filling the skies over the Pacific never materialized. Kessler solved the mystery by explaining that while the Japanese were dedicated to the integration of jet aircraft, they cautiously avoided any technology that involved the manufacture of highly developed precision instruments, especially electrical avionics. Reports from Tokyo to Berlin were "drastic and desperate in their description of Japanese capabilities," prompting the Air Ministry in Berlin to conclude that much of the information extended to the Japanese would be worthless because the technical basis for its proper exploitation was nonexistent.[24] As a result, Japan

petitioned Germany not only for the technical and manufacturing expertise to mass-produce the aircraft but also for assistance in developing
proficiency in jet-fighter tactics as well.

Kessler pointed out that although the Luftwaffe had never been able
to deploy large numbers of jet fighters against the Allies, it nonetheless
had developed a system of fighter tactics specifically for the ME 262
and 163. U.S. Army Air Corps (AAC) officials agreed with Kessler's contention that despite the weakened state of the Luftwaffe,[25] and despite
the fact that American fighter escorts typically outnumbered attacking
German fighters, by 1945 Germany's airborne defenses remained quite
effective. Col. Leslie Peterson of the AAC, who participated in the interrogation of Kessler, recognized the similar operational deficiencies of
both the weakened German and Japanese air forces and found their
respective strategic predicaments compelling. As a result, Peterson
questioned Kessler about which, if any, Luftwaffe tactics the Japanese
might employ.

Kessler provided Peterson with both a comprehensive description of
the Luftwaffe's defensive order of battle and his own personal assessment of Japanese plans to combat American B-29 raids. Earlier in the
war German squadron commanders had determined that massive
fighter attacks, both on the frontal and tail axes of the enemy aircraft,
were the most effective method of attacking enemy bomber formations. However, these tactics proved ineffective against large formations and eventually were easily countered by new escort fighters such
as the American P-51 Mustang. Kessler proposed that coordinated
attacks by small groups of up to four planes per target would be more
successful. These elusive groups would attack the enemy plane from
all directions, as frontal attacks took too long to deliver sufficient firing
and tail attacks subjected the attacker to the enemy's greatest concentration of firepower. However, while Kessler's tactics helped the Luftwaffe hold its own against American B-17 and B-25 bombers, they were
ineffective against the British Mosquito bomber. There was simply no
aircraft in the Luftwaffe's inventory that could counter the Mosquito's
combination of speed and altitude, a challenge that encouraged the
development of Germany's jet fighters.[26]

Once the ME 262 and ME 163 were operational, the Luftwaffe planned
to use their speed and maneuverability to disperse and destroy Allied
bomber formations. Kessler described a typical Luftwaffe jet attack as
a formation of either ME 262s or ME 163s that would initiate the main
attack from below, pass the enemy in vertical flight, then reattack from
above.[27] In addition, Kessler revealed that these attacks were to be

ground-vectored by radar rather than by the interception of voice communication. The Japanese were notorious for their use of enemy voice
communication to direct their attacks, a practice that U.S. Navy pilots
successfully countered by adhering to radio silence. A Japanese combination of jet aircraft and radar control would render this tactic useless and could offset the numerical advantage enjoyed by the air forces
of the United States in the Pacific.

The immediate concern of Army Air Corps officials was Japan's
efforts to counter American B-29 operations. Kessler recalled that in
1944 the Luftwaffe felt that the ME 262 could have retarded the Allied
aerial bombardment of Germany had Hitler not demanded that the jet
be converted from an interceptor to an attack bomber. In 1942, upon
seeing the first ME 262, Hitler had agreed to allow a percentage of the
aircraft to remain as interceptors; however, by 1943 the paranoid *Führer*
had decided that he had been deceived about the number of 262s that
had been converted to bombers and subsequently flew into a "frantic
fury, [ordering that] all of these planes be converted, threatening that he
would with his own hands tear the guns out of every 262 that he could
find and have the responsible officers court-martialed."[28] Kessler
unequivocally stated that the Japanese suffered no intervention by the
imperial government into the strategic deployment of the turbojets and
were likewise depending on the ME 262, as well as the ME 163, to combat the raids in the immediate future.[29] However, successful integration of the German jets remained in the future; in the interim, Japan
would attempt to augment its depleted fighter squadrons with the
rocket-powered Ohka suicide aircraft.[30]

Kessler traced the evolution of the Ohka, or Baka, to the early-1944
development of a German remote-controlled rocket known as the Mistel.[31] Although the Japanese showed little interest in the Mistel because
of their inability to reproduce the aircraft's remote-control guidance
systems, the idea of an independently controlled missile prompted
Japanese scientists to develop a manually piloted, rocket-powered
bomb. Kessler pointed out that the Baka never matched the success of
the conventional kamikaze, and by 1945 the Baka's inconsistency had
proven too costly. Still convinced of the necessity for a human-piloted
bomb, Japan turned to Germany to supply a more effective vehicle. In
March 1945 a V-1 rocket modified to carry a pilot had been captured by
Allied ground forces advancing through Germany. Doubting the existence of Nazi suicide squadrons, Kessler attributed this particular
incarnation of the V-1 to Germany's attempt to provide Japan with an
improved suicide vehicle.[32]

Kessler did, however, acknowledge that while serving in Norway he had been "astonished to hear . . . of more than sixty [Flying] Fortresses destroyed by ramming during an operation over Northern Germany."[33] Although he told his interrogators that he and his fellow Luftwaffe officers "could not believe it," he did admit that Hitler, Göring, and Dönitz were incessantly pressing the Luftwaffe to emulate the Japanese and employ suicide tactics. On the basis of what Kessler had told them, AAC officials formulated a chilling theory. If the American bombers had indeed been the victims of a mass suicide attack, then the utilization of the V-1 rocket as a suicide vehicle had been proven effective. The Japanese Bushido code of warfare, embodied by the dreaded kamikaze, joined to the effectiveness of German rockets was a fearful combination that the U.S. Army Air Corps would prefer not to face. However, Kessler's testimony proved of mixed value: although the ONI and AAC were now aware of a heretofore unknown Japanese threat, no one knew of any effective countermeasures against these weapons.

In addition to describing Japanese integration of German weaponry, Kessler also provided insight into the rumored transport air route used by Japan and Germany. He stated that to his knowledge no flights between the Axis partners were ever completed, although two Italian officers had embarked on a flight to either Tokyo or Manchuria in early 1942. Also, Japan had initiated a flight to Europe via India, but the aircraft and its crew were never heard from after the departure and were presumed lost. However, the absence of an active airborne trade route did not mean that one was not desired.[34]

Kessler revealed that the activation of air transport flights between Germany and the Far East had been anticipated since the beginning of the war and had intensified since Germany's invasion of Russia. As early as 1943 the Luftwaffe General Staff was contemplating the establishment of regular air traffic between Germany and Japan, with the intention of sending information, models, designs, and, if possible, technical innovations in exchange for scarce materials such as tungsten and rubber. This intention reached the planning stages to the extent of modifying three Junkers 290 four-engine transports so as to enable the aircraft to cover the long journey and return to Germany with 2 tons of cargo. The mission's hand-picked pilots, former Lufthansa airline pilots accustomed to the rigors of long flights, were already in training for the journey. Had the proposed flight taken place, Kessler and his party would have traveled to Japan aboard one of the JU 290s instead of in the belly of *U-234*.[35]

The flights never materialized, an outcome that Kessler considered "astonishing, but typical of the Luftwaffe." At the center of the failure lay the Japanese government, which had signed a nonaggression pact with the Soviet Union. Japanese officials feared that a flight over the Soviet Union might be forced down in Soviet territory, putting Japan in the unenviable position of having to explain why it was shepherding German personnel and war material across Soviet airspace. The probable outcome would be a break in diplomatic relations, followed by a declaration of war, which would force Japan to defend its empire along two fronts. As a result, Japan vigorously objected to any arrangement that might violate Soviet airspace. Still, Kessler seemed puzzled as to why the Luftwaffe would dispose of the aircraft and cancel the mission without ascertaining whether a clandestine arrangement could be reached with the Japanese. Instead of regular journeys, such an arrangement might result in occasional flights, which, though secretly condoned, would be publicly condemned if discovered.

Japan expected the proposed flights to proceed; however, in the fall of 1944 Soviet generalissimo Josef Stalin publicly railed against the "aggressor nations" of Germany and Japan, prompting the Japanese to err on the side of caution by disassociating themselves from the German plan.[36] However, the Japanese diplomatic entourage in Berlin—Ambassador Oshima and his aids Admiral Abe, Admiral Kojima, and General Komatsu—remained in favor of the air route, even if the journey did violate Soviet territory. Admiral Koshima suspected that Tokyo's fear of a crack in the nonaggression pact would result in the Soviets allowing the United States to put air bases on Russian soil, from which the Americans could easily attack Japan. Koshima believed, however, that this reasoning was preposterous; whether the Germans violated Soviet airspace or not was of little consequence, for the Soviets would never allow the Americans to use their airfields to attack Japan. Koshima further pointed out that the disagreements between Moscow and Tokyo were negligible compared with those between Moscow and Washington; indeed, Japanese and Soviet intelligence agents in Turkey regularly exchanged intelligence concerning the United States.[37]

Ulrich Kessler was an internationally regarded diplomat and military strategist; however, his failure to secure a staff-level command was due primarily to his differences with Hermann Göring. The enmity between the two was well known within the Luftwaffe's inner circles, leading some to wonder how Kessler stayed alive throughout the war. Now, in June 1945, while Göring was incarcerated in Nuremburg awaiting trial, the ONI sought to gain a more definitive image of the former *Reichsmarschall.*

Kessler revealed Hermann Göring to be an odd, somewhat comical character who did not necessarily agree with the hard-line National Socialists with whom Hitler surrounded himself. Luftwaffe officers such as Field Marshal Manfred von Richthofen and General Bieneck, who knew Göring during World War I, categorized him as a "catastrophic phenomenon" who "should have become an actor," a reference to Göring's habit of "studying Napoleonic gestures before the mirror in [a] compartment of his private train." In addition, Kessler revealed that Göring had an infamous passion for outlandish jewelry and was "effeminate to such a degree that he would often attend meetings . . . dressed in an Oriental dressing gown fastened with a large brooch." One of Göring's cousins once characterized the *Reichsmarschall* as a cross between a fake Prussian officer and a Persian shah, though Kessler always thought him "more of a Nero type."[38]

Göring was rumored to have performed "brave and daring" accomplishments during World War I and was even awarded the Pour le Mérite for valor while flying with the infamous Flying Circus of Baron Manfred von Richthofen. During the 1920s, however, when the survivors of the Flying Circus formed the Richthofen Society, many of the veterans voted against Göring's admission on the grounds of "proven cowardice." In addition, a later addiction to narcotics further alienated Göring from his contemporaries. His relationship with Hitler was ambiguous; while Göring was deathly afraid of the *Führer,* he nevertheless despised the "Jew-baiters . . . and Hitler's mishandling of the war." However, Göring's fear of Hitler dissuaded him from ever opposing the *Führer* on matters of military significance. Kessler believed, as did many, that Göring merely assented to Hitler's wishes, and that although he declared himself to be "Hitler's most loyal paladin," Göring actually wished the *Führer* dead. General von Waldau characterized Göring's role in Hitler's government by stating that Göring's post of chief of the General Staff would best be filled "by an attendant at a lunatic asylum."[39]

Despite Göring's foibles, he was immensely popular with the German people, who valued his moderating influence on Hitler and his opposition to the fanatical fringe within the party. Indeed, Göring's eccentricities stood in stark contrast to the rigors of National Socialism and further endeared him to most Germans as a "jolly good fellow" who possessed a sense of humor. In the presence of superiors Göring often enjoyed assuming the role of the butt of humorous stories and jokes. However, in situations in which he was the superior officer he seriously guarded his reputation, as evidenced during prewar naval maneuvers.

During the fall of 1938 Göring boarded the pocket battleship *Deutschland* to oversee the year's naval maneuvers. Göring was a notoriously bad sailor, which explained in part his intense hatred for the navy. As a result, he spent his time aboard ship trying to avoid seasickness by feeding the fish that trailed the warship, a task that did not go unnoticed. During the farewell festivities that accompanied the conclusion of the maneuvers, two naval junior officers approached the *Reichsmarschall* and informed him that on behalf of the Kriegsmarine they wished to present him with yet another title to add to his lengthy list of honors. Because Göring was already known as Reich Master of the Hunt, the Kriegsmarine now wished to bestow upon him the title of Reich Fish-Feeding Master, which came with the authorization to wear a tunic woven from a fisherman's net. Göring flew into a rage and demanded that Admiral of the Fleet Erich Raeder arrest the two officers. When informed that such discipline was contrary to the tradition of the navy, Göring pressed and cajoled Raeder until he was able to secure three days' restriction for the guilty officers.[40]

Although Kessler steadily advanced through the ranks of the Luftwaffe, he maintained that he had sacrificed his military career to his political convictions. As a result of his distaste for the ruling National Socialists, Kessler soon became involved in the plot to overthrow Hitler. Between September 1943 and the spring of 1944, various conspiracies organized at least six attempts to assassinate the *Führer* and gain control of the German government through a coup d'état; however, none of these materialized. For his part, Kessler became affiliated with the Goerdeler Group, one of the original anti-Hitler factions, which was headed by Carl Goerdeler.

Goerdeler was the conservative Protestant mayor of Leipzig who, like many conservatives, harbored monarchist sympathies. In 1936 Goerdeler, who despised Hitler's anti-Semitism and the alarming rate of rearmament, broke with the party and was soon dedicating his energies to the removal of Hitler and the National Socialists. By late summer of 1938 Goerdeler had succeeded in enlisting the aid of disaffected army officers such as Gens. Franz Halder and Ludwig Beck, who believed that in order to shield Germany from a European conflict that would ultimately destroy it, the *Führer* must be overthrown.[41]

Vital to the conspiracy's success was the approval and complicity of the Allied Powers. To this end, Goerdeler dispatched Berlin financier Jakob Wallenberg to London to negotiate a post-Hitler armistice with the British while simultaneously maintaining contact with the Americans through Allen Dulles, who headed the Office of Strategic Services (oss) in Switzerland. Goerdeler's representatives in London and Bern outlined the conspirators' plans for a post-Hitler Germany, even pronouncing that Louis-Ferdinand, the oldest surviving member of the Hohenzollern royal family—who in 1941 was a five-year employee of the Ford Motor Company's assembly plant in Dearborn, Michigan—would emerge as the heir to the German throne. However, the Allies remained noncommittal, prompting Goerdeler's representatives to warn Dulles that, in the event that the United States and Britain refused to consider a favorable peace with the proposed Goerdeler government, the conspirators would turn to the Soviets.[42] Both Allied governments, however, refused to offer guarantees of a negotiated peace and regarded such discussions as presumptuous at best.

The Goerdeler Group initiated its first attempt on Hitler's life in February 1943, in what came to be known as Operation Flash. The conspirators discovered that Hitler would be traveling to Smolensk in occupied Russia and planted a British-made bomb aboard his aircraft.[43] However, the plan failed because the bomb's detonator did not activate. In November 1943 a twenty-four-year-old infantry officer, Alexander von dem Busche, volunteered to hide a bomb underneath a new infantry overcoat that he would be modeling for Hitler's approval. Busche's plan was to grab Hitler as the *Führer* closely inspected the coat and sacrifice his own life for Germany by blowing the two of them to pieces. However, Hitler continued to lead a charmed life; Allied bombing raids destroyed both the new overcoats and Busche's bombs. A subsequent plan for the assassination was thwarted when at the last moment Hitler decided to forgo a rescheduled inspection and travel to Berchtesgaden for the Christmas holidays. Because the suspicions of Heinrich Himmler and the ss were making it increasingly difficult to gain access to Hitler, by the spring of 1944 the Goerdeler Group had joined forces with other conspiracy factions, one of which included Count Berthold von Stauffenburg. It was Goerdeler's affiliation with von Stauffenburg that linked Kessler to the 20 July 1944 attempt on Hitler's life.

Kessler's involvement with the Goerdeler Group began in February 1943 when he was approached by one of his wife's friends, Frau Hanna Luecke-Kallenberg, who had maintained contact with various anti-Hitler factions throughout the war. Luecke-Kallenberg, aware of Kessler's convictions, urged him to contact a Leipzig lawyer named Perkuhn, who would "have something very important to tell him." Kessler met with Perkuhn at the Esplanade Hotel in Leipzig, where he was informed that Goerdeler's primary purpose was to "avoid mob rule when the Nazi government was removed after the war was lost." As the conversation proceeded, the issue of Hitler's assassination was brought to Kessler's attention, with Perkuhn explaining that while the conspirators already included important army officials, they still needed "an important personality from the Air Force." Kessler stated that he was convinced that his own officers and units would support his decision, and he would try to "sound out" Field Marshal Albert Kesselring, whom Kessler knew opposed Hitler's handling of the war.[44]

Kessler became further informed about the scope of the assassination plans through his brother-in-law, Dr. Kurt Weber, the mayor of Königsberg, East Prussia. Weber—who, Kessler revealed to his interrogators, "hated the Nazis intensely"—had been a close friend of Kessler's since 1925. Now, as one of Goerdeler's confidants, Weber was able to give Kessler details of the Goerdeler Group's post-Hitler plans. He revealed, for example, that Kessler was earmarked for the post of secretary of state for air under the new government.[45] However, because Kessler was becoming increasingly important to the success of the conspiracy, he was also becoming a target of Gestapo and ss suspicion.

Both Weber and Kessler remained apprehensive about the possibility of arrest. Weber, who was in constant contact with Goerdeler himself, kept vials of poison for himself and his family within reach. Kessler was alarmed to discover that the conspiracy, and particularly his role in it, was the subject of conversation of "other smaller fry, like former secretaries of labor unions . . . his chauffeur [and] a former orderly." In addition, a former friend of Kessler's, Dr. Jürgen Riensberg, met with Kessler on the ferry at Warnemünde and warned him that a client of his had been visited by a Luftwaffe major who spoke openly of the Luftwaffe's role in a rumored overthrow of the government. The major had said that because of uncertainty about the convictions of the Luftwaffe hierarchy, Kessler was regarded as the only suitable official to lead the revolt. Kessler now realized that the discovery of his complicity was only a matter of time, and that he needed an alibi. He attempted to camouflage his involvement by writing a letter to his parents in which he reported that "in compliance with the sound will of the people, the whole breed of vipers and conspirators has been eradicated, down to their children, and their children's children." Kessler was fully aware that the Gestapo was reading and censoring his mail, and this remark might serve to throw the hounds temporarily off his trail.[46]

While in Berlin, Kessler had become acquainted with Japanese naval attaché Rear Adm. Kojima Hideo. In July 1944, after the failed attempt on Hitler's life, a worried Kessler confided to Kojima the depth of his involvement. Kojima, who was genuinely fond of Kessler, spoke with his army counterpart in Berlin, Colonel Komatsu, and the two decided to request Kessler to replace the current air attaché in Tokyo, with whom the Japanese were not pleased. Kojima and Komatsu visited Göring to explain the urgent need for Kessler's appointment to this post, stressing Kessler's experience in air warfare, which was needed to help Japan fend off the advancing Americans. Both attachés realized that, in light of the events of 20 July, their request would likely fall on deaf ears; surely Göring would not release a conspirator in the assassination plot, especially one against whom he harbored such personal animosity. However, Göring, who was in fact, not unaware of Kessler's involvement in the plot, saw the Japanese request as a final opportunity to rid himself of Kessler, and he eagerly agreed. Kojima and Komatsu's intercession thus derailed the Gestapo's investigation of Kessler and, by diverting his destiny from the gallows to *U-234*, ultimately saved the general's life.[47]

On 21 May 1945 the director of the ONI received a letter from Miss Louise W. Boothe, of Lenox, Massachusetts. In this letter Boothe recounted that she had read that one of the German prisoners aboard *U-234* was Gen. Ulrich Kessler, the same Ulrich Kessler whom she had met while he was a member of a delegation to the 1932 Disarmament Conference in Geneva. Boothe and her mother, who had been staying at the same hotel as the German delegation, became acquainted with Kessler. At that time, she said, he had indicated that he had "no use for the Nazis" and that he regarded the level of German rearmament as a precursor to a war that would "end in the complete ruin of Germany." Boothe stated that she and others who met Kessler at Geneva regarded him as an "honorable, straight-forward fellow" who deplored both the upcoming war and the mistreatment of the Jews. In closing, Boothe said, "It would not be right to class Kessler as a Nazi or place him among Nazi criminals."[48] This assessment led ONI investigators to give credence to Kessler's claim that while he had performed his duty to Germany according to his orders, he had nevertheless opposed the National Socialists and had planned to aid in their overthrow.

Ulrich Kessler provided the ONI with testimony from one of the highest-ranking German officials not interned at Nuremburg. While he revealed information concerning the rise of National Socialism in Germany, its worldwide political aspirations, and the postwar plans of the victorious powers in Germany, his most valuable contribution was his identification and assessment of Germany's technical and material aid to Japan. Granted, Allied knowledge of these innovations did not eliminate the threat, and the United States remained far from victory in the Pacific. However, if Kessler's testimony did not provide American servicemen with a solution to the problem of Japanese integration of German weaponry, it nevertheless provided some clue of what to expect should the anticipated invasion of Japan actually take place.

U-234 at the time of her launching, Kiel, 23 December 1943. The scaffolding served as camouflage from Allied bombers. U-Boot Archiv

Lt. Cdr. Johann Heinrich Fehler
U-Boot Archiv

Two ratings hoist the Kriegsmarine ensign from *U-234*'s *Winter-garten*. U-Boot Archiv

U-234's officers on Commissioning Day. *Left to right:* Lt. (jg) Karl Ernst Pfaff, 1st Lt. Albert Klingenberg, Fehler, Lt. Cdr. Horst Ernst, 1st Lt. Günter Pagenstecher. Fehler later replaced Klingenberg with Lt. Cdr. Richard Bulla. U-Boot Archiv

The crew and officers of *U-234*, Commissioning Day, 2 March 1944
U-Boot Archiv

Johann Fehler and his wife, Liseota, at *U-234*'s ceremonial dinner.
U-Boot Archiv

Fehler salutes his crew as *U-234* is commissioned. U-Boot Archiv

1st Lt. Erich Menzel
Erich Menzel

Cdr. Dr. Heinz Schlicke
Heinz Schlicke

Lieutenant (jg) Pfaff ready for
action. U-Boot Archiv

Karl Pfaff *(center)* dines with two unidentified members of the Marinesonderdienst-Ausland at *U-234*'s prevoyage ceremonial dinner. U-Boot Archiv

The surrendered *U-234* sails for Portsmouth, New Hampshire, under the guns of the USS *Sutton*. U-Boot Archiv

U.S. Navy guards from the *Sutton* search *U-234*'s crew.

U-Boot Archiv

Lt. Col. Fritz von Sandrart boards the *Sutton.* U-Boot Archiv

General the Air Force Ulrich Kessler ponders the future at Portsmouth.
Archives and Special Collections, University of New Hampshire

Aboard the USS *Sutton*. *Left to right:* Kay Nieschling, Franz Ruf, Heinrich Hellendorn, Ulrich Kessler, Fritz von Sandrart (with cigar).
U-Boot Archiv

U.S. Navy tugs escort *U-234* into Portsmouth Harbor. Mrs. Edward Pauls

U-234's crew muster aboard the USCG cutter *Argo*. Mrs. Edward Pauls

Dr. August Bringewald arrives at Portsmouth. U-Boot Archiv

"Get the hell off my ship!" Fehler departs the *Argo* after admonishment from Lt. Charles Winslow, USCG (center with clipboard).
Mrs. Edward Pauls

An unidentified official hoists one of the cargo containers from the forward mine tubes. *U-234*'s cargo of uranium oxide was reportedly stored in one of the six forward tubes. National Archives, Northeast Region, Waltham, Mass.

U-234 at rest in Portsmouth. The raised area on the foredeck and the circular figures amidships are the mine tubes. National Archives, Northeast Region, Waltham, Mass.

U-234's *Schnorchel* is raised into position. Archives and Special Collections, University of New Hampshire

Last gasp of the leviathan, 20 November 1947. Torpedoes from the USS *Greenfish* (SS-351) explode amidships, sending *U-234* to the bottom off Provincetown, Massachusetts. Mrs. Edward Pauls

The 1984 reunion of *U-234*'s surviving personnel. *Left to right, front:* Horst Ernst, Hein Fehler, Franz Walter. *Second row:* Fritz Möstl, Georg Lühmann, Herbert Jasper, Kurt Pagel, Franz Wiedenhöft, Helmut Hauthal, Paul Kegel, Wolfgang Hirschfeld. *Third row:* Lothar Winter, Helmut Richter, Herbert Rauhe, Otto Distler, Otto Engelhardt, Heinrich Hellendorn. *Back:* Hubert Lehrmann, Ernst Steffen, Siegfried Schramm, Rolf Bender, Werner Wintermeyer, Günter Walter, Werner Bachmann, Erich Menzel. U-Boot Archiv

6

The
Problem of
Air Defense

U-234's CARGO WAS of menacing potential, but Allied military intelligence could only speculate as to its practical application. In addition, intelligence analysts had little concrete evidence regarding Japan's capacity to manufacture such advanced weapons. The presence of military and civilian technical personnel on board the submarine provided American intelligence officers with an unexpected bonus, and the information gleaned from these individuals proved as valuable as the captured armaments and hardware. The military contingent of passengers consisted of the Luftwaffe's 1st Lt. Erich Menzel, an air communications, reconnaissance, and radar expert, and Lt. Col. Fritz von Sandrart, an antiaircraft specialist.[1] The ONI interrogations of these individuals provided insight into the organizational and technical framework of the ground-based and airborne defense systems deployed by Germany and, by proxy, Japan.

A comparison of German and Japanese antiaircraft defense reveals a polarity, for while German defenses were consistently effective until overwhelmed by sheer numbers of Allied aircraft, Japanese defenses were consistently ineffective. One reason for this disparity was each country's perception of tactical probability and reality. For example,

Germany, though not anticipating the magnitude of the Allied strategic bombing campaign, did not discount the possibility of bombing raids over the Reich; the relative proximity of England to Germany and the obvious potential of the United States made such raids all but inevitable. Therefore, in 1943, when British bombers attacked Hamburg, Germans were justifiably shocked by the ferocity of the campaign; however, the attack itself was not unexpected.

The incendiary bombing of Hamburg jolted the Japanese as much as it did the Germans.[2] Prior to the attack, the majority of Japanese civil-defense and military officials refused to consider the possibility that the Japanese home islands might someday suffer similar devastation.[3] Radio Tokyo exhorted Japanese civilians to disregard the Allied bombing threat: "Why should we be afraid of air raids? The big sky is protected by iron defenses. For young and old it is time to stand up. We are loaded with the honor of defending the homeland. Come on, enemy planes! Come on many times!"[4] However, by August, Japanese foreign minister Shigemitsu Mamoru, despite accusations that he was overestimating the Allies' bombing capability in the Pacific, instructed Ambassador Oshima Hiroshi in Berlin to obtain "all the information we can get on defense against air raids."[5] Consequently, the defense of the home islands would depend largely on the success of German antiaircraft technology.

The Royal Air Force (RAF) launched its first bombing attack on Germany in 1940 in retaliation for the Luftwaffe's bombing of London. These early-daylight raids, in which the RAF employed conventional explosives, were met by the combination of German radar, antiaircraft guns, and excellent fighter defense and were subsequently rendered untenable by excessive losses.[6] However, by 1942 the British were conducting successful nighttime bombing missions over Germany, primarily thanks to the introduction of the Lancaster and Mosquito bombers, advances in British radar, and the introduction of the Pathfinder system, whereby designated aircraft flew ahead of the bombing mission to mark the target.[7] One result of these advances was the first thousand-plane raid, which was launched against Cologne in May 1942 and inflicted as much damage as was rained on London throughout the entirety of the war.[8] Allied success during this period culminated in the incendiary bombing of Hamburg, in which forty thousand to sixty thousand people were killed and 4 square miles of the city torched.

By late 1943, however, advances in radar, the introduction of night-fighter squadrons, and improved ground defenses had turned the tide in Germany's favor. As a result, by mid-1943 Allied bomber losses had risen from negligible numbers to over 5 percent, and by early 1944 up to 10 percent of Allied attacking forces were being destroyed by German antiaircraft defenses.[9] In August 1944, at the peak effectiveness of German antiaircraft defenses, the Luftwaffe employed thirty-nine thousand antiaircraft batteries manned by over one million men.[10] Allied casualties mounted; an August 1943 raid on the ball-bearing factories at Schweinfurt resulted in losses of more than a quarter of the Allied aircraft and men, and in a March 1944 raid on Nuremburg, 12.5 percent of the British attacking force was destroyed—losses "horribly reminiscent of Passchendaele."[11] American forces suffered similar losses. Sixty bombers of the U.S. Army Air Forces (AAF) were lost in twin raids on Schweinfurt and Regensburg in August 1943, and sixty more were lost in a second sortie against Schweinfurt two months later. During October 1943 the AAF lost 9.2 percent of its aircraft. Within six months of the Hamburg raid, Allied bombers had been driven from the night skies, a ringing endorsement of Germany's defensive acumen.

The German success was short-lived, however. The introduction of external fuel tanks, which permitted Allied bombers to complete their missions with fighter escort, and the Allied offensive into Europe as a result of the Normandy invasion, had the dual effect of depleting the ranks of the Luftwaffe's best pilots and crippling Germany's French-based antiaircraft batteries. As a result, the Allied strategic bombing campaign gained full effectiveness only after Germany's peripheral air defenses had largely been destroyed.[12]

However, perhaps the primary reason for the dwindling effectiveness of German air defense was the sheer weight of the Allied bombing offensive. During one week in February 1944, Allied bombers flew over six thousand sorties, delivering nearly 20,000 tons of ordinance, with a loss of 420 aircraft.[13] With the number of Allied sorties continuing to rise unabated, the Luftwaffe could not counter every bombing mission and had to surrender control of the skies to the Allies; in February 1945 the Allies launched the incendiary bombing of Dresden practically unopposed. German antiaircraft fire control and radar countermeasures remained effective, primarily because of their longevity compared with the aircraft of the depleted Luftwaffe; in fact, many Allied pilots attributed more damage to German flak than to Luftwaffe fighters. However, the German antiaircraft system was a triad, and without the fighter aircraft, the other elements were ineffective. Attempts to compensate for the loss of fighter aircraft with turbojet and rocket-powered interceptors, as well as new ground-to-air missiles, fell short, and German ground batteries, while innovative and somewhat effective, collapsed beneath the weight of the massive Allied raids.

In Japan, Foreign Minister Shigemitsu's fears proved justified; on 15 June 1944, sixty-eight American B-29 bombers left Bengal and attacked Tokyo in the first air assault on the home islands since the 1942 Doolittle Raid. The frequency of B-29 missions over Japan increased in proportion to America's encroachments into the Japanese sphere of influence. With the fall of Saipan on 8 July 1944, the United States now possessed a closer platform from which to accelerate the bombing of the home islands; the first conventional raid from the Marianas hit Tokyo on 24 November 1944. The Americans' occupation of Iwo Jima in February 1945 and subsequent expansion of the island's airfields provided an intermediate base for the long-range B-29s, as well as a station for fighter escorts.[14] As a result, by early 1945 the AAF was attempting to disrupt Japan's ability to wage war by destroying its industry by means of large-scale nighttime bombing.[15]

However, because Japanese industrial capacity was relatively small and widely dispersed, and practically impossible to hit at night, the results of the campaign were deemed unsatisfactory. In February 1945 Gen. Curtis LeMay assumed command of the B-29 Twenty-first Bomber Command and immediately switched tactics from high-level precision bombing to low-level incendiary attacks. On the evening of 9 March 1945, 325 B-29s attacked Tokyo. By morning, 16 square miles of the city lay in ruins, 267,000 structures had been burned to the ground, and at least eighty-nine thousand people had ceased to exist.[16] The firebombing of Tokyo was merely a prelude; during a six-day period from 23 May to 29 May 1945, American bombers devastated Osaka, Nagoya, Kobe, Yokohama, and Tokyo with incendiary raids.[17] By now even the most reluctant Japanese officials had to admit Japan's vulnerability to air strikes.[18]

The increased allocation of Japanese armaments to the remnants of the Greater East Asia Co-prosperity Sphere to counter the steady encroachment of the Americans is reflected in the increased inadequacy of Japan's home air defenses. During the 9 March raid on Tokyo, American bomber losses amounted to less than 2 percent, and by the 23 May raid the B-29s were dropping their bombs with impunity, for "the antiaircraft guns had long since ceased to operate."[19] As American bombing missions escalated, AAF losses to equipment and personnel diminished; in late spring 1945, Japanese air defenses accounted for only one-fifth of all B-29 losses, the rest being attributed to mechanical failure and other causes. Meanwhile, the toll exacted upon Japan reached staggering proportions: by midsummer 1945, 60 percent of the ground area of Japan's sixty largest cities had been incinerated.[20] The failure of Japanese home defense was serious enough to prompt Baron Hiranuma Kiichiro, president of the Japanese Privy Council, to remark at a summer 1945 Imperial Council that the "Japanese do not retaliate in any way against [American] air raids. . . . The enemy do as they please. There are absolutely no counterattacks against enemy air raids."[21]

Comparative figures show that German defenses exacted a far greater toll upon the AAF than did those of Japan. In numbers of aircraft alone, the AAF lost 8,325 bombers over Europe but only 414 over Japan.[22] The success of German antiaircraft methods was not lost on the Japanese. In 1944, acknowledging at last the ineffectiveness of their antiquated radar and air-defense systems, Japanese officials sought to acquire German antiaircraft technology.

Japan petitioned the Luftwaffe for the services of Germany's leading air-defense authorities, a request that Germany granted. On 3 May 1945 a German Admiralty message to Tokyo disclosed that "an expert in aerial defense" and "a specialist in radar and infra-red ray . . . and radio-controlled weapons" had left Europe for the Far East in late March on board *U-234*.[23] These two individuals were 1st Lt. Erich Menzel, a radar and communications expert, and Lt. Col. Fritz von Sandrart, the former head of the antiaircraft defenses of Bremen. The two Luftwaffe officers were not only to evaluate and update current Japanese systems but also to facilitate the training of Japanese technicians in the manufacture and integration of the German systems.

Erich Menzel was a twenty-four-year-old native of Radebeul, near Dresden in Saxony. A bachelor who spoke German, French, and English with ease, Menzel was valued by his ONI interrogators for his "good and solid education." In Radebeul, Menzel received his primary and secondary education: five years of *Volksschule* followed by eight years of *Gymnasium*. However, upon graduating from the *Gymnasium* in 1939, Menzel passed up the opportunity to advance to a university degree, opting instead to volunteer for military service with the Wehrmacht.[24] Menzel was content in the military, which satisfied both his sense of adventure and his intellect by allowing him to begin studies in the new field of radio and radar warfare.

Menzel's advancement through the ranks of the military exemplified the Wehrmacht's rapid promotion of bright young men to the upper reaches of the military hierarchy. Menzel's success in the army was apparent from the earliest stages; his basic-training unit, stationed in Silesia, was awarded the honor of serving in the Nürnberg Abteilung and was selected to participate in the National Socialist Party festivals in

Nürnberg. On 1 October 1939 Menzel was assigned to the Fourteenth Training Unit and was soon transferred to Potsdam for basic training in radio and radar as a junior officer. Upon completing the course in 1940, Menzel served with the signal communications corps during the German invasion of France and was later stationed at a Luftwaffe airfield in Orléans.[25]

In November, Menzel began training as a combat radio/radar operator, and eventually he journeyed to Nordhausen to receive his flight training. In February 1941 he graduated as an aerial operator and was commissioned a lieutenant in the Luftwaffe. By May, Menzel had completed training at the Officer's Candidate School in Mecklenburg, receiving his rating as a combat navigator and bombardier. He was next transferred to Brittany, where he prepared to join the Luftwaffe for combat flying over England. However, in one of the few black marks in his career, he was denied combat status because of an argument with his commanding officer and was assigned as an instructor to ground crews. After six weeks a disappointed Menzel requested and received a furlough.[26]

In June 1941, while Menzel was at home in Silesia, Hitler launched his invasion of Russia, and because of his proximity to the eastern front, Menzel was sent to Bobruisk. There Menzel finally acquired aerial combat experience, flying missions against the Soviets until his unit rotated to Hannover for reequipping in October. In January 1942 Menzel's crew returned to combat duty, this time in Focşani, Romania; however, his duty in the Balkans was brief. His reputation had preceded him: his expertise in the fields of radio control and radar was rare, and his experience as an instructor superseded his value as a combat operator. As a result, he was assigned as an instructor at the Luftwaffe's Night Flying School in Erfurt for a one-year tour.[27]

In February 1943 the Luftwaffe's director general of signal communications determined that Menzel's expertise was best suited to research, and he assigned Menzel to the Technical Testing Station of the Luftwaffe in Wernenchen near Berlin. At Wernüchen emphasis was placed on radio developments, and work centered on the development, design, and testing of radio equipment for the Luftwaffe. Stations were set up for the examination of captured enemy radio systems—a captured B-24 Liberator was used for testing British and American radar equipment—and research was conducted with technicians from such electronic contractors as Siemens, Telefunken, and Lorenz.[28]

During the next two years Menzel developed expertise in several fields by contributing to the development of new radar systems, bombsights, radar reconnaissance methods, and radio-controlled weapons.

His work did not go unnoticed; in January 1945 he was named advisory officer in matters concerning communications and radar to the new military air attaché in Tokyo, General of the Air Force Ulrich Kessler. Once in Tokyo, Menzel would also be at the disposal of the Luftwaffe Personnel Department to act as a liaison with the General Staff, and he was subsequently assigned diplomatic credentials. His mission being regarded as a high priority, Menzel immediately reported to Horten, Norway, where he boarded *U-234* for his journey to Japan.[29]

Menzel's Luftwaffe ratings as navigator and bombardier, as well as his substantial combat experience against the British, Soviet, and American air forces, made the information obtained during his interrogation immensely valuable to the ONI because of its operational, rather than theoretical, nature. In addition, Menzel's operational experience in airborne reconnaissance and his subsequent duties as a combat intelligence officer inclined the ONI to regard his testimony as "very reliable"; it was noted that "full credence can be placed in his information."[30] Menzel surprised his interrogators by exhibiting an attitude more representative of the civilians on board *U-234* than of the military contingent. One ONI official observed, "[He] believes the war was useless in the first place, and being somewhat of a scientist, he feels that any knowledge he has is to be used for the good of all."[31]

The primary question facing the ONI was exactly how much of the expertise that Menzel embodied already existed in Japan. Menzel was in a position to make this assessment. During a 26 July discussion of naval reconnaissance, his interrogator noted that because "little is known of what the Japanese actually may have received from the Germans, . . . [Menzel's account] may be of interest, since it may be of tactical value to our Pacific forces in their counter-reconnaissance work."[32] In addition, the ONI was interested in learning from Menzel the extent to which the Japanese had adopted German tactics of aerial reconnaissance—tactics that would presumably have been of great value to the Japanese because of the "tremendous task [they] faced in reconnoitering the huge water mass of the Pacific." Again, knowing what tactics the Japanese might have adopted could be of enormous tactical value to the Americans.[33]

Menzel revealed to ONI investigators that part of his mission had been to give lectures in the various fields of his expertise, as well as to direct Japanese efforts to develop and integrate new communications and radar systems and to provide advice on the tactical and technical utilization of these systems in combat. Menzel was to evaluate the entire scope of Japanese air defenses through an assessment of organization, methodology, and effectiveness. To accomplish this, he was to examine such areas as Japanese antiaircraft artillery, naval reconnaissance, airborne communications, and air-to-ship combat.[34]

Because of the potential for a massive amphibious landing that would accompany an invasion of the home islands, one area of interest to the ONI was sea-borne reconnaissance, both along coastal areas and over the open sea. Menzel informed his interrogators that the various German methods employed to gather intelligence of coastal convoys, fleet anchorages, and coastal shipping had all been judged successful, albeit to different degrees. Luftwaffe engineers had equipped all German reconnaissance aircraft with the FUG 200 Hohentwiel radar; plans to replace the Hohentwiel with newer models such as the Berlingerät and FUG 225 had never materialized.[35]

The Hohentwiel had an effective range of about 60 kilometers (37 miles), although factors such as swells, changes in altitude, and ship size directly affected this range. The effects of ship size were an important consideration: because of their low surface profile, submarines could be detected no further away than 35 kilometers (22 miles), while large convoys increased this range to 80–90 kilometers (50–56 miles). However, overall the Hohentwiel was an exceptional radar and a challenge to Allied countermeasures because of its ability to change frequencies easily.[36]

To accommodate the Hohentwiel airborne radar, the Germans employed two antenna systems, the *Grossantenne* and the *Kleinstantenne,* which were normally placed in the nose of the aircraft. The larger of the two, the *Grossantenne,* was deployed on slower, older aircraft. The *Kleinstantenne,* more compact and finer in resolution, was installed in faster aircraft. Because of its success and its smaller size—it was only a third the size of the *Grossantenne*—the *Kleinstantenne* was produced in greater numbers and outfitted on all newer radar installations.

Menzel informed his ONI interrogators that the Germans used both parallel and perpendicular reconnaissance patterns when searching a coastal area. However, as the war progressed the parallel method was employed only when the seriousness of the situation required that pilot and crew be exposed to extreme enemy countermeasures and coastal defense, and the perpendicular method became the standard system. The main difference between the two methods was the length of time for which the Hohentwiel was operational: the longer the radar was turned on, the greater the chance of detection. The perpendicular method required the Hohentwiel to operate only when the aircraft was flying perpendicular to the shoreline, and not during course adjustments or turns. In contrast, the parallel method required that the Hohentwiel operate continuously as the aircraft flew a continuous linear course parallel to the shore.[37]

The perpendicular method required that an initial course be flown parallel to the coast at an outboard range of 70 kilometers (44 miles) and at a minimum altitude, normally 40–50 meters (131–64 feet), to avoid detection. The aircraft would then climb to an optimum search altitude of 800–1,000 meters (2,625–3,281 feet) while changing course to initiate the search. Here, at a course 90 degrees to the coast, the Hohentwiel was engaged until the image was interrupted by ground interference. At this point the aircraft would turn off the radar and fly a course away from the coast. Once back at the origination point, the pilot would extend his flight path to incorporate a new area of the coast and repeat the search course.

Menzel assessed the perpendicular method as "good and successful."[38] It obtained results "with minimum enemy interference."[39] The method owed its success largely to the short operating time of the Hohentwiel—normally, a scanning time of less than three minutes—as well as to the use of minimum flight altitudes when applicable, both of which reduced the chances of detection. However, when operating over an uneven or irregular coastline, such as a bay or inlet, the Hohentwiel had to be left on, increasing the chance of fighter or flak detection. In addition, the irregular nature of the coast added to ground clutter; a ship could be spotted only if she was closer to the aircraft than the aircraft was to land. To help alleviate this problem, German engineers had developed antennas to be deployed along both sides of the aircraft in addition to the nose set. Because the operator could now alternate between antenna sets, a close sweeping of an irregular coast was now allowable, even though the Hohentwiel still had to operate continuously; the increased risk of detection was deemed acceptable in view of the results that could be obtained.

In the course of his work at the Technical Testing Station at Wernüchen, Menzel had been exposed to new radar systems as well as evaluations of captured Allied sets. During the final months of the war in Europe, German technicians had begun research into a rotating antenna system, whereby the *Kleinstantenne* was rotated by hand. Menzel judged this method "more convenient, and good results were obtained." He also rated the new German radar Berlin as "better than the Rotterdam"[40] but considered Allied radar "far superior and far ahead of its German counterparts."[41] The Meddo system with its photographic cathode ray tube, the British ASV night-fighter radar, Allied radar bombing devices—all these, Menzel claimed, were superior to anything the Germans possessed.

American fighter and bomber pilots who had engaged Japanese night fighters over Japan reported that since November 1944, Japanese night-fighting aircraft had been equipped with a radar-controlled inclined cannon, which had been installed in the aircraft's nose. Owing to the success of similar devices used by the Luftwaffe, the ONI questioned Menzel as to whether the radar-controlled cannon had originated in Germany or Japan. Menzel replied that although experiments involving the principle of a radar-guided cannon had been performed at Wernüchen, the results were judged insufficient to merit use in combat. As a result, little of this information was passed on to the Japanese; indeed, the Japanese commission stayed at Wernüchen for only one day. However, Menzel pointed out that the commission did include some "crack radar experts," and he saw no reason why these scientists could not have elaborated on the radar-controlled cannon on their own.[42]

On 19 May 1945 the chief of the AAF's Armament Section, Lt. Col. Edward Elliot, submitted a questionnaire to Menzel addressing the matter of German bombsights that might have been acquired by the Japanese. Asked to identify various bombsights, Menzel pointed out that the German *Bombenzielabwurfgerät* (BZG), model 1, was an old sight that had not been used since 1941, and its successor, the BZG-2, was "cheaply produced . . . [and] did not have a good reputation among bombardiers."[43] While Menzel professed no knowledge of the *Sturzflugvisier* 5-B or the IVR bombsight computer, he did report at length about Germany's most popular and effective system, the Lufternrehr, or Lufte, series.

The Lufte series, which was manufactured by Zeiss, was the most commonly used bombsight in the Luftwaffe and was so proficient that, rather than develop new sighting systems, German engineers simply improved on the Lufte. As a result, the Lufte sight underwent a continuous evolution that encompassed the series 7B, 7C, and 7D. Menzel informed the ONI that the Lufte sight was designed along the lines of the tremendously effective American Norden bombsight—a claim that Menzel admittedly could not completely verify, since he himself had never seen one of these top-secret American devices. However, as far as practical experience was concerned, Menzel had used the 7C, and later the 7D, in radar-controlled bombing runs at sea when the 7B was phased out of service. As proof that Germany was sending the latest in German technology to Japan, Menzel had carried with him on *U-234* detailed drawings for the manufacture of the Lufte 7D; consequently, Lieutenant Colonel Elliot's questioning focused on Menzel's knowledge of the model 7D.

The model 7D was the most modern and effective of the Lufte line, and it included all of the cumulative improvements that had been tested on its predecessors, such as an automatic drift-angle compensator. Menzel pointed out that the new 7D was designed to compensate for advances in Allied bombsights and had optical, electrical, and gyroscopic features that rendered it the most technologically advanced bombsight that the Axis powers possessed. The Lufte 7D used radar to assist in ranging control and had an effective angle of vision that ranged from 20 degrees to the rear of vertical to 80 degrees forward from vertical. Menzel surprised Elliot by stating that the graduations on the Lufte bombsight had no practical value; the only scale used in aiming was cross hairs, which were activated automatically once the bombardier had sighted the target along the plane of a straight line.[44] Clearly, the 7D was an advanced bombsight, and even though inferior to Allied sights, it could prove menacing to Allied antiaircraft defenses, especially at sea.

For all its advanced features, the Lufte 7D did have limitations. For example, Menzel pointed out that the sight provided "extremely poor results" at altitudes below 1,200 meters (3,937 feet); acceptable accuracy began at about 1,500 meters (4,921 feet), with optimum results obtained at 4,000–5,000 meters (13,123–16,404 feet) at airspeeds of 300 kilometers per hour (186 miles per hour).[45] With the Lufte sight, the Germans used the tactic of *Gleitbombenwurf,* or bomb release in a steep glide. With this innovation, the bombsight could be effectively used in a steep glide at a vertical speed of 2–3 meters (7–10 feet) per second. The result was a shorter, more accurate bomb run. The desired length of a standard run was forty to fifty seconds; with the *Gleitbombenwurf,* this time was considerably shortened.

Bombing accuracy was another of Elliot's concerns. Menzel pointed out that under combat conditions, accuracy with the Lufte 7D was quite adequate. He reported that in Russia, bridges had been destroyed from altitudes of up to 6,000 meters (19,685 feet) with all bombs falling within an area of 50 meters (164 feet). In addition, the Lufte could be synchronized with a radar system to improve performance under bad weather conditions. However, this method was not to be considered "blind bombing"; although the target could be tracked with radar during the targeting phase, it had to be physically visible at the moment of bomb release.[46]

Arguably the most important testimony given by Menzel involved his knowledge of and operational experience with the Henschel (HS) 293 remote-controlled glider bomb. Among Menzel's documents on *U-234* were an instruction book and drawings for the latest version of the HS-293—the first evidence Allied intelligence had ever received about Japan's possession or knowledge of this early incarnation of the guided missile.[47] The Luftwaffe had experienced some early success with the HS-293 in the Mediterranean Sea; in fact, the HS-293 held the distinction of being the first airborne guided missile to sink an enemy ship, having sunk the British sloop *Egret* off the Spanish coast on 27 August 1943.[48]

The HS-293, designed in 1943 by a Professor Kramer,[49] was an air-dropped radio-command guided weapon, intended to replace air-launched torpedoes for antiship use. The HS-293 resembled a small aircraft, with a wingspan of 3.1 meters (10 feet 3½ inches), and carried a 500-kilogram (1,100-pound) warhead.[50] Upon release from its parent aircraft, a liquid-fuel rocket accelerated the missile to speeds in excess of 560 kilometers per hour (350 miles per hour), in about twelve seconds. At this point the rocket engine shut down, and the bomb continued flight in a glide. The effective range of the HS-293 depended on its altitude at release; when released from 1,370 meters (4,500 feet), it had a range of about 8 kilometers (5 miles).[51]

The HS-293 was guided to its target by an operator who from the parent aircraft manipulated the missile with a joystick steering device. The operator could visually track the missile by means of a flare located in the tail of the missile and could transmit roll and/or yaw course corrections to an on-board receiver. However, the HS-293 had little penetrative power; therefore any violation of the hull integrity of a surface vessel had to come from an HS-293 that had been released from a relatively high altitude.[52]

At first glance the HS-293 did not appear to the ONI to be much of a threat. However, Menzel informed his interrogators that the Japanese planned to use the missile against ground targets, which he called "pin points." Menzel had planned to instruct the Japanese in the operational aspects of the missile, providing descriptions of the missile and its avionics, conducting detailed training on the interface between the control units in the parent plane and the receiver in the missile, and helping to make the necessary adjustments needed to deploy the missile.[53]

Because the Japanese had little experience in remote-controlled weapons, they required instruction in the basic flight characteristics and tactical applications of the missile. Consequently, Menzel was to instruct the Japanese in such rudimentary areas as proper release distance from target, characteristics of the missile in parallel flight to its target, and behavior of the missile after release, as well as provide instruction to the crews who would be releasing the bomb and steering it in flight. After proficiency had been shown in these areas, Menzel would work with the Japanese to devise tactics such as formation bombing with the HS-293.[54]

In the hands of an experienced operator, the HS-293 constituted a deadly menace to both ground and sea targets and would be an ideal weapon with which to repel an amphibious force. Menzel informed the ONI that the bomb was "100 per cent accurate when correct and trained personnel handled it," and the addition of an armor-piercing projectile would eliminate the need for a high-altitude release. However, although the Japanese had previously obtained knowledge of the functions and principles of the missile, they lacked detailed drawings and the most vital element: the frequency by which the HS-293 was controlled.[55] These deficiencies were to be addressed and corrected by Erich Menzel.

Menzel was to evaluate both the visual and radar reconnaissance methods of the Japanese as well as instruct them in German torpedo and bombing tactics and the use of German instruments.[56] He was also charged with training the Japanese to evaluate captured Allied radars and to effect their deployment.[57] However, once he was established in Tokyo, his duties would expand to encompass all activities involving Japanese problems of air defense, reconnaissance, air-to-sea attack strategy, and radar.[58] His ultimate responsibilities were to introduce, manufacture, and incorporate German equipment into Japanese defenses, if at all possible.[59] To facilitate this, a Hohentwiel naval early-warning radar system and two airborne systems, the 1 B/3 and the 39 FUG X, accompanied him on *U-234*.[60] In addition, a new Kiel 2 system was to follow on a subsequent submarine, along with the expertise to reproduce these systems in the person of one Dr. Mahlfeldt, a leading German electronics expert.[61]

The Luftwaffe's Lt. Col. Fritz von Sandrart was the former head of the German air defenses at Bremen and had recently taken part in the design and testing of Germany's latest antiaircraft weapons.[62] Von Sandrart joined the army in 1913 and spent the years following World War I (1919–37) in Argentina.[63] At the time of *U-234*'s surrender he was attached to Flak Regiment 26 at Bremen. Von Sandrart was considered an expert in antiaircraft defense strategy. His duties in Japan were to focus on the introduction and tactical application of Germany's newest defense systems. His perceived lack of technical expertise would be compensated for by Menzel and by other technicians who were set to follow *U-234* on subsequent missions.[64]

Germany had been an innovator in antiaircraft defense since World War I. Von Sandrart recounted attempts in 1914 to shoot down enemy observation balloons and aircraft by mounting 7.7- and 10.5-caliber field howitzers on wooden platforms, an innovation so successful that by 1917 the guns were placed on trucks, thus becoming mobile. The Germans addressed the problem of accuracy by providing each gun with a firing table that was calibrated on the distance given by a 1.5-meter range finder, the angular height of the object, and its estimated speed.[65] Although crude by the standards of 1945, these innovations were the beginnings of German antiaircraft expertise, and they ultimately led to such sophisticated devices as fire-control computers, two of which were on *U-234*.[66]

As early as 1933, von Sandrart explained, Germany had realized that it was surrounded by potentially hostile states that had highly developed air forces and antiaircraft capabilities. In order to catch up, Germany would have to accelerate rearmament in the areas of both the air force and air defense. In 1941, however, the Luftwaffe discovered that its existing antiaircraft systems were inadequate, prompting research into more effective methods. In 1942, improved radar bolstered the effectiveness of the antiaircraft batteries, and German military planners elevated air-defense research and development to a higher priority, third behind aircraft and tank production.[67] This emphasis on antiaircraft technology explained why German air defenses had exacted such a heavy toll on Allied bombers conducting raids over Europe, losses that Allied planners did not wish to experience again over Japan.

The extent to which the Japanese had integrated German antiaircraft and countermeasures technology into their own systems continued to concern the ONI and the AAF. General Kessler had addressed these concerns by pointing out that prior to the spring of 1941 no formal military liaison existed between Germany and Japan. He also stated that no "ballistics experts, ordnance men, AA [antiaircraft] tactics experts, or other specialized personnel" had preceded those captured aboard *U-234* to Japan.[68] However, by 1943 Germany had indeed initiated the transfer of German technology to Japan. In June 1943, Japanese officials received technical drawings of the Würzburg D radio direction-finding system, which could be applied to existing Japanese antiaircraft armament, accompanied by a Henschel radio engineer (Pohl), who assisted the Japanese with the mass production of the

Würzburg.[69] Still, the Japanese perceived no need for any substantial improvement in their antiaircraft technology, because they believed the home islands invulnerable to enemy attack. However, Germany did not suffer from such delusions about the Japanese home islands. Consequently, the impetus to develop an efficient antiaircraft defense system for Japan came not from Japanese strategists but from the Germans.

Japan's reluctance to consider and subsequently adopt modern antiaircraft technology was emblematic of the antiquated state of the Japanese military-industrial sector. Japanese officers in Germany had received instruction in the theory of Germany's air-defense system, and had even observed its effectiveness by witnessing the tactical deployment of fighter aircraft in the defense of Berlin's regional headquarters, as well as ground defenses against Allied bombing raids on German installations at Leuna and Merseberg. In addition, Germany's Krupp armory had provided the Japanese navy with designs for a naval version of the excellent 88-millimeter dual-purpose artillery and antiaircraft gun, and in 1942 a Japanese submarine had arrived in Japan with a Zeiss artillery director, or primitive fire-control system.[70]

As long as these German antiaircraft systems remained based on mechanical technology, the Japanese made efforts to integrate them into their existing systems. However, once the Germans began developing electronic means of guidance and fire control, which made the components more sophisticated, the Japanese found themselves unable to continue incorporating German technology. Japan's war industry simply lacked the technological basis to reproduce the components of Germany's state-of-the-art fire-control computer systems and radar; it was unable to meet "the most primitive demands," unable even "to produce reliable radio tubes." The Germans recognized that this inability to develop electronic equipment was the "deadlock of the entire Japanese armament program." A confidential March 1945 OKM report from Naval Attaché Paul Wennecker's office in Tokyo concluded that Japan would be unable to counter an Allied air attack. Its land defenses were even weaker than its notoriously bad naval defenses. In fact, its entire air-defense system was obsolete, and it was incapable of evolving beyond that stage without an infusion of technological expertise. It was this realization that led to the transfer of German technical specialists to Japan on missions like that of *U-234*.[71]

One matter about which Allied air commanders were curious was the absence of German fighter cover during heavy antiaircraft barrages. Von Sandrart explained that by 1945 the Luftwaffe was experiencing a shortage of qualified pilots (a situation the Japanese faced

now). Using fighter defense in close proximity to antiaircraft fire carried the risk of ground forces shooting down their own planes. Because
Luftwaffe officers regarded their pilots as too valuable to expose to a
Fliegerabwehrkanonen, or flak, barrage, they deployed their fighter
aircraft sparingly, usually either to meet an incoming bomber formation before the commencement of ground fire or to chase the retreat-
ing survivors. This strategy of economy explained why fighter aircraft
were not deployed in zones of heavy antiaircraft concentrations, thus
allowing ground batteries full freedom to fire.[72]

By virtue of his work in Germany with experimental equipment, von
Sandrart was able to provide information regarding the latest German
developments in antiaircraft and air-defense systems, some of which
were destined for Japan. For example, German munitions experts had
steadily increased shell caliber to achieve higher muzzle velocity in
order to compensate for the higher altitude of Allied bombers. However, the increased size of the explosive charges required to attain sufficient velocity caused excessive wear on the gun barrels and forced
German engineers to ponder other methods of achieving altitude. To
address this problem, subcaliber guns and shells were being introduced and tested as the war in Europe ended. As a result of the experimentation, muzzle velocities of 1,300 meters (4,265 feet) per second
had already been attained, and higher velocities were not out of the
realm of possibility.[73] Another innovation, the *Pfeilgeschoss,* or arrow
shell, designed to be fired from a conically shaped tube, had been
deployed on a trial basis to antiaircraft batteries in the Frankfurt area.[74]
AAF officials expressed concern about these weapons, the deployment
of which by the Japanese could eliminate the B-29's tactical advantage
of high-altitude bombing.

One successful tactic employed by the Germans was the deployment
of dummy installations to counteract Allied reconnaissance missions.
According to von Sandrart, dummy installations were centrally directed
by a divisional commander, who telephoned operational commands to
the installation's resident commander. The effectiveness of this tactic
was proven by mock installations that represented the Oslebshausen
freight yards and the Focke-Wulf aircraft factory in Bremen, both of
which drew frequent bombing. Daylight camouflage was not employed
in the Bremen area, but night camouflage was employed with great
success and helped save the Oslebshausen yards and the Focke-Wulf
factory from complete destruction by enemy bombing raids. To enhance
the decoy effect, large fires that simulated Allied ground markers were
set, and the results were likewise highly successful.[75]

AAF officials were also curious about reports by American and British bomber pilots of multicolored explosions mixed among regular flak over Germany in late 1944. By April 1945, American B-29 crewmen were reporting similar sightings over Japan. On 13 April seven aircrews claimed that "balls of fire" had traced across the sky, with some hitting the ground and exploding. A 16 April report stated that one B-29 had been attacked four times during the same raid: the first fireball "came at us from 3 [o'clock] . . . but our speed took us past him"; the second appeared aft of the aircraft after crossing Tokyo Bay and eventually exploded in the ocean; the same fate greeted a third, which appeared about 240 kilometers (150 miles) from the Japanese mainland; and the final attack had the same results.[76] Suggested explanations for these anomalies ranged from rocket-powered suicide missions to a new magnetic antiaircraft device designed to attach itself to a bomber before exploding. Allied intelligence reported that the Japanese were attempting to buttress public morale by announcing new defensive weapons, one of which involved an "atomic discharge" that would paralyze the enemy aircraft. Such a weapon could possibly appear in the form of "a colored ball of some sort shot into the air."[77]

Wing Commander H. Priestly of the Royal Air Force, eager to clear up the mystery, had requested that the ONI secure information on the identity of the "colored balls of fire." ONI interrogators put the question to von Sandrart, who professed knowledge of the fireballs that had been reported over Europe and identified them as experimental weapons that, while distracting, had nonetheless been determined to be impractical. The device, which had been developed by the Luftwaffe and was not intended for ground antiaircraft units, was released from an aircraft that had climbed above the ceiling of the enemy bomber formation. The bomb was equipped with a time fuse that would theoretically detonate at the altitude of the attacking formation. The new weapon was of limited success, however, and was therefore sent back to the experimental laboratories.[78] As to the reports concerning the use of the device over Japan, von Sandrart could only refer his interrogators to the Luftwaffe's technical and experimental branch, leading the ONI to suspect that the Japanese were using German air-to-air missiles.

Knowing that Japan lacked the industrial capacity to mass-produce antiaircraft weapons, American officials wondered how the Japanese allocated their scarce resources among their various defense priorities. Von Sandrart revealed that Germany had faced a similar problem. The Kriegsmarine had traditionally followed a strategy of "stationary protection batteries" (a strategy embodied, for example, in Admiral

Dönitz's repeated requests for increased antiaircraft protection for the shipyards at Kiel and Bremen, at least one thousand guns for each).[79] However, the sheer number and range of bombing targets within Germany reduced the usefulness of that strategy. As von Sandrart revealed, the concentration of resources in nonmobile batteries denied protection to other targets that might actually be more important.[80] In addition, with nonmobile batteries, it was impossible to shift defense resources to match Allied bombing pressure, which often changed daily. As a result, the General Staff of the Luftwaffe adopted the *bewegliche Kriegsführung,* or mobile strategy. Because Japanese antiaircraft specialists were known to be familiar with the overall German antiaircraft defense system,[81] AAF officials speculated that the Japanese would likewise adopt a strategy of mobility.

Von Sandrart told his interrogators about the link between the Bremen early-warning communications network and antiaircraft defense, as applied under the mobility system. As Allied air raids increased in early 1944, the Luftwaffe reorganized Germany's early-warning network, placing it under the operational command of the *Jagddivision,* or aircraft intercept command, which simultaneously introduced a fighter grid location system designed to integrate fighter cover with antiaircraft batteries. Tactical disposition of "filter centers," which received and processed air situation reports from systematically distributed early-warning stations, was established across the country and in all major cities; on the coastlines, these centers were augmented by long-range interceptor radar such as the Giant Würzburg. The filter centers were likewise responsible for lateral liaison with adjoining stations to guarantee a constant situation update. For example, the local antiaircraft commander of the Bremen defense district received continuous air situation reports from the Bremen filter center. In the event that Bremen was threatened by an incoming formation, the Bremen commander received additional situational and position updates from the Second Aircraft Intercept Command in nearby Stade, whose radar would "paint" the identical contact as Bremen, albeit from a different bearing. In addition, long-range Freya early-warning systems, located along the Bremen periphery, would begin operation, further enhancing the accuracy of the contact. This cross-reference of information allowed aircraft and antiaircraft commanders to form an accurate estimation of the threat, to which they could economically deploy the applicable countermeasures.[82]

In the event of an incoming attack, a coordinated series of defense measures were activated, all designed to meet the threat with effectiveness and economy. In the event that a radar contact containing more than ten aircraft violated the 350-kilometer (217-mile) defense perimeter, a full alarm would be issued for the immediate area under threat—for example, the Bremen metropolitan area. If only a single aircraft approached, a partial, or district, alarm would sound. In either case the alarm would have to sound far enough in advance of the estimated arrival of the contact to allow the populace time to evacuate to air-raid shelters, some of which might be as much as twenty minutes from the target area. Early-warning advance timing was of great importance; time was needed not just to clear the target area of civilians but also to staff the defense batteries and prepare all guns, fire-control mechanisms, and radar. These defense systems, as well as a divisional command post, were usually activated as soon as the 350-kilometer perimeter was reached by an incoming formation.

Because energy became a premium commodity as the war progressed, electrical current was not supplied to all of the immediate area defense systems on a full-time basis, except for the radar stations along the 100-kilometer (62-mile) perimeter. These stations also served as transformers, effecting a timely current switchover to the area defenses. To transfer the current, German engineers discovered that high-wire conveyance systems were preferable to underground cables, as they provided better resistance against the concussion of a bomb blast. In addition, in case of transfer failure, it was far easier to locate a downed line than search for it underground, and consequent quick repairs were usually possible. However, in the case of an electrical failure, the lateral liaison communications network remained at least marginally operational, as auxiliary systems permitted the transmittal of radio traffic, as well as continuous Freya readings, to the individual battery command posts.[83]

Von Sandrart pointed out that the primary purposes of an area antiaircraft command were to prevent uncoordinated antiaircraft fire, to engage and attack approaching bombers as soon as possible, and, after a bomb release, to reengage the returning bombers while simultaneously attacking any secondary aircraft. The basis for success in this system was the quick and efficient location and designation of targets. Once the incoming formation had been identified and its position marked on a location, or "spotter" grid, overlapping forward batteries initiated a flak saturation, a tactic that generally proved successful, although premature bomb-drops reduced the chances of downing a bomber with antiaircraft fire. The resulting strategy of deploying high concentrations of coordinated firepower as early as possible proved effective; however, changes in Allied strategy severely disrupted its continuity.[84]

As the war progressed, the increased number and range of Allied bomber raids proved "exceptionally annoying" to antiaircraft commanders.[85] Particularly annoying was the increase of range in Allied radar, which, according to von Sandrart, would have eventually forced the German defense network to dissipate by rendering early-warning systems ineffective. Von Sandrart expressed surprise that the Allies had not made greater use of this advantage, rather than simply increasing the number of aircraft, and lives, lost over Europe.

German antiaircraft measures were substantially reduced by RAF night attacks featuring the Mosquito XVI attack bomber. The Mosquito's great speed (668 kilometers, or 415 miles, per hour) and ceiling (11,887 meters, or 39,000 feet) confounded German radar and rendered early detection difficult, especially at night.[86] The altitudes that the Mosquito could attain hampered ground air-defense batteries because of the longer firing range required; British pilots discovered that the higher they flew, the less they were affected by German ground fire.[87] The RAF even began to find ways to dilute German antiaircraft measures using day flights; von Sandrart explained that an attack from the sun, in partial cloud cover, was particularly effective because it made optical aiming and firing of antiaircraft guns "practically impossible."[88]

Perhaps von Sandrart's most valuable revelation concerned the development and design of the *Grossbatterie* air-defense system. Standard antiaircraft defenses had proven their worth throughout the war, but their effectiveness was limited by the availability of guns and ammunition. As the war evolved from a series of short, blitzkrieg-style engagements into a drawn-out conflict on two fronts, Germany's war industry proved unable provide sufficient numbers of antiaircraft weapons to protect all of Germany's priority targets. As a result, Luftwaffe officials determined that a system of priority defense locations would be designated to receive a system of multiple-gun batteries, operated by a central fire-control system. The development of the Kommando Geräte fire-control computer pushed the project from the theoretical to the practical stage, and the increased number of massive Allied bombing raids forced the Germans to implement the system operationally.[89]

The *Grossbatterie* system was calibrated on an incoming aircraft at an estimated bombing level of 8,000 meters (26,246 feet) and traveling at an airspeed of 110 meters (361 feet) per second. The gun formation consisted of three batteries of 8.8- and 10.5-caliber antiaircraft guns, staggered in a triangular formation, which were set up in a triangular formation.[90] Within the triangle, two batteries were directed to the main avenue of approach, with the remaining battery at the apex of the formation. The batteries were placed 150–200 meters (492–656 feet) from the fire-control station and 400–500 meters (1,312–1,640 feet) from each other, proportionally distanced so that their fire overlapped. Typically, this design provided effective defense for its particular area; however, in extensive defense areas such as Bremen, the overlapping of fire batteries was not always possible because of shortage of guns and personnel. Von Sandrart explained that the *Grossbatterie* theory was based on the assumption that regardless of the direction from which a bomber formation might approach, it would be engaged and subsequently covered by the fire of at least two *Grossbatterien* prior to reaching its drop zone. The predictability of an Allied formation consistently approaching from one or two fixed directions over a particular area enhanced the accuracy and effectiveness of the system. For defense, the batteries themselves were protected by earthen revetments, and thus could be destroyed only by a direct hit.

The *Grossbatterie* system proved effective, in terms of both the destruction of enemy bombers and the forced early release of their bomb loads. However, this effectiveness, though substantial, was eventually negated by Allied countermeasures. Increased jamming of German active and passive radar, for which the Germans had no remedy, and the increased number of bombers eventually overwhelmed the batteries, which, according to von Sandrart, were soon "rendered helpless in the face of overwhelming air power."[91] However, Germany had demonstrated its resiliency throughout the war and expected to return the *Grossbatterie* to its previous level of success.

Von Sandrart believed that only new weapons and tactics—some slated for release in early 1946, others ready for immediate deployment—could return the *Grossbatterie* to its early effectiveness. Some of the operational weapons included improved fire-control computers to compensate for high-speed bombers such as the Mosquito, more sensitive proximity fuses for flak projectiles, antijamming devices to counter Allied interference with active and passive radar, and radar-guided rocket projectiles fitted with homing devices. In addition, the Krupp armament works was experimenting with subcaliber guns as well as newer weapons featuring an improved muzzle velocity; von Sandrart claimed that muzzle velocities of 1,300 meters (4,265 feet) per second had already been achieved, with even higher speeds expected.[92]

The interrogation team in Washington noted with alarm that all of these devices were aboard *U-234*, and hence destined for deployment by the Japanese.[93] However, von Sandrart showed little concern for Japan's deployment of German antiaircraft defense measures. Although he was perhaps the leading flak authority in the Luftwaffe, he revealed that he "never had any idea about Japanese Flak," and what little he did know led him to the conclusion that the Japanese "were far behind in Flak equipment compared to the Germans."[94] As to the prospects of American air success over Japan, von Sandrart replied that because air superiority was the key to Allied victory in Europe, the Japanese "do not stand an earthly chance. . . . They will be taken apart far worse than Germany."[95]

7

Dönitz's
Naval
Mission

BY LATE 1944 Grand Admiral Karl Dönitz had concluded that the best opportunity for the Kriegsmarine's officers to gain operational experience in large-scale fleet maneuvers was to learn from the Japanese. German naval operations, which had once been of imposing potential, with surface vessels such as the *Bismarck* and *Tirpitz*, were now limited to U-boat operations and coastal engagements; in contrast, Japan's war in the Pacific had been a primarily naval affair since 7 December 1941. Therefore, on 3 December 1944 Dönitz announced to Hitler his intention of transferring German naval officers to assignments with the Japanese Imperial Navy for the purpose of acquiring experience that could later be used to revamp the decimated German fleet.[1]

In addition, a naval technical mission to Japan had been previously considered. In 1943 German naval attaché Paul Wennecker requested an information exchange, but it was postponed because of its low priority. However, Dönitz's desire to send naval officers to Japan, coupled with Hitler's desire to accommodate the Japanese, prompted the OKM to revive the plan, although preparations for the mission's departure were not finalized until December 1944.

The naval mission to Japan was distinct from the mission of the other specialists aboard *U-234*. Because of the magnitude of Japanese fleet operations, the OKM perceived a need for German observation of Japanese "developments, methods, equipment, etc. of value," information that could be returned to and utilized by the Kriegsmarine. On the other hand, mission members were instructed to reveal as little as possible to their Japanese hosts; their packages were all marked "Not to be handed to Japanese subjects," and all material belonging to the members of the naval contingent was to be screened by mission chief Gerhard Falcke and Wennecker's staff before being exchanged with the Japanese.[2]

Dönitz had originally intended to send ten to fifteen officers to Japan. However, because of space limitations, he could send only four aboard *U-234*. In December 1944 the four were issued orders to report to Falcke in Berlin. Falcke, who had been in contact with Wennecker as to exactly what to bring to Japan, coordinated the accumulation of the necessary technical information for the journey, and by February the contingent had arrived in Kiel. Finally, on 25 March 1945, naval aviator Richard Bulla, antiaircraft specialist Heinrich Hellendorn, and naval judge Kay Nieschling joined Falcke in Kiel, where they boarded *U-234*. After first traveling to Norway while *U-234* completed her sea trials, Falcke's mission finally departed in April on the long voyage to Japan.

Commanding the naval contingent to Japan was forty-eight-year-old Gerhard Falcke, a naval construction engineer and electrical welding expert. Upon the conclusion of preliminary POW interrogations, the ONI assessed Falcke as "well-informed, reliable, intelligent, [and] cooperative"—a "high-type" man who, despite professing no "active interest in things political," nevertheless exhibited allegiance to National Socialism.[3] The OKM had regarded Falcke as the ideal officer to head the technical mission to Tokyo; before completing his training as a naval engineer, he had served as the Kriegsmarine's foreign liaison, coordinating cooperative naval efforts with the Soviet Union, Italy, Bulgaria, Spain, and Japan. His combination of diplomatic and engineering experience provided him with unique qualifications for this mission.

Falcke was one of the oldest of *U-234*'s passengers. Born in 1897 near Merseburg, he attended *Volksschule* at Koburg and *Gymnasium* in Cologne, graduating in 1915. After completing secondary school, Falcke immediately joined the Imperial German Navy, serving at sea until resigning his commission as *Leutnant zur See* (lieutenant [jg]) in 1919. Like Kessler, Falcke left the navy after the war to resume his education and subsequently entered the technical *Hochschule* (university) at Aachen to study electrical engineering, welding, and machine and tool construction.

Falcke received his degree in 1925 and immediately began his career as a production engineer with the Siemens Company in Seimensstadt. By 1928 he had advanced to section manager and was transferred to research and development, where he specialized in electrical welding methods. In 1935 he left Siemens to establish himself as an independent contractor. Falcke quickly received orders to install electrical welding processes for the Messer facility in Frankfurt/Main as well as the Müller plant in Cologne; however, he was accused of nonfulfillment of his contracts in both instances and subsequently left after a short stay. In 1936 Falcke went to work for the fledgling Luftwaffe, serving as a technical adviser with the Air Force Technical School near Berlin. At the academy Falcke brought his expertise in electrical welding methods to bear on standard production procedures to produce airframes with superb structural integrity.[4]

On 15 March 1938, with the situation in Europe worsening, Falcke was recalled to duty with the Kriegsmarine. In view of his engineering experience he was immediately advanced to the rank of lieutenant commander and assigned to the Shipping Branch (Flottenabteilung) Branch) of the OKM in Berlin. There he coordinated the procurement of material and equipment for the navy's Construction Office (Konstruktionsamt) and, upon obtaining the necessary items, also determined priority for the allotment of these materials for the construction of new weapons and equipment for naval surface vessels. In 1940, however, Falcke was reassigned when the Shipping Branch and the Construction Office were combined to form the Department of Warship Construction (Hauptamt Kriegsschiffbau).[5]

In 1940 Falcke was named chief of the Liaison Section of the Department of Warship Construction. In this capacity he was the liaison for naval technical representatives from countries within Germany's sphere of influence.[6] Although his duties required diplomatic and technical visits to these countries, Falcke himself never ventured from his Berlin office; his staff members handled all travel to foreign locales while he received visits from foreign technical and shipping representatives. As a result, Falcke gained extensive knowledge pertaining to the exchange of naval-related materials, plans, documents, and personnel with these countries.[7] Of all the countries with which Falcke was familiar, he was the most interested personally in Japan; indeed, Falcke spoke fluent Japanese and was a student of Japanese culture.[8] Consequently, when the OKM sought an officer with the diplomatic and engineering proficiency to head up Wennecker's naval technical section in Japan, Falcke was the logical choice.[9]

Because of his liaison with the Japanese, and particularly the Imperial Japanese Navy, Falcke was able to provide the ONI at Portsmouth with details of German and Japanese naval cooperation. According to Falcke, the Axis powers had maintained political connections through their respective foreign offices prior to the Tripartite Pact. After the conclusion of the pact, subsequent evaluations indicated to Japanese officials that Germany's command structure, weapons technology, and armaments industry were more advanced than their own. Consequently, the Axis powers ratified supplemental agreements concerning the exchange of military and economic information; the idea was that such information would be conveyed to the appropriate officials who would then acquire proficiency in their particular areas.[10]

Falcke also guided his ONI interrogators through the OKM's confusing chain of command as it applied to Japanese affairs. The Oberkommando der Wehrmacht (OKW), or Wehrmacht High Command, provided general directions and decisions pertaining to Japanese liaison involving the Wehrmacht. The Foreign Office coordinated matters on a political level, and the Ministry of the Office of Armament Industry directed industrial matters, both military and civilian. In addition, the Group for Industry and various civil officials worked together to provide cooperation between the military and the private sector. Finally, the OKM itself was divided into two separate departments: the Sea War Directorate, which coordinated Japanese and German military matters, and the Department of Warship Construction, which handled access to German shipyards as well as the sending of reciprocal missions to Japan.[11]

Another department of interest to the ONI was the Marinesonderdienst-Ausland (MSD), which coordinated all overseas shipping and receiving for the Reich. As part of his liaison duties, Falcke maintained a close working relationship with the MSD and was able to provide the ONI with an overview of its command structure, as it existed at the time of *U-234*'s departure. By the spring of 1945, because of Allied penetration into Europe, the MSD had relocated from Bordeaux to Kiel. At Kiel the MSD had its Naval Warfare Executive Office for Foreign Navies, which was commanded by a Commander Eiffel, with a Dr. von Hanfstengel serving as his adjunct. Directly under the Executive Office was the Navy Transportation Department–Kiel, which was headed by Commander Becker, who employed Lieutenant Commander Longbein as his executive officer; these two individuals would coordinate and supervise the loading of *U-234* at Kiel.

The MSD also had officers stationed in Japan as part of the German-Japanese attaché group. In the spring of 1944 this group consisted of

Commanders von Krosigk, van Wuellen-Schloten, Ross, and Souchon, First Lieutenant Koch, and Inspector Boreck.[12] Of these, von Krosigk and Souchon were assigned to coordinate, from the Japanese perspective, the loading and arrival of *U-234*, Germany's final cooperative effort in her official affiliation with Japan.[13] According to Falcke, *U-234*'s aborted mission was the culmination of a long and frustrating attempt to arrange cooperation between allies positioned half a world apart.

Because Falcke worked closely with the Japanese naval contingent in Germany, he was able to provide ONI investigators with details of German-Japanese naval cooperation. He told them that during the early stages of the war, having recognized Germany's superior war-making capabilities, the Japanese government convened a "Military Tri-Pact Commission" to be sent to Europe. In early 1941 the commission, which consisted of military, technical, and economic experts and was headed by Adm. Nomura Naokuni, arrived in Berlin with orders to explore the possibilities of material and technological exchanges between Germany and Japan. According to the provisions of the pact's supplemental protocols, each branch of the German armed forces was to prepare a lecture series and inspection program to familiarize the Japanese commission with German manufacturing and research techniques.[14] The commission would receive a comprehensive up-to-date review of Germany's wartime command structure and armaments technology within the designated parameters.

Once the lecture schedule was agreed upon, instruction began immediately, covering all aspects of Germany's naval war experience. Officials from the OKM's Naval War Leadership lectured on the individual branches of naval warfare, especially those that had been involved in the invasion of Norway, as well as the auxiliary cruiser program. Naval personnel issues, such as finances and training, were addressed by officers from the Personnel Bureau. Various aspects of ship engineering, such as mechanized and high-voltage electrical engineering, ship construction, and shipyard organization and efficiency, were covered by officials of the Department of Warship Construction, including Falcke. Armaments issues and weapons technology, such as communications and radio defense networking, were handled by the responsible weapons offices, while financial issues were covered by the Office of Armaments Economy of the Supreme Command. A major goal of this endeavor was the transfer of German industrial technology to Japan. Material procurement, processing methodology, standardization, and fuel and lubrication issues were handled by the appropriate offices by way of a group interactive consortium, in which experts from Reich offices, as well as private German industry, were selected to speak.[15]

Because members of the Japanese commission attended only those sessions that pertained to their particular area of expertise, lectures in different areas (for example, weapons technology and ship construction) were scheduled to occur simultaneously. As a result, despite the great scope of the lecture program, the entire series was completed within two and a half weeks.[16]

Although Nomura's legation investigated all forms of German naval technology, they were primarily interested in U-boat construction. Falcke later recalled that the Japanese were "quite surprised" at the difference between German and Japanese construction, especially regarding the size differential between comparable submarines. For example, the German Type VII submarine, a 769-ton boat, carried the same firepower as the Japanese 2,500-ton vessel. However, there proved to be a practical reason for the disparity in size; because the expanse of Japan's operating area required larger interior storage spaces, Japanese naval engineers sacrificed speed and maneuverability for extra room. Regarding stability and durability, Nomura noted that whereas Japanese submarines were riveted, German U-boats were welded and therefore possessed greater structural integrity.[17] All of this information was evidently of great value to Nomura, who upon his departure expressed his appreciation to Falcke in a letter acknowledging the efforts Falcke had made in Nomura's behalf despite his demanding schedule at the Department of Warship Construction.[18]

Although the informational exchange program was advantageous to both Germany and Japan, a growing distrust between the parties was evident. The distrust was due in part to the lack of bilingual personnel who could translate Japanese into German. To guarantee a complete understanding of the proceedings, the Japanese members requested a written transcript, so that details could be translated at a later time. While a number of the Japanese present had some command of German, having earlier spent substantial amounts of time studying in Germany, relatively few of the Germans involved could read or write Japanese. Those who did have some knowledge of the language still had difficulty understanding military or technical expressions. In dealing with their Japanese counterparts, German officials were further disadvantaged by their ignorance of Japanese culture. This ignorance, coupled with the language difficulties, fostered the impression that the Japanese could not be trusted to maintain "absolute secrecy."[19] Consequently, German personnel involved in the exchange program were

instructed to exercise discretion when delivering lectures or conducting tours; Falcke was instructed to "withhold information of . . . high
importance from [Nomura's] mission," on the assumption that "the
Japanese were not [being] entirely above board."[20]

This assumption was not altogether unfounded. During the early
months of the cooperative exchange, the Japanese had sent the Germans data concerning American battleships, principally consisting of
cross-section drawings of the widest part of the ship, in return for German data on British warships. However, the drawings that the Japanese provided, though remarkably accurate, proved to be of little value
because they all were of older-model ships.[21]

The Japanese too harbored justifiable suspicions that their German
counterparts were being less than completely honest. Nomura and
other members of the commission had expressed an interest in certain
matters that the OKM regarded as sensitive. The High Command and
the Foreign Ministry therefore issued simultaneous orders stating that
whereas all German officials involved in the exchange program were
to provide the Japanese commission with the benefits of their expertise, there were nevertheless restrictions on the nature and extent of
the instruction they could provide. Specifically, instruction would be
limited to German weapon systems and devices that were already
deployed at the front.[22] In his interrogation by ONI officials, Falcke confirmed that the Germans had withheld certain types of information. He
reported that whereas the Germans had received orientation on all of
the Japanese naval weaponry that was in operational use, as well as
some items still in the developmental stage, they had withheld information about recent developments such as torpedo and U-boat pressure boxes and circulating motors. In addition, as "a matter of principle," they had not furnished research results to the Japanese.[23]

Although German leaders were reluctant to reveal the extent of
their technology during the early years of the war, the once-stringent
limitations on cooperation were amended as Germany and Japan both
began to suffer losses at the front. Falcke, whom the ONI regarded as
having "knowledge of what was expressly for exchange with Japan,"
revealed that he was escorting hundreds of pounds of drawings and
plans, with which the Japanese could develop their own naval armaments industry.[24] Included in these documents, which were stored in
mine container 30550-27 on *U-234*, were drawings for the German battleship *Bismarck*, the new 36C and Z51 destroyers, and the Type 43 M-
boat, along with new S-boat designs.[25] Perhaps most important were
drawings of Germany's new submarines, which included plans for the

manufacture of the Types II, VII, IX, X, and XI conventional U-boats, along with the Types XXI and XXIII boats. In addition, Falcke was to draw upon his naval construction expertise to provide the Japanese with specialized directions for the manufacture of the new boats, beginning with the Type IX.[26] To ensure continuity with German manufacturers, Falcke also carried copies of the construction licenses and patents, which would resolve any questions as to Japan's right to build the boats.[27]

Falcke's ONI testimony also provided investigators with an inside view of the workings of what had been considered an efficient German naval bureaucracy. Primarily because of the multiplicity of Falcke's talent and expertise, his duties at the Department of Warship Construction were far-ranging—so much so that Falcke repeatedly complained about the position's demands on his time. During the early months of the war the department was inundated with requests from Germany's allies and dependents, a flood that Falcke's understaffed office was ill prepared to handle. As early as November 1939 Falcke notified his superiors that he and his staff were overworked to the point that even vacations and furloughs were not being granted.[28] Throughout the war Falcke, who was also expected to maintain his research assignments as a naval engineer, complained of debilitating personnel problems brought on by the manpower demands of the war. In addition, the ever-increasing demands of foreign countries meant "too much work [and] not enough sleep"; the situation was "ruining his health."[29] In April 1943 Falcke claimed that organizational red tape and continued staffing problems had contributed to health problems in the form of an ear infection;[30] however, his pleas for replacement personnel were ignored.

Falcke was also responsible for the welfare of German personnel sent overseas on behalf of the Department of Warship Construction. Because of wartime demands on the Kriegsmarine budget, Falcke did not have sufficient funding to properly finance the department's network of liaison personnel, and consequently he spent many hours pleading for reimbursement of his representatives, who were forced to dip into their personal funds in order to complete their missions. Many times, upon refusal of reimbursement, Falcke reimbursed his personnel out of his pocket, which added to the frustrations of his position.

Falcke's difficulties with the logistics of overseas travel and assignments were typified by the experience of Chief Engineer Hermann Lange, who traveled to Japan in August 1943. Lange, a naval designer, had expected an allotment of Japanese yen prior to departing Europe;

however, he received neither German marks or Japanese yen as compensation. In addition, logistical difficulties delayed his departure from Bordeaux for two weeks, a period of time for which he did not have sufficient funds. As a result, he was forced to borrow 250 marks from MSD chief Becker. Upon arriving in Japan with no reserve of Japanese currency and his own private funds much depleted, Lange complained to Falcke that he could not perform his assignment properly. The 3,000-yen clothing allotment that he had received from the naval attaché in Tokyo was "not enough money with Tokyo's economy"; he could neither dress himself nor entertain Japanese dignitaries in a style befitting German diplomatic personnel. The effectiveness of his position was suffering, Lange claimed; it was up to Falcke to rectify Lange's fiscal deficiencies.[31] By this time, after four years of bureaucratic squabbles, fiscal misadventures, and run-ins with temperamental allies, Falcke had had enough, and in April 1944 he requested a transfer, stating that despite his best efforts his office was nonetheless incompetent.[32]

In addition to his administrative duties, Falcke also coordinated the transmittal of requests from military planners to their research and development departments. There were problems in this area, Falcke said, most of them due to miscommunication between research personnel and military leaders; there was often a gap between what the military wanted and what the technicians and scientists could actually provide. Falcke told his ONI interrogators that he assumed that such confusion did not occur in the U.S. military, where there was surely much less bureaucracy and officials surely did not demand what was "not technically possible."[33]

Like his contemporaries, Falcke was interned at Fort Meade, Maryland, until his transfer to the interrogation center at Fort Hunt, Virginia, in June 1945.[34] He remained at Hunt for the remainder of the summer, at which time he was placed under the jurisdiction of the provost marshal general of the army. Despite his National Socialist leanings, Falcke was designated an "anti-Nazi" and was subsequently relegated to internment at a facility designed to segregate ardent followers of Hitler from their less fanatical compatriots. As a result, on 27 August 1945 Falcke was transferred to the "anti-Nazi" prisoner-of-war facility at Ruston, Louisiana.[35] In December the provost marshal general announced the closure of the Ruston facility, and Falcke, along with 213 fellow officers, was transferred to Dermott, Arkansas.[36] His later whereabouts are not clear; although his fellow officers were repatriated to Germany in late 1946, a 1949 newspaper article claimed that Falcke performed "several years' work for the United States Navy" before returning to Germany.[37]

Gerhard Falcke exemplified the midlevel National Socialist bureaucrat trained in diplomatic as well as technical matters. Ambitious and devoted to National Socialism at the beginning of the war, Falcke was unique in that his disenchantment was brought about not by the political and military failure of the Reich but rather by the decimation of his command by bureaucratic inefficiencies.

While Falcke spent the majority of his service in an administrative role, he nonetheless remained proficient in matters of naval engineering as well as naval procurement. He was the ideal choice for a liaison mission to Japan, which desperately needed someone of his social and intellectual skills. For his part, Falcke regarded his mission to Japan as his final chance to fulfill what he considered his destiny.

Lt. Cdr. Richard Bulla had been ordered to Japan to observe rather than instruct. During the war the Kriegsmarine was deficient in the development of carrier-borne naval aviation, an area in which the Japanese Imperial Navy excelled. By late December 1944 a desperate German High Command had come to recognize the importance of naval aviation to the success of its submarine offensive and sought to rectify this deficiency by learning the secrets of Japan's success. To this end, on 28 December, Grand Admiral Karl Dönitz ordered Bulla to board *U-234* and travel to Japan.[38]

Bulla had the unusual distinction of serving as an officer in both the Luftwaffe and Kriegsmarine simultaneously. Although he had enlisted in the regular navy in April 1935, he was nonetheless transferred to the Luftwaffe, still functioning as a naval officer, in December 1938. Bulla served as the adjutant of Wing Group 206 until the September 1939 invasion of Poland, when he rejoined the Kriegsmarine. In December he received orders to report to the cruiser *Atlantis* to serve as the raider's flying officer and torpedo officer.[39]

The *Atlantis*'s commanding officer, Capt. Bernhard Rogge, was intrigued by the use of aircraft aboard naval vessels, regarding aircraft as vital to the protection of the raider. Bulla confirmed Rogge's opinion and proved invaluable as the "eyes" of the *Atlantis,* patrolling vast expanses of the Indian Ocean in his Heinkel (HE) 114 patrol craft.[40]

Initially successful as a reconnaissance pilot, Bulla nonetheless became dissatisfied in his duty as an observer and pressed Rogge to allow him to develop a combat role for his plane. With Rogge's permission, Bulla outfitted his HE 114 with two 110-pound bombs and a 20-

millimeter cannon, complete with 120 rounds of ammunition. In addition, he suspended a grapnel from the aircraft, the purpose of which was to catch an enemy ship's radio aerial before it could transmit an emergency signal.[41] Bulla's innovations proved highly effective, and they helped the *Atlantis* become one of the most successful German raiders of the war, with a total of 145,697 gross tons destroyed to her credit.[42]

In late December 1944 Bulla was ordered from his assignment at an artillery officers' school and instructed to report to Berlin, where he was presented with orders to proceed to Japan. In the interim prior to his departure, Bulla spent his time in briefings held by Dönitz, the chief of naval personnel, an Adm. K. Balzer, and the Japanese military attaché, Oshima Hiroshi. On 1 February 1945 Bulla arrived in Kiel, where he reported to his former *Atlantis* shipmate Lieutenant Commander Fehler and boarded *U-234*.[43]

Bulla informed ONI investigators that his mission to Japan called for him to spend two to five years studying Japanese naval aviation, after which he would return to Germany to establish a similar branch in the German navy in peacetime.[44] This revelation surprised navy officials; during the war the Kriegsmarine had been conspicuous for its lack of a naval air arm. Many observers believed that after the sinking of the German battleship *Bismarck*, partially by British carrier-borne aircraft, the Germans would expedite the formation of a fleet air force. In February 1943, however, construction of the sole German aircraft carrier, the 23,000-ton *Graf Zeppelin*, was halted because of changing strategic priorities.[45] As a result, the Kriegsmarine was converted to a submarine navy,[46] prompting ONI officials to question Bulla's mission and its implications as to the Kriegsmarine's aborted plans for postwar Europe.

ONI officials were relieved when Bulla revealed that he had been the only naval officer ordered to Japan for the purpose of studying Japanese naval aviation, an indication that the German High Command had realized too late the importance of carrier-based aviation.[47] However, the length of Bulla's proposed mission—two to five years—caused intelligence officials in Washington to speculate that Germany had been relying on Japan to continue the war, as evidenced by cooperative missions such as that of *U-234*. Bulla's expectation of returning to Germany and creating a naval air force in peacetime further convinced intelligence officials that German military planners planned to use the alliance with Japan to buy time in which to perfect secret weapons and technology of mass destruction.[48]

Bulla revealed that the technical exchanges between Germany and Japan had been minimal, for while the Japanese were eager to obtain the latest German scientific developments, they were reluctant to part with their own developments or materials.[49] On the other hand, regular submarine service between the two allies had existed for some time. Bulla recounted that as a Luftwaffe pilot during the summer of 1942, he had rendezvoused with the Japanese submarine I-30 in the Atlantic and escorted it to the submarine base at Lorient, France. As to the purpose of the submarine service, Bulla stated that while he was of the opinion that "some of the latest German developments which [were] actually under production in Germany found their way to Japan via these submarines," Japanese plans for the mass production of jet aircraft were pending the arrival of *U-234*.[50]

Many of Bulla's most valuable revelations, however, did not come as answers to investigators' questions but were overheard in monitored conversations between him and his cellmates. Even in the supposed privacy of his cell, Bulla proved to be the consummate soldier; while other prisoners complained about prison life or speculated about postwar Germany, Bulla engaged in conversations about military matters. One ONI monitor reported that "[Bulla] seems to have been a flyer and knows a lot about German planes [and talks about] missions over London and also aerial combat."[51] During one conversation Bulla told about engaging a small British vessel in the Atlantic, which, though heavily armed, "I sank in a masterly way, without incurring any loss or damage."[52]

ONI investigators were surprised to discover that Bulla's expertise extended to armaments and new weapons. Room monitors listened intently as he and Hellendorn discussed the different calibers of Germany's latest ship-borne antiaircraft guns, which ranged from 28 to 88 millimeters and were electrically controlled. Many of the newest 88-millimeter guns were equipped with a new arming device, which accelerated the rapid-fire capability of the weapon. Bulla and Hellendorn also compared the range of the new weapons, mentioning that most of the latter-day German vessels had turned to the 38-millimeter antiaircraft gun as their primary air-defense system[53]—a development that prompted Hellendorn's mission to integrate the new guns into the Japanese inventory.

Like Bulla, Heinrich Hellendorn had traveled to Japan primarily as an observer rather than an instructor. In January 1945 Admiral Dönitz personally addressed *U-234*'s naval contingent and instructed Hellendorn to offer the Japanese his expertise in shipboard antiaircraft defense while simultaneously studying the Imperial Navy's tactics at sea. Dönitz informed Hellendorn that upon the completion of their mission he was to return to Germany—which must have come as a relief to the young first lieutenant, for he had never desired to depart in the first place. ONI interrogators regarded the twenty-six-year-old Hellendorn as a "frank, sincere . . . intelligent . . . non-political individual [who] gives his information readily."[54]

Born in October 1919 in Bentheim, Hellendorn completed his compulsory education of four years of *Volksschule* and six years of *Mittlelsschule* at Bentheim, with a final three years of *Oberschule* at Norden. In September 1939 the Kriegsmarine summoned Hellendorn to Stralsund, where he underwent basic military training; in December he was assigned to the *Schleswig Holstein* for five months of seaman and signal training. Upon completion of his sea training, he spent three months as a cadet at the Naval School at Flensburg, graduating in April 1940 as a *Fähnrich*, or midshipman.

In August 1940 Hellendorn was assigned to Antwerp, where he spent three months training naval reserve troops. In October he attended the Ship Artillery School in Kiel, where he was instructed in artillery firing and aiming techniques. Upon completion of this two-month training, he reported to Swinemünde, where he was trained in tactical artillery aboard the ships *Drache* and *Fuchs*. In February 1941 he was ordered to report to Hamburg, where he was assigned to the battleship *Bismarck;* here he received his first experience as an artillery officer. In May he returned to Swinemünde to the Flak Artillery Coastal School for further training, and in June he was named third flak artillery officer to the *Bismarck*'s sister ship, the *Tirpitz.* In August 1944 he was promoted to second officer. However, he was wounded in action and subsequently granted convalescence leave until January 1945. Late in January he was summoned to Berlin, where he received orders to report to Admiral Dönitz's headquarters. It was there that he learned of his assignment to Japan.[55]

Hellendorn was unable to provide the ONI with any information regarding naval artillery that it did not already possess. However, he did shed light on the makeup of the Kriegsmarine during the closing months of the war. Hellendorn informed his captors that the German navy consisted mostly of merchant and luxury vessels; German leaders had always believed that England would never declare war on Germany, therefore the Kriegsmarine's fleet never underwent a sizable increase. In regard to tactics, Hellendorn confirmed Germany's deficiency in large-scale fleet actions with his admission that German naval strategy focused on coastal defense patrol; it was this deficiency that prompted Dönitz to send his officers to Japan for training.[56]

Because of their common interest in ordnance and artillery, Bulla and Hellendorn compared "recipes" for effective armor-piercing projectiles during their discussions in captivity. While contemptuous of early German attempts at antiship shells, they agreed that the high-explosive character of antiaircraft shells, combined with the armor-piercing power of an antitank shell, provided the most effective projectile. Bulla expounded on this theory, stating that his most effective projectile consisted of "one high-explosive antitank [shell], one armor-piercing shell, one high-explosive incendiary, one M [mine], and one D [delay]."[57]

Bulla also surprised ONI monitors when he revealed the existence of a new aircraft that was able to "climb and descend vertically and can take off or land on a plate of five meters. . . . The [German] Navy wanted eighty of these planes for use on destroyers." Bulla further stated that the new aircraft could fly in inclement weather when standard aircraft could not and were outfitted with a new bomb release, which, unlike previous unreliable German releases, operated on a relatively "simple principle."[58]

Although Bulla proved to be a valuable source of information for ONI investigators, doubt remained as to the extent of his knowledge. Bulla repeatedly claimed that he knew little of the submarine's mission, or of German technology in Japan. When Hellendorn mentioned to Bulla that he had told the interrogators that he knew nothing about Japanese rockets, Bulla responded, "Yes, the Japs were smart enough never to tell about it to the Germans."[59] However, upon returning from his 24 May interrogation, in which he claimed little knowledge, Bulla privately informed Hellendorn that he knew about the first Japanese U-boat to visit Germany, an event that had been shrouded in secrecy.[60] In addition, it had been Bulla, with confirmation by Hellendorn, who had provided the identity of Shoji and Tomonaga, the two Japanese officers on board *U-234*.[61] Bulla's claim that he knew little is questionable, for he had convenient access to Japanese diplomats in Berlin; indeed, he lived across the street from Oshima Hiroshi, who had been elevated from military attaché to ambassador.[62] Whatever the extent of Bulla's involvement, he did appear to appreciate his good fortune in having landed in America, telling Hellendorn, "we can learn something here."[63]

Whereas Falcke, Bulla, and Hellendorn were operational naval officers, Kay Nieschling was not. Nieschling was a naval judge, ostensibly sent to Japan to provide jurisdiction to the numerous German naval personnel stationed in Japan. In addition, he was charged with helping to clear the German diplomatic corps in Japan of the remnants of the

Richard Sorge spy ring, which at its height had crippled the effectiveness of the Naval Attaché's Office. Nieschling, like Falcke, was proficient in political matters and, though admittedly committed to National Socialist idealism, surprised his captors with his relatively objective views of the global situation following Germany's capitulation.

By 1945 the German presence in Japan had reached such proportions that Wennecker petitioned Berlin for help in the legal administration of the German legation. The OKM looked to its corps of young, ambitious officers and found in Kay Nieschling a suitable candidate. Consequently, on 24 December 1944 Nieschling received orders to report to staff judge Admiral Rudolph in Berlin, who subsequently informed the younger judge of his assignment to Tokyo.[64]

Nieschling's assignment to Tokyo came as no surprise to Kriegsmarine observers, for Wennecker needed both a junior naval officer and a military judge. Wennecker's contacts in the Japanese navy were limited to admirals and staff officers, which restricted his perception of the overall state of the Japanese navy.[65] The OKM believed that Nieschling, who had acquired a reputation as an effective diplomat during an assignment in Norway, would help broaden the Kriegsmarine's knowledge of the Imperial Navy through his interaction with Japanese junior officers.[66]

Nieschling's official duty was to serve as the judicial and investigative officer for the two-thousand-man German naval contingent stationed in Japan.[67] By November 1943 the Allied naval blockade had prevented the movement of German blockade-runners between Japan and Europe. As a result, any German naval personnel arrested for violations of military or civil law could not return to Germany for trial and therefore had to stand trial in Tokyo. Nieschling was assigned to establish a system of German military courts to address this problem. However, his primary assignment was to examine the records of the German Foreign Ministry and purge those German Communists who had participated in the Sorge spy scandal.[68]

Richard Sorge was a German journalist assigned to the Japanese bureau of the *Frankfurter Zeitung* who simultaneously served as a spy for the Soviet Union. From his arrival in Tokyo in September 1933 until his arrest in October 1941, Sorge headed an espionage ring that infiltrated both the German and Japanese diplomatic communities. Sorge's base of operations was the German embassy, which he penetrated so thoroughly that he became a virtual staff member of two German ambassadors during his eight-year operation.[69] Upon his arrest in 1941 Sorge boasted, "The fact that I successfully approached the German

Embassy in Japan and won absolute trust by people there was the foundation of my organization in Japan. . . . Even in Moscow the fact that I infiltrated into the center of the embassy and made use of it for my spying activity is evaluated as extremely amazing, having no equivalent in history."[70]

Indeed, Richard Sorge commanded one of World War II's most successful espionage organizations. However, two incidents emerge as his most vital communiqués to the Soviets. Thanks to his high-level contacts within the Japanese military's inner circle, Sorge was able to obtain information that enabled him to warn Moscow of the June 1941 date of Operation Barbarossa, the German invasion of the Soviet Union. Josef Stalin, however, was skeptical of Sorge's reliability and ignored this vital intelligence. When Sorge's prediction was realized, his credibility was restored. His next report was treated with more respect.

By the late summer of 1941 Stalin felt the pressure of the German invasion in the west, in addition to the threat posed by the Japanese presence in Manchuria. A Japanese invasion would be a strategic nightmare, forcing the Soviets to fight on two fronts simultaneously. However, Sorge was instrumental in alleviating Stalin's concern; in September he notified Moscow that the Japanese had decided not to invade the Soviet Union through Manchuria, opting instead for a movement south against Indochina and the colonial possessions of the Western powers. Consequently, Stalin was able to transfer his Siberian troops to the German front, where they aided in the defense of Moscow.

Such monumental leaks of intelligence were sure to attract the attention of Japanese and German officials, and in October 1941 Sorge and thirty-five of his operatives were arrested by the Tokko, or Thought Police. After a lengthy trial Sorge was imprisoned for three years in Tokyo until his execution in 1944. However, the repercussions of his spy ring did not end with his death, and German officials in Berlin feared that high-ranking diplomatic personnel, including Wennecker, might be continuing Sorge's work. Consequently, the OKM sent the ambitious Nieschling to investigate and prosecute the remnants of Sorge's organization.

The ONI determined that among the passengers and crew aboard *U-234*, Nieschling was one of the most conspicuous in his dedication to National Socialism; indeed, he was assigned the duty of political officer aboard the submarine during the voyage to Japan. Although his enthusiasm had wavered during the early 1930s, the outbreak of war in 1939 restored his loyalty, as high-ranking Wehrmacht officers convinced the young judge that it was beneficial to Germany that he remain devoted to National Socialism and Adolf Hitler. Consequently, Nieschling rose within the ranks of the Kriegsmarine, making important contacts as he advanced his career. By the time he arrived in Berlin for briefing on his mission to Tokyo, he was the subject of discussion concerning "his possibilities as a future [Nazi] leader in Japan."[71] Indeed, Nieschling had developed a reputation; American intelligence described him as a "high-ranking naval judge, well-informed on German personalities in Japan and Japanese personalities in Germany."[72]

ONI monitors noted that "this man [Nieschling], without a doubt, is a hopeless case, 100% Nazi," an observation supported by Nieschling's admission that he "carried *Mein Kampf* wherever he went, it being [his] Bible."[73] Nieschling stated that National Socialism and Germany were "one and the same . . . 80 percent of the German people are still Nazis . . . and will remain Nazi until they die."[74] Nieschling further argued that the United States should not consider National Socialism dangerous, provided American assessments did not include the "terror, destruction, and resistance movements like 'Werewolf'" or the rogue military courts of "impure Nazis" in American POW camps.[75] However, should the United States attempt to eliminate German National Socialism, it would "have to police the world for at least two generations."[76] Although investigators dismissed this pronouncement as meaningless dogma, it nonetheless proved prophetic: Nieschling had unwittingly foreshadowed American efforts to bring to justice suspected war criminals who avoided trial.

The ONI was naturally curious about the operative effectiveness of its counterpart, the Seekriegsleitung (SKL), or OKM Intelligence. However, Nieschling's appraisal of the SKL led the ONI to conclude that the organization's reputation for ruthless efficiency was more legend than fact. Nieschling described the SKL as being infected with sectional rivalry and jealousy as well as infiltrated by elements of the resistance. Vital departments were directed by political appointments, as exemplified by Capt. Norbert von Baumbach, head of 3SKL (Intelligence Evaluation), whom the OKM did not consider an officer of "capabilities and brains."[77] Nieschling revealed that situations such as von Baumbach's were not isolated, leading the ONI to conclude that the SKL was less than effective, and surely not the intelligence juggernaut of rumor.

Although Nieschling stated that the overall mission of *U-234* was to "keep Japan active in the war and to increase Japanese war potential," he also revealed that because of Japanese secrecy and refusal to cooperate, Germany had no idea just what that potential was.[78] Not only did the Japanese withhold secrets from Germany; they also were notoriously distrustful of their ally. To illustrate this point, Nieschling related the story of a German naval attaché in Tokyo who, upon departing on a mission, discovered that he had forgotten some vital papers. When he returned to his office, he found the place "swarming with Japanese police and officials." The embarrassed Japanese claimed that they had made a mistake—they had intended to search the office next door—and apologized profusely.[79] Incidents such as this were emblematic of the mistrust between the Axis partners, and the ONI concluded that German-Japanese relations, though active, were nonetheless strained.

Nieschling provided valuable information on Japan's diplomatic relationship with the Soviet Union, a point of contention between Germany and Japan that was of vital interest to the United States. The Allies had been pressing the Soviets for the formation of a second front against Japan but were uncertain of Stalin's veracity regarding the relationship between Moscow and Tokyo. Because of his prominence within the German diplomatic corps, Nieschling was privy to secret OKM documents that outlined the nature of the Soviet-Japanese relationship, and was therefore able to shed some light on Stalin's intentions.[80]

The OKM believed, correctly, that Moscow would never start a two-front war, having absorbed devastating losses while resisting the 1941 German invasion. From interviews with Soviet prisoners of war, the Wehrmacht learned of the existence of Siberian combat units on the eastern front, an indication that the Soviet Union had withdrawn a large percentage of its Siberian defenses to fight the Germans, once the threat of a Japanese offensive was removed. In addition, at the time of the OKM report there existed "no enmity" between Japan and the Soviet Union, and therefore no plausible reason for war existed. Nieschling also pointed out that the OKM had observed that in the few disagreements between the two, the Soviet Union, although quite obstinate, always "backed down in the end."[81]

To further illustrate the Soviet-Japanese relationship, Nieschling related a conversation he had had with Lieutenant Commander Shoji, one of the two Japanese passengers on *U-234*. During a discussion regarding Moscow's violation of the Soviet-Japanese nonaggression pact, Shoji, who had been stationed with the Japanese Foreign Mission Office in Stockholm, recalled that the Japanese ambassador in Moscow had been "treated badly," presumably to satisfy the United States.[82] Shoji nonetheless praised the effectiveness of the Soviet Foreign Office, stating that Japan could never tell what Russia had in mind. . . . Stalin was [always] cleverer than the Japanese."[83]

Perhaps the most alarming information gleaned from Nieschling was his appraisal of the state of the German nation during the final months of the war. Nieschling revealed that as late as January 1945 the German High Command was determined to end the war "in ways which were more or less . . . acceptable," even if it required resorting to a *levée en masse* for one final resistance.[84] Hitler's generals were counting on an outpouring of nationalist fervor to sustain such an effort, but as Nieschling pointed out, there was also a strong practical basis for continuing the war. First, Germany's food supply had suffered no significant damage and appeared good for at least another year.[85] In addition, despite heavy air raids against the civilian population, basic needs for clothing, fuel, and transportation were apparently being met. The reichsmark remained strong and healthy, and the danger of public unrest had been effectively controlled by the Gestapo. Finally, Nazi propaganda minister Joseph Goebbels had convinced Hitler that the Allied propaganda "war-of-nerves" could be fought with "intensive and clever counter-propaganda."[86] These were ominous claims, but ONI officials dismissed them as an attempt on Nieschling's part to salvage some dignity in the aftermath of defeat.

Nonetheless, even as late as January 1945 the battered German war machine was not totally beaten.[87] Nieschling revealed that he had seen OKM documentation to the effect that the U-boat corps "stood to receive a very important fresh impetus very shortly." Germany's munitions industry had revitalized the U-boats with improved weapons such as stealthier, more powerful mines and precision acoustic torpedoes. In addition, recent technological advances such as a long-range anti-position-finding device, the *Schnorchel,* and an untraceable radio transmitter promised to render German submarines virtually invisible to Allied antisubmarine countermeasures. Finally, a new defense system designed to protect the submarine from its most dangerous enemy, the depth charge, would reduce the effectiveness of the Allied hunter-killer groups that by 1944 had severely weakened the U-boat menace in the Atlantic.[88]

Nieschling verified rumors of additional "new weapons"—the specifics of which he admittedly had no knowledge of—that would inflict heavy losses on advancing Allied troops and foreshadow a renewed German offensive that would "shock" the Allies with its "immense troop and material concentrations."[89] The strategic deployment of these weapons earlier might have reversed the direction of the war in Europe. Although there was no longer a threat in Europe, the existence of such weapons presented American intelligence with a twofold dilemma.

First, the ONI concluded that if other German missions like that of *U-234* were successful, American troops participating in the proposed invasion of Japan might face weapons against which they had no defense. The second concern was voiced by Nieschling, who reminded the ONI that the Americans and British were not the sole victors privy to the new weapons; no one could be certain how much of Germany's technology had been seized by Soviet troops during their advance on Berlin.

Although the ONI investigators noted that Nieschling had "an unreasonable fear of Russia,"[90] they were nonetheless interested in hearing his account of Germany's assessment of the American-Anglo-Soviet alliance. According to Nieschling, German leaders could never understand why the English and Americans would not cease their advance and allow Germany to fight the Bolsheviks.[91] The High Command expected to negotiate a last-minute agreement that would form an anti-Soviet Anglo-German-American alliance, based on the premise that the "complete ruin and absolute reduction of Germany to chaos could not be in line with . . . English policy." Nieschling predicted, with considerable foresight, that should the effort to secure such an alliance fail, a schizophrenic postwar Germany would emerge, torn between the "intolerant total dogmatism" of the Soviet Union and the "constructive, democratic West."[92]

Many Germans believed that an alliance between the forces of democracy and communism was inherently polarized, and therefore impossible to maintain. Soviet aggression threatened world peace; therefore, rather than fight alone, the Allies should side with the German nation, regardless of "its militarism and National Socialism."[93] Nieschling expressed concern that the United States and Great Britain would have to begin this fight against communist aggression in the near future, the same fight in which Germany had seen its "culture, fortunes, and holiest ideals fallen to the ground and cruelly crushed."[94] For the most part, ONI officials dismissed Nieschling's predictions as scare tactics and propaganda, designed to sow suspicion and mistrust in American relations with Moscow.[95]

Paranoid or not, Nieschling raised issues for which the ONI had neither satisfactory answers nor explanations. The United States contended that in the event of a Soviet uprising in Europe, the U.S. military force there possessed eighty-five thousand aircraft with which to preserve the peace. Nieschling challenged this claim, inquiring whether the Americans had calculated the date at which the operational effectiveness of these aircraft would cease. Furthermore, Nieschling said that he doubted that the United States understood the "terrible and unimaginable" possibilities of the existing V-2 and proposed V-3 rockets, with their "unlimited range and boundless potential."[96] Nieschling also correctly surmised that the Americans possessed little knowledge of the abilities of the Soviet Union's armaments industry and scientists. Another matter of potentially grave consequence to the Allies was the Soviet Union's possession of vital German experimental installations.[97] Nieschling was convinced that the Soviets would not hesitate to exploit any German technology they could acquire.

Whether Nieschling was an astute observer of world politics or merely a demagogue spouting Nazi doctrine, his predictions proved remarkably accurate. He predicted that an immediate consequence of an American victory over Japan would be a free China, which would subsequently fall to communism.[98] When the Allies decided upon the Elbe River as the line of demarcation between the Western and Soviet spheres of influence in Germany, Nieschling commented that this could only result in the future division of the German Reich, in which "very painful and nerve-shaking elements of the coming struggle are already in formation."[99]

Nieschling also correctly surmised that the Soviet Union would cause the Western Allies trouble in the near future.[100] While the United States and England represented the bastions of freedom in the postwar world, Moscow's refusal to aid the Americans by fighting the Japanese would leave the United States standing "alone and weak opposite a still-powerful Russia."[101] To preserve the peace, it was imperative that the United States possess both a resolute will and strong weapons. Nieschling pointed out that although America had "put these weapons in iron," it was vital that "God grant the United States more wisdom . . . in its leadership than Germany had."[102] Germany had indeed been defeated, but, Nieschling suggested, perhaps the historical significance of Germany's final resistance would prove to be that it had strengthened the United States.

Given the ominous implications of *U-234*'s mission, none of Nieschling's comments, dogmatic as they were, could be regarded as completely unimportant. Nevertheless, the ONI evaluated his musings as little more than a defeated staff officer's desire to see Germany freed of Soviet occupation and open to the return of German national identity and Prussian militarism.[103] But before Kay Nieschling is dismissed as merely another by-product of Hitler's failed Third Reich, it must be remembered that as a high-ranking naval, diplomatic, and political officer he was privy to military and political decisions and other developments unavailable to most. He was a knowledgeable and candid observer whose suspicions of Soviet geopolitical designs and whose revelations concerning Soviet possession of German weapons technology can arguably be viewed as a forewarning of the coming ideological struggle between the Soviet Union and the West. He addressed his detractors with uncanny accuracy when he warned, "Woe to the German, the defeated! But thrice woe to the conquerors of today!"[104]

8

The Scientist

ON 24 MAY 1943 Maj. Gen. Okamoto Seigo, Japan's military attaché in Berlin, implored his superiors in Tokyo to consider "the part that science is playing in this war."[1] Okamoto was referring particularly to German and Allied development of devices that used "electric waves to detect moving objects" as well as "more powerful airplanes [with] higher speed"—devices that would, he said, "decide the outcome of this war." Indeed, in its haste to establish dominance in the Pacific, Japan had sacrificed research and development in modern military technology in favor of a conventional military juggernaut. Japan's strategic investment certainly paid immediate dividends, but as the war progressed the Imperial Army and Navy found their technical capabilities to be markedly inferior to those of their German allies, and, worse, to those of the Americans. As Okamoto put it in his message to the Imperial Command, "When battles hang in the balance, and we are found wanting in this respect, who knows what will happen?"[2]

Okamoto suggested that Tokyo initiate discussions with the Germans concerning the exchange of technical and scientific information, but, cognizant of the difficulty of shipping actual samples and prototypes because of Allied control of the Atlantic, he pointed out that any such sharing must be limited to an exchange of technical experts and the procurement of scientific data in the form of documentation and blue-prints.[3] Because the Kriegsmarine's once-reliable blockade-running surface vessels had been decimated by Allied naval forces, Germany's only reliable mode of transporting contraband to Japan was the submarine.[4]

U-234 was not the first U-boat to ferry German technicians and scientists to Japan,[5] but she was certainly one of the most anticipated. In January 1945, while discussing *U-234*'s mission with General Kessler, Oshima informed the general that "Japan is most anxious that you and your party of . . . military men and technicians should arrive in Japan as soon as possible."[6] On 14 April 1945, in compliance with Japanese wishes, the OKM disclosed to Tokyo that on board *U-234*, already en route to the Far East, were "two German civilian engineers who are experts in the mass production of the ME-262 turbo-jet fighter" as well as "a specialist in radar and infra-red ray."[7]

The civilian engineers were August Bringewald and Franz Ruf of the Messerschmitt Corporation, and the radar and infrared specialist was Dr. Heinz Schlicke. Of all the passengers aboard *U-234*, ONI officials at Portsmouth considered these individuals to be the greatest threat to American security, for although the weapons systems on board the submarine had ominous implications, without the proper experts to manufacture and deploy them they were nothing but inert machines. To facilitate Japanese integration of the latest German technology, Berlin had charged Bringewald, Ruf, and Schlicke with the task of converting these objects into weapons for the defense of the Japanese homeland. However, with the defeat of Germany, all technologies intended for the use of the friends of the Third Reich now became prizes of war for the victorious Allies.

The United States quickly learned that it was not the only Allied power actively seeking German technology and its creators. On 2 January 1945 Lt. Cdr. J. H. Marchant informed Rear Adm. Luis de Flores that "all key personnel, together with documents and equipment, of the *Technische Hochschule* [technical university] and assorted laboratories in Vienna had been removed to Moscow . . . for continued work in the field of ram jets." Marchant revealed the location of "several hundred" technical colleges, staffed by German personnel, that were being established in the Soviet Union, and he reported that the Soviets had assumed direction of the full-scale production of the Jumo 109-400 jet engine at the Junkers Engine and Aircraft Works in Muldenstein. Marchant further revealed that prominent aeronautical engineers Helmut Schelp and Herwath Schwabl, then working for the U.S. Navy in

Munich, had been propositioned by Soviet agents on several occasions.[8] With such bold advances by the Soviets becoming commonplace, American officials decided to monitor the situation more closely.

On 14 December 1945 Marchant informed Flores that "most of the first class German technical personnel who resided in the Russian zone of occupation have been transported to Russia." The Soviets had stepped up their recruitment efforts and were continuing to entice Germans working for the Americans with "excellent working conditions, pre-war salaries, and comparative freedom." Marchant pointed out that whereas Soviet agents had recruited several key scientists and technicians in the field of guided missiles, "German technology in this field has not been exploited by any U.S. agency."[9] The United States had, of course, mined the talents of several German scientists, but the fact remained that these men were classified as prisoners of war, and would therefore have to be repatriated back to Germany because of the provisions of the Geneva Conference. Upon their return to Germany, it was anybody's guess where they might end up.

Fears that the "best" German scientists might be spirited away to the Soviet Union after repatriation prompted H. Struve Hensel of the Navy Department to press Secretary of War Robert P. Patterson for an American exploitation policy. "The United States should seek . . . all outstanding German scientific personnel who can be persuaded to come," Hensel stated. "Our national security requires that we obtain the fullest possible benefits from . . . the most able German scientists." While reports indicated that most German scientists would rather return to the United States to work, attractive offers from the Soviets and the lack of a formal U.S. exploitation policy were prompting many to relocate to the Soviet Union instead. Hensel besought Patterson for help: "We will be taking a definite risk if we do not . . . form a plan for bringing these scientists to the United States . . . both for the material gain from their efforts and for insurance against their talents being turned against us."[10]

While the issue was being considered at the diplomatic level, the military decided that time was of the essence, and the individual services took matters into their own hands. In late May 1945 Robert Staver, the U.S. Army's head of jet propulsion research and development in Europe, cabled his superiors in Washington to suggest that captured German weapons could be used against the Japanese, and that "a hundred German specialists should be sent to the United States . . . with all of their documents, plans, and equipment."[11] After some discussion, Staver's idea was approved; on 21 July the U.S. Naval Technical Mission's intelligence section in Germany reported to the War Department that the American Chiefs of Staff, along with their British counterparts, had "approved shipment [to the United States] of outstanding German specialists . . . for research related to [the] Japanese War."[12] Thus began a competition among the American services, as well as between America and its allies, for the apprehension of the "best" German scientists. While the U.S. Army and Air Corps had initiated preliminary discussions on sending German "brains" to the United States, the U.S. Navy, in "great secrecy," was able to forge ahead of its sister services with the introduction of "three German scientists" into the United States.[13] However, these scientists did not traverse the Atlantic on American initiative; they came on the orders of the Third Reich, aboard *U-234*. They were the radar and infrared specialist Dr. Heinz Schlicke, and August Bringewald and Franz Ruf of Messerschmitt. We will return to Bringewald and Ruf in the next chapter; let us first consider the technical mission of Schlicke.

By 1945 Japan's scientific capabilities were virtually obsolete, consisting of technology that trailed that of the Allies by a full three years.[14] Whereas Erich Menzel had been charged with instructing the Japanese in the application and production of existing radar technology, both German and Allied, Dr. Heinz Schlicke was to help them in the development of new radar, infrared, and countermeasures systems. This revelation came as no surprise to the ONI; intercepted Axis dispatches had outlined the scope of Schlicke's mission. However, ONI officials considered Schlicke to be one of Germany's leading electronics experts, and they were suspicious of the claim that a scientist of his stature should be limited simply to helping the Japanese decipher blips on a radar screen.[15]

Born in December 1912 near Dresden, Schlicke grew up during the confusion of World War I and, like most Germans, suffered from the consequences of Germany's defeat.[16] Nevertheless, he excelled academically and entered the mathematics-physics branch of secondary school, where he endured the demanding regimen of the "hard sciences." He later studied under Dr. Heinrich Barkhausen at the *Technische Hochschule* in Dresden, where in 1937 he earned the first of three doctoral degrees in engineering science in the uncommonly short span of nine months.[17] In 1939 he went to work in research and development at the Telefunken Transmitter Laboratory in Berlin and ultimately received the second of his doctorate degrees. However, the outbreak of war in that year changed the direction of Schlicke's research, and ultimately of his life.[18]

After several research assignments, Schlicke was named director of the Naval Test Fields in Kiel, an assignment in which he directed research pertaining to, and the repair and testing of, radar, infrared, and direction-finding equipment.[19] In 1941 he joined the Kriegsmarine with the rank of *Marinebaurat* (naval engineer) and was placed in charge of the communications unit at Kiel, which was responsible for the maintenance, repair, and installation of all naval communications throughout Norway, Denmark, and the Balkans. In January 1943, because of his success in solving German problems with high-frequency antennas, Schlicke was transferred to the OKM in Berlin, where he was assigned to serve as a research coordinator for a Dr. Kuepfmueller, the overall director of naval research.[20] In this capacity, Schlicke was in charge of the development of infrared equipment operating in the 0.1- to 300-meter range and communications equipment in the 10- to 30,000-meter range. In Berlin, Schlicke did not work directly with radar and radar intercept equipment, but he had become peripherally familiar with German advances in this area as a result of his membership on Kuepfmueller's Scientific Research Naval Operations Staff. Because of the changing direction of the naval war and the Kriegsmarine's increasing reliance on its submarine corps, the focus of Schlicke's research changed from radio and radar technology to developing countermeasures to Allied antisubmarine devices.

By the spring of 1944 Germany's U-boat situation was desperate, with an average of one out of three submarines being sunk monthly. As a result, Schlicke and his colleagues, in conjunction with various naval laboratories, were charged with researching the entire electromagnetic and sound spectra in an attempt to find a way to mask the presence of a submarine electronically. Schlicke described these sessions as a "strenuous battle of wits, measures, countermeasures, and counter-countermeasures," often conducted during Allied bombing raids.[21] By the fall of 1944, however, the approach of the Allies and the scarcity of both time and materials forced the OKM to acknowledge its Japanese allies as an increasingly important source of help for relieving the pressure on Germany.

By 1943, Japan's requests for aid in electronics had become continuous. As a result, Kuepfmueller sent one Chief Engineer Steckert and an aide to Japan, along with the plans for a Würzburg Riese radar set, a radar receiver of the Athos model, and plans for various German submarines. However, the Japanese "failed to take advantage of this information," and the mission was considered a failure. In October 1944 Chief of Naval Ordnance Admiral Bachenköhler, upon the advice of Dr.

Kuepfmueller, decided once again to send an officer to Japan to aid the Japanese in electronic matters. Consequently, Schlicke was ordered to report to Adm. Paul Wennecker in Tokyo, to work with Japanese electronic engineers.[22]

Schlicke's primary contact in Japan was Commander Ito, the chief of Japanese naval radar research. Ito, like Schlicke, had been a student of Dr. Barkhausen at the *Technische Hochschule* and had received his doctorate in 1937. In 1938, at the behest of the Japanese government, Ito had invited Barkhausen to Tokyo to instruct Japanese scientists in the field of high-frequency technology;[23] however, German priorities prevented the distinguished Barkhausen from leaving Germany. In 1944 Barkhausen recommended that Schlicke be sent to Japan and, upon the issuance of Schlicke's orders,[24] gave his former student a formal letter of introduction to Dr. Ito. Because of Ito's prestige, the OKM determined that Schlicke need not formally meet with any other Japanese scientists; it was assumed that he would form working relationships with others upon his arrival.[25]

Schlicke was originally scheduled to go to Penang, the German submarine base in Indonesia, where he would join a group of naval engineers who were developing installations in the Far East, but at a 6 January 1945 conference the OKM decided to send him to Tokyo instead.[26] Schlicke was due to depart for Japan in February 1945, but the designated submarine was sunk before she reached the departure port of Bergen.[27] As a result, Schlicke and his equipment were assigned to the next available submarine, Fehler's overcrowded *U-234*. In late February, Schlicke boarded the submarine at Kiel and departed for Kristiansand, *U-234*'s last port of call before heading to Japan.

Schlicke, like most of the *U-234* passengers taken into custody, was imprisoned at Portsmouth; however, he did not remain there for long. Having learned of Schlicke's prominence from intelligence reports, the ONI classified him as a "Category I" enemy alien scientist and transferred him to Fort Meade, Maryland.[28] At Fort Meade, Schlicke was given private quarters and by his own admission was "treated well."[29] However, he was soon transferred to Fort Hunt, Virginia, where the ONI learned that his assignment in Japan was more complex than originally believed.

Schlicke revealed that his mission consisted of five primary goals involving German advances in radar and radio communications, submarine warfare, and a rare instance of reciprocity on the part of the Japanese. His first duty was to acquaint himself with Japanese research in communications and direction finding. Schlicke revealed that the Japanese had developed their own magnetron in 1933 and had since performed a great deal of research with hollow transmission lines and long-distance wave propagation.[30] Japanese scientists' theoretical applications of magnetron tubes and hollow transmission were of "great interest" to the Germans, and Schlicke was instructed to familiarize himself with the technology. The magnetrons were of particular interest to German scientists because they were considered to be superior to German versions. Britain and the United States had also utilized hollow-line transmission. Schlicke explained that upon receiving the first captured Allied Meddo system, German engineers were unable to calculate the size of the transformers inside the hollow lines and, for lack of theoretical data, were unable to duplicate the apparatus. Because Japan had experienced some success with hollow-line transmission, German engineers were "highly interested" in Japanese developments.[31]

Schlicke's second duty involved monitoring the Allied high-frequency radar technique, which was being employed against the Japanese. Schlicke planned to gain a thorough understanding of the Allied technique by relying on "presumably good" Japanese intelligence as well as on his own observations. To help intercept and analyze enemy radar transmissions, Schlicke brought with him aboard *U-234* the equipment necessary to construct receiving stations that would be able to intercept frequencies in the 0.8- to 10-centimeter range. Schlicke planned to intercept transmissions at the 1.2-centimeter mark, the frequency thought to be used by the Americans; the information gained would be vital for German countermeasures in relation to early warning and radio camouflage.[32]

Schlicke had also been instructed to construct radio navigation stations in Japan and Indochina. Of a type code-named Goldweber, these massive stations operated between 20 and 80 meters using the Wullenweber antenna system. Placed in a circle, the Wullenweber antennas evolved through a coupling, which, when transmitted to a stationary vertical antenna, transmitted a "narrow, powerful, rotating beam" within short wavelengths, which could be used as either a navigational direction finder or a vessel location device.[33] Germany had originally intended to erect three such stations, one each in Norway, Italy, and Japan, but by the spring of 1945 only the Norwegian station was functional.[34] As a result, Schlicke was to direct the construction of stations in Japan and Indochina while a replacement for the Italian leg of the triad was being sought.

Prior to his departure from Germany, Schlicke had attended the Luft-waffe Radio Consultation Center in Leoberdorf, near Vienna. Here he participated in experiments involving long-distance wave propagation, the purpose being to determine the optimum transmission time for various times of the day. Schlicke would continue these experiments in Japan using a 50-hertz quartz-controlled transmitter as well as an impulse transformer. However, he did not have these items among his possessions on *U-234;* he explained that they were to have been brought to Japan on the next submarine. Any other equipment he needed to perform his experiments would have to be constructed in Japan.[35]

Schlicke's final assignment involved experiments with the Kurier transmission system, which employed a self-destructing millisecond radio signal that submerged submarines could use to relay undetectable messages, as well as a direction-finding apparatus. The Kurier system transmitted high-speed impulses of 250 hertz within a period of 0.44 second, all during off-frequencies. Because the speed of the impulse was such that Allied equipment could not detect it, Germany planned to outfit its newest U-boats with the Kurier. By the spring of 1945 Allied intelligence had begun to fear that the experimental Kurier might become operational at any time, thus rendering the new Type XXI U-boats undetectable by preventing detection of their direction-finding signals and radio transmissions.[36]

Schlicke was to supply the Japanese navy with other elements of German radio technology. Among the items he carried on *U-234* was a search receiver capable of receiving transmissions on a 1-centimeter wave band; this receiver was intended for use by the Japanese navy as an early-warning radar device.[37] Schlicke also planned to instruct the Japanese in the construction and operation of the German Goliath long-wave transmitter, which when coupled with Schlicke's own retractable antennas would allow submarines to receive signals at a depth of 20 meters (66 feet).[38] When implemented, this technology would provide the Imperial Navy's submarines with greater stealth as well as more secure communications at sea.[39]

The ONI discovered that Schlicke had also worked in the armaments industry, albeit briefly, and therefore was able to provide valuable information concerning the use of bombs in submarine warfare. Schlicke revealed that Germany had feared that the Allies had developed remote-controlled bombs, prompting the Kriegsmarine to initiate efforts to develop countermeasures. As a result, Germany was forced to scrutinize its own remote-controlled-bomb program. According to Schlicke, Germany had developed three remote bombs, which were in the testing stages at the war's end: the "Fritz" X falling bomb, the HS-293 gliding bomb, and the BV-143 gliding bomb. Schlicke also provided details regarding German developments in the remote detonation of warheads, in aiming and computing devices for remote-controlled missiles and rockets, and in passive acoustic homing devices for torpedoes.[40] Although he did not know if the Japanese had shared in the development of these bombs, or if Germany had shipped them to Japan, he was able to provide the ONI with his assessment of other areas of Japanese research and development.

Schlicke also provided Allied intelligence with an assessment of Japanese capabilities to develop and manufacture electronic devices. The ONI had suspected that the Japanese were deficient in this area, but the extent of their inability to develop specific items had been unclear. From Schlicke the ONI now learned, for example, that the Japanese had experienced "great difficulty with their radar development [and] had great difficulty in production even though they were acquainted with the theoretical information." They possessed no high-grade insulating material for radar construction, a deficiency that Schlicke had sought to make up for by bringing his own, which was among his possessions on *U-234*. Schlicke also informed his interrogators that the Japanese navy was "practically blind at night, since it possessed no high grade detection gear . . . [and] what little they did have was of a very poor grade." Addressing the ONI's curiosity about Japanese advances in guided missiles and infrared fuses, Schlicke reported that, should the Japanese receive any information on such missiles and fuses, they "would find [them] impossible to produce because of the lack of properly trained scientific personnel."[41]

Schlicke's overall assessment revealed that the Japanese had "felt [a] deficiency of electronics since the beginning of the war . . . which [had cost] them a great deal of ships and men." In addition, he pointed out that Japan had "strongly" asked both the OKM and the OKW for help and information concerning electronics. These requests were consistent in their content: Japan wanted to know "all electronic progress Germany had made [and] all electronic progress Germany knew the Allies had made."[42] On the whole, Schlicke regarded Japanese scientists as inferior to their German counterparts and quite incapable of producing products requiring extensive research in areas such as chemistry and physics.[43]

During 1944 a Professor Falkenhagen, a physicist at the Institute of Technology in Dresden, had worked with Japanese scientists on an absorption material that, when applied to the outer hull of submarines, would theoretically render the U-boat invisible to both radar and infrared search devices. This early experimentation into stealth technology became known as *Schwartze U-Boot,* or black submarine.[44] As part of his mission, Schlicke was to gather information on Japanese progress in sound and electric absorption materials.

This aspect of Schlicke's assignment, code-named Schornsteinfeger (chimney sweep), focused on Japanese experiments with ferrites, an artificial element with insulating properties.[45] Ferrites had been developed by two Japanese scientists while researching their doctoral dissertations under the direction of Dr. Barkhausen, who had also been Schlicke's mentor years before in Dresden.[46] Schlicke discovered that ferritic materials had a magnetic insulating property that conceivably could be used as a radar masking agent, rendering surfaced submarines undetectable.[47] Such a development could revive Germany's decimated wolf packs, a consideration that prompted Schlicke to designate ferritic research as a matter of highest priority.

Schlicke revealed that Germany had investigated four separate methods of camouflaging U-boats. To combat Allied radar, Germany had developed the *Schnorchel* and the *Schwarze U-Boot* and had experimented with geometric deflection of radar beams. As countermeasures against near infrared detection, the Kriegsmarine had developed *Wärmetarnung,* or heat radiation camouflage, and camouflage paints. When faced with ultraviolet detection, which had afforded Allied submarine hunters success when tracking submarines that were leaking fuel, Kriegsmarine engineers worked with the German industrial giant I. G. Farben to develop a lightweight diesel oil that would not fluoresce on the surface of the water when exposed to searchlights. Finally, German engineers had hoped to counter sound detection with the application of sound absorption materials.

Schlicke revealed that "a great deal of research [had] been done" in the field of *Elektrischer Sumpf,* or electric absorption materials. Basically German engineers sought to reduce the detection range of Allied countermeasures by conditioning the submarine's hull through application of a covering that would absorb incoming radar waves "of the largest possible frequency range." The problem was to locate a suitable substance that had the proper permeability as well as adequate dielectric constants to provide maximum absorption. Schlicke reported that once test materials had been located, a further difficulty arose in the attempt to attach the material to the hull of the submarine: some materials used air bubbles as agents of absorption, and these bubbles either collapsed or filled with water when the submarine submerged. To address this problem, the material was coated with a special wax repellent, which proved satisfactory when tested on U-boat *Schnorchel* heads; tests revealed that a *Schnorchel* coated with the substance could be detected only from a range of 5 kilometers (3 miles). Schlicke also revealed that he had carried samples of this material with him aboard *U-234*.[48]

As a result of German experimentation, two absorption methods were developed, code-named *Fafner* and *Alberich*. The Fafnir method was based on the theory of the underwater reflection and absorption of sound. To attain a sufficiently "feeble" reflection of sound waves, a layer of absorbent material approximately 10 centimeters (4 inches) thick was applied to the outer hull of the submarine. The primary insulating material contained air particles that absorbed the compressive energy of the sound waves. To aid further in sound deflection, the material was applied in a ribbed fashion. The result was reflected sound energy, within a relatively wide range of frequencies, of less than 10 percent.[49] However, although the *Fafner* method was desirable because of its effectiveness over a wide frequency range, it was regarded as impractical for operational use on German U-boats. In addition to application problems due to inconsistent adherence underwater, the 10-centimeter thickness of the coating substantially decreased the speed of the submarine.[50] Whatever its deficiencies, however, the *Fafner* method was the only insulating technique that had been revealed to Admiral Kojima and the Japanese Naval Commission.

In the search for an effective absorbent material that would not impair the submarine's performance, German engineers developed the Alberich method. With this method, the insulating material was applied at a more efficient 4-centimeter (1.6-inch) thickness, and it was substantially easier to apply to the submarine's outer hull. Alberich was regarded as superior protection against Allied ASDIC (sonar) devices.[51] However, the method was based on the theory of the absorption of specific resonance frequencies. It was assumed that an enemy would be using only one or two particular frequencies, and so the insulating material was designed to absorb only those two frequencies.[52] For this reason, the method was effective only within a narrow frequency band.

Clearly, there were advantages and disadvantages to both Fafnir and Alberich. Dr. Kuepfmueller, who had conducted research into the use of various geometrical shapes to hinder underwater detection, concluded that the most effective counter to Allied submarine detection consisted of a combination of three methods: use of the *Schnorchel* to avoid radar contact; use of geometrical angles and shapes to deflect radiation; and application of absorption materials.[53] As a former colleague of Kuepfmueller's, Schlicke would have known of this countermeasure triad, and because German officials had never revealed the Alberich method to the Japanese, the ONI assumed that Schlicke had intended to use this knowledge as "a means of bargaining with his captors."[54]

As a prominent figure in the field of infrared (IR) technology, Schlicke proved to be invaluable to the ONI as a source of information on this subject. From 1942 to 1944 he had been assigned to the Kriegsmarine's Naval Chief of Staff Signal Ordnance Office, where he was in charge of the development of IR equipment.[55] As a result, he was eminently qualified to instruct naval personnel in the area of German advances in IR.

Schlicke informed his interrogators of several basic problems German engineers had encountered in the development of IR equipment. Of primary concern to the Kriegsmarine were the absorption of IR beams when passing through water vapor and the tendency of the moisture of fog or sea spray to disperse the IR beams that were not wholly absorbed. Schlicke stated that under excessively moist conditions, such as a fog, IR transmission became substantially less sensitive depending on the size of the water droplets. Another area of concern was the lack of efficient IR filters. Schlicke explained that his organization had sought to develop a filter for IR transmitters that would not be affected by reflected light, such as moonlight on the water at night.

By the spring of 1945 Germany was anticipating a revival of its U-boat corps, primarily through the operational introduction of new submarines such as the Type XXI and XXIII U-boats. However, because the Allies were now using IR as an effective detection device for U-boats transmitting with radar, the success of these new boats depended on decreasing the amount of radiation that was emitted from their signal transmissions. One solution was the development of IR detection equipment, which was desirable because no radio signals were emitted from the boat.[56] By 1945 Germany had lost up to 80 percent of its operational boats; hence, any development that protected precious U-boats and experienced crews was of enormous value.

Schlicke also revealed German developments in IR detection techniques. One such innovation was the *Warmepeii Geräte,* an instrument that could detect large enemy ships at up to 50 kilometers (31 miles) and submarines at up to 16 kilometers (10 miles) by tracing the vessel's heat signature. However, a major drawback to this instrument was that although the direction of the vessel could be determined, precise distance could not. Another IR device was the evaporograph, which employed passive IR direction finding. The evaporograph formed actual images of the source of long-wave heat radiation without the aid of a scanning device. The source's heat signature reflected into a parabolic mirror, which in turn projected the image onto a glass screen. The screen was coated with an oil film only a fraction of a wavelength thick and encased within a vacuum to ensure that the image was projected in an environment whose pressure was below the outside atmospheric pressure. After approximately six seconds a vague outline of the subject would appear; after ten seconds the full image would be visible. If human, the subject's stomach would be the first part to register, followed by the nasal area; non-heat-emitting items such as buttons appeared as dark spots. The evaporograph was effective up to 100 meters (328 feet) and was virtually undetectable because no radiation was projected from it. In addition, experimentation showed that water vapor did not affect the sensitivity of the instrument, primarily because of the long wavelength on which it operated.[57]

German methods of IR detection were marginally successful; however, the most effective instruments were constricted by narrow survey fields. As a result, engineers also sought to enlarge the field of vision for IR detection.[58] Schlicke revealed that work had been progressing on the *Bildwandler* and the second-generation *Grobildwandler*, both of which were designed for aircraft as well as naval vessels. Schlicke had worked with a Dr. Schaffernicht of the German electrical conglomerate AEG (Allgemeine Elektrizitats Gesellschaft) on the *Bildwandler* detection unit; however, the pair experienced "considerable difficulty" due to lightning interference. These difficulties led to the *Grobildwandler*, which originally operated with a scanning disk similar to those employed on early television sets. In an effort to reduce both motion and radiation, the improved *Grobildwandler* was outfitted with a set of vibrating reeds, which scanned the appointed area. Schlicke stated that the latter method met with substantial success; the improved unit was intended for installation on small surface vessels and U-boats.[59]

One of the more ambitious attempts at IR detection was code-named Flamingo. The Flamingo project consisted of a series of three separate revolving IR warning receivers, Flamingo I, II, and III, which were waterproofed for installation on U-boats. U-boat commanders had informed the OKM that prior to an attack by an enemy destroyer or aircraft, a red disk would appear near the attacking vessel. This was a definite indication that enemy searchlights being employed at close range were using IR filters to compensate for the fact that ocean clutter made radar ineffective at such close range. As a result, the Flamingo I warning device was installed on U-boats to detect the presence of the IR beam that emanated from the filtered searchlight. The Flamingo I was effective against a 100-watt searchlight equipped with an IR filter up to 8 kilometers (5 miles) away; it was also considered advantageous as a "fairly accurate" direction-finding device because of its deviation of only 5 degrees. In addition, the device exhibited no reaction to interference from outside sources of nighttime radiation such as stars.[60]

The Flamingo II was an IR detector intended for passive use. The device was developed to locate an aircraft by detecting the aircraft's exhaust gases. Earlier experimentation with rotating devices had proved successful; however, difficulty was encountered when attempting to pressure-proof the device. In addition, the wide sweep of the 45-degree rotating antenna caused problems with loss of direction, a difficulty common to panoramic observation. These problems were solved in the Flamingo II, which used mercury switches as well as an enhanced housing that could withstand the pressure of depth. To solve the directional-loss problem, changes to the antenna rotation were effected. The Flamingo II, which searched for radiation rather than actual heat, had an effective range of up to 8–10 kilometers (5–6 miles) against medium-sized military aircraft.[61]

In 1944, IR receivers in Kiel had reported that enemy aircraft that had previously been detected at a range of 10–15 kilometers (6–9 miles) with conventional IR direction-finding equipment could no longer be located with that equipment. Allied aircraft engineers had discovered that aircraft exhausts were being "read" by the German IR receivers, and consequently they began to shield those exhausts. As a result, work began on the Flamingo III, which would read the actual heat signature of an aircraft rather than its radiation. However, Schlicke told the ONI that work on the Flamingo III had not been completed when he visited the laboratory in February 1945.[62]

Schlicke also revealed that the Germans had been looking into the use of IR for homing purposes. In 1944 work began on a homing device for an explosive boat known as the Linse. The Linse was a small vessel that was directed to its target by means of IR detection devices. From a range of 5,000–1,000 meters (16,404–3,281 feet), the boat would effect steerage through the line-of-sight principle, using the *Bildwandler* unit. From 1,000 meters, a homing device would take over guidance. The homing device had a wide aperture, which gave it a wider range of coverage. Because the actual temperature of the target could not be determined, a default temperature of 100°C (212°F) was assumed. Schlicke reported that research conducted at Neubrandenburger See had been deemed successful, the boat's performance rated "excellent."

Although it was too late for the Germans to make operational use of the Linse, Schlicke stated that the Japanese might try to integrate the new weapon into their program; he had carried complete details of the device with him aboard *U-234*.[63]

Perhaps Schlicke's most alarming revelation concerned the existence of IR proximity fuses. In February 1945 Schlicke had been informed by a Dr. Preikschot that German IR proximity fuses were to be installed in ground-launched or air-to-air missiles; twenty thousand of the fuses had been ordered, and operational deployment of the missiles was planned for March 1945. The missiles were extremely accurate, with a projected deviation of only 5 degrees. However, their effectiveness was dampened by the use of the IR fuse. When targeting a large, scattered group of aircraft, the fuse would seek a position between aircraft because of the conflicting heat registers of the target planes; the fuse would seek the average direction and explode harmlessly in midair.[64] Nevertheless, the possible use of IR proximity fuses as homing devices for both missiles and rockets was a cause of concern to ONI officials, who recognized that Schlicke would be a valuable asset if the need arose for the development of countermeasures.

Schlicke's knowledge of existing technology was of immense value to ONI officials, but while imprisoned at Fort Meade he provided an even more valuable service to his captors by giving a series of lectures at the Navy Department designed to summarize his electronic research for the Kriegsmarine.[65] His first lecture, delivered on 19 July 1945, was entitled "A General Review of Measures Planned by the German Admiralty in the Electronic Field in Order to Revive U-Boat Warfare." This initial lecture provided the navy with a comprehensive review of German communications and radio location techniques covering both active and passive detection, camouflage, search reception, deception, radar jamming, counterjamming, remote control, and anti-direction-finding measures within the entire frequency field of electromagnetic and ultrasonic waves.[66]

Schlicke's expertise impressed even the most skeptical American scientists and military leaders, many of whom had protested the exploitation of German scientists.[67] However, much of Schlicke's lecture material was strange to even the most astute American officials, which, combined with the language barrier, made for an air of confusion. Schlicke tried to clarify the material by providing a series of sketches to illustrate such concepts as the "Damping Components of a TE-20 Wave in Relation to the Frequency" or the "Development of the Distant Field from the Hollow-Line Field."[68]

Schlicke continued his cooperation with naval officials until 25 June 1946, when he, along with other German scientists, was repatriated to Germany. Many of the repatriated German scientists were offered the choice of remaining in Germany or continuing their research in the United States. Although a sizable number chose to return home, many were worried about conditions in postwar Germany, particularly those like Schlicke whose homes lay in the Soviet sector. Schlicke chose to return to the United States, and on 7 October 1946 he resumed his work at the Office of Naval Research facility at Sands Point.[69]

During the summer of 1945, as Schlicke and the other former passengers of *U-234* adjusted to life as prisoners of war in the United States, Allied technical missions in Europe were uncovering the secrets of German research into numerous technologies. On 6 July, cognizant of the value of such information to America's continuing war in the Pacific, the Combined Joint Chiefs of Staff proposed guidelines for American exploitation of a "minimum number of German scientists" in the United States.[70] The results of the ensuing program would have a profound effect on Dr. Heinz Schlicke's life.

Field reports from Europe validated the navy's interest in German research in the field of pilotless aircraft and guided missiles. Lt. Cdr. J. H. Marchant of the Naval Technical Mission had made a survey of German facilities and concluded that "the Germans were probably further ahead of the U.S.A. in the field of guided missiles than in any other field"; it was a field, he said, that "has only been superficially scratched" by American researchers. Marchant pointed out, however, that American appropriation of German technology would be merely a prelude to further work; a comprehensive understanding and deployment of German technology would require an understanding of German scientists' "fundamental progress and projective thinking." On the basis of his observations, Marchant recommended that "unstinted support be given to the exhaustive exploitation" of scientists working in "this all-important field."[71]

Another area of German research in which the navy expressed interest was infrared technology. On 9 August 1945 Cdr. H. G. Dyke of the Naval Office of Research and Development, in an effort to determine which German scientists would be of maximum exploitation value, sought the advice of physicists at the Massachusetts Institute of Technology. Nine days later, MIT responded with a report on German progress in IR research.

The MIT report was prefaced with an acknowledgment that at the time of the German surrender, "the Germans were well ahead of us in military infra-red developments, both in fundamental research and in the production and military use of equipment." The report offered several reasons for this discrepancy, with two emerging as most prominent. First, Germany had the advantage of a considerable head start on IR development for military purposes, with research dating back to the rearmament programs of the 1930s. Second, German "shortcomings" in the field of radar development had led scientists to place emphasis on other physical properties that might counter Allied radar systems. The MIT report further acknowledged that while German combat applications of IR were "considerably more extensive" than American applications, they were nonetheless of relatively little importance at the time of the German surrender. However, during the closing months of the European war, German leaders had "become keenly aware of the advantages of IR [and] had learned . . . that IR devices will be a *sine qua non* of combat troops in future wars."[72]

The navy's Bureau of Aeronautics (BuAer) was interested in practical applications of both pilotless aircraft and IR technology and sought out those scientists who could help develop masking techniques for guided missiles. On 24 October 1945 the chief of the bureau notified Lt. Cdr. W. H. van Benschoten of the Special Devices Division of the navy's Office of Research and Inventions that BuAer desired to initiate research into "methods for camouflaging supersonic pilotless aircraft against radar detection . . . This study might be conducted with reference to the German V-2 missile."[73] BuAer soon discovered that the ONI had "in its custody the man who [had been] in charge of electronic research of the German Navy," and who was thus "eminently qualified to undertake the investigation." The bureau therefore requested that Dr. Heinz Schlicke, then at Fort Hunt in Virginia, be "procured and assigned to the project," code-named Project 77.[74] On 31 October, van Benschoten formally requested that Schlicke be moved to the Project 77 Experimental Laboratory at Sands Point, Long Island.[75] However, Schlicke was classified as a prisoner of war, and thus fell under the jurisdiction of the provost marshal general of the army. Consequently, Rear Adm. H. G. Bowen, chief of research and inventions, filed a formal request with the War Department that custody of Schlicke be transferred from the army to the navy, a request that was ultimately approved.[76] Schlicke's subsequent work was of such value that the ONI decided upon a long-term exploitation of him.

Because of the uncertain status of alien civilians, all German nationals were scheduled to be returned to Germany by 15 July 1946; Heinz Schlicke was no exception. However, on 30 April of that year the naval Office of Research and Inventions informed the officer in charge of

Project 77 that although Schlicke would have to be repatriated to Germany, a newly instituted program would "provide for the future employment of German scientists and technical personnel," thus offering the navy the opportunity to retain Schlicke's expertise after his repatriation. The new program would allow the navy to reemploy any scientists who met certain criteria; because the navy had expressed continued interest in Schlicke's work in the field of electromagnetic radiation, he was designated as a desirable candidate for the exploitation program, known as Project Paperclip.[77] In addition to the opportunity to continue his research in the relative freedom of the United States, a Paperclip contract also offered a scientist inducements such as legal status in the United States, the eventual transfer of his family to America, and patent protection.[78] Schlicke thus became one of the Paperclip scientists, his work deemed so sensitive that America's Soviet allies were denied access to it.[79]

At Sands Point, Schlicke, along with his assistant, Erich Menzel, pursued theoretical work on radar camouflage and infrared research, fields in which the ONI considered him to be "outstanding."[80] After the defeat of Japan, he worked on classified projects for the Office of Naval Research until 1 September 1950, when his personal-services contract with the Navy was terminated.[81] However, he had already requested to be released from his work with the navy in order to accept a job offer from the Allen-Bradley Company of Milwaukee, which he did in 1950. In 1964 Schlicke finally completed the voyage he had begun in February 1945 when Allen-Bradley sent him to Japan on a business trip. A noted lecturer, author, and inventor, Schlicke today believes that "the USA was well compensated for the money spent to bring me here. . . . I feel my work is a 'thank you' to America for restructuring and reviving a devastated Germany through the Marshall Plan and for being instrumental in its reunification."[82]

9

The Men from Messerschmitt

THE DISASTROUS JUNE 1942 Battle of Midway prompted the Japanese to reevaluate their wartime manufacturing priorities, placing the production of aircraft above other munitions concerns. Upon assessing their weakened air force, Japanese military officials discovered that Japan trailed the Allies not only in numbers of combat aircraft but also in airborne technology. Indeed, Japanese pilots who compared their aircraft with those of the Americans were convinced that they were flying vastly inferior machines. According to Cdr. Nomura Ryosuku, staff air operations officer for the Eleventh Air Fleet at Rabaul, Japanese pilots lived in "horror of American fighters" and conceded that their Mitsubishi Zero fighters, while comparable to the American Curtiss P-40 Warhawk, were no match for more modern fighters such as the Grumman F4-U Corsair. In addition, in aeronautical engineering the Japanese lagged from one to one and a half years behind other combatants, and actual aircraft production trailed yet another year.[1] Cognizant of the desperate condition of their aircraft industry, the Imperial Army and Navy determined that the immediate solution was to request operational combat aircraft from Germany, along with the appropriate aeronautical, technical, and engineering expertise to help develop manufacturing proficiency.

The origins of Japan's aircraft industry date to the end of World War I. In 1920 the aircraft division of Kawasaki Shipbuilding began the construction of French-designed aircraft and aircraft engines. By 1926 other Japanese firms such as Nakajima, Mitsubishi, Aichi Tokei, Kawanishi, and Tashikawa had followed Kawasaki's example and formed aircraft divisions, specializing in airframe and power plant construction. However, despite the optimism that surrounded the fledgling industry, Japan's aircraft manufacturing ambitions remained limited in scope and of relatively small significance.[2] Japan was not compelled to establish a larger air force until 1937; however, diplomatic events in that year forced Japanese leaders to reevaluate the need for an expanded air force. Japan's intervention in China prompted a shift in the foreign political position in eastern Asia and alerted the West to the potential of Japanese aggression. Simultaneously, the Western democracies began introducing aircraft into their own arsenals, primarily in response to Germany's Luftwaffe. As a result, Japanese leaders realized that to be considered a world power, Japan would have to expand its army and naval air forces and equip them with the proper armament and other apparatus.

Japan began to intensify the output of its aircraft industry; the number of aviation workers increased from approximately 50,000 in 1937 to over 150,000 in 1941. By 1941 Prime Minister Tojo Hideki's government had also begun to encourage the growth of Japan's domestic aircraft industry by subsidizing the expansion of smaller companies and enlarging existing facilities; by 1944, 90 percent of airframes and 80 percent of all engine production originated from Japan's "privatized" firms.[3] However, whereas Japanese firms were quite proficient in the manufacture of foreign aircraft, they could not adequately design and build their own.

Originally, Japanese companies did not possess the expertise to design and manufacture their own aircraft, and so they relied heavily upon foreign firms for research and development. Japanese officials diligently sought foreign licenses to benefit from the experience of European and American manufacturers, in hopes of eventually being able to develop their own design and manufacturing facilities. In addition to soliciting foreign designs, Japanese firms also began to import design and manufacturing specialists and technicians to oversee the integration of Western production methods into Japanese factories as well as the organization and construction of new plants. Japan's gradual expansion and modernization of its aircraft industry, the licensed construction of foreign models, and the exploitation of foreign specialists' experience characterized the early development of Japan's army and naval air forces.[4]

Despite the impressive performance of Japan's air forces during the early stages of the war, production of even its most successful aircraft, such as the Mitsubishi Zero, was fraught with difficulty. Because of the relatively rapid rise of industry in prewar Japan, aircraft manufacturers could not rely on a heavy industrial background like that of other highly industrialized nations.[5] In addition, individual factories had practically no reserves of trained workers; as skilled workers were conscripted into the military, the bulk of available manpower remained in an unskilled, largely agrarian workforce.[6] Japan's ability to rely on foreign firms, which was substantially threatened by the outbreak of war with the United States in 1941, was further compromised by the isolation of Germany in the middle of 1941; this interruption of trade practically stopped the importation of vital German machine tools to Japan. These and other difficulties prompted German officials to label Japan's aircraft industry as "backward" in certain respects.[7]

While Japan did not substantially trail the other industrialized nations in airframe and engine construction, it was greatly deficient in the development of avionics and other equipment. The reliance on foreign licenses for aircraft instruments meant that Japanese manufacturers were dealt a lethal blow when foreign expertise was either eliminated, as was the case with the United States, or denied, as was the case with Germany. Japanese engineers were now forced to design and build their own instruments, which, while sufficient, were not equal to the ever-improving products of Allied avionics. A 1944 United States Strategic Bombing report stated that "[Japanese] aircraft instruments are inferior to . . . German, English, and American instruments. . . . All-metal airplanes, generally of good design, are inferior in performance, armament, and equipment to similar British and American types."[8]

Japanese military leaders were well aware of their dependency upon foreign expertise in the field of aviation. However, the signing of the Tripartite Pact and its subsequent secret military aid protocols provided the admirals and generals some relief; as long as Japan remained allied with Germany, it would be able to counter, and in some cases master, Allied innovations. Japanese reliance on German firms was evidenced by the pre-1941 flow of German equipment to Japan through the Soviet Union; electrical equipment from Bosch, navigational instruments from Siemens and Askania, and radio equipment from various German firms were regularly shipped across the Trans-Siberian Railroad.[9] These shipments ceased with the German invasion of Russia in

June 1941; however, Japanese demand for German equipment did not abate.

By December 1944 Japan's hopes for remaining competitive in the air rested primarily on the availability of German aid. However, German observers in Japan were frustrated by what they perceived as an ignorance of efficient construction methods, as well as by the lack of standardization, technical personnel, and machine tools. Japanese officials sought to address these deficiencies by buttressing their own antiquated manufacturing processes through the acquisition of modern German equipment, securing the production rights to German innovations, facilitating the training of Japanese engineers in Germany, and obtaining the services of German technical and manufacturing personnel. A December 1944 report from the Reich Chief Engineer's Office summed up Germany's goal by stating that, through the transfer of material and personnel, Germany hoped that "Japanese aircraft production will be substantially aided for a long time by a proper manufacturing set-up and improvement in factory organization."[10] However, Japan's needs for assistance were too immediate to be met by a revamping of its antiquated manufacturing processes. Japanese leaders sought not only to acquire the wherewithal to produce Germany's modern aircraft but to purchase the aircraft themselves.

Surprisingly, the initial inquiries about the availability of German aircraft did not come directly from the Japanese military. Because there was no official protocol concerning technical exchanges between the two allies, Japanese industry began to analyze which German aircraft could be most easily duplicated using existing Japanese production facilities. In 1942 the Berlin field office of the Mitsui Bussan Machinery Company queried its Tokyo head office: "[Because] no Fokker-190 single seat fighter has been shot down [in Europe] . . . would you consider purchasing a sample after talking it over with the Nakajima Aircraft Company?"[11] In December 1942 Japan and Germany signed a supplementary agreement to their economic pact that specifically addressed "the delivery of certain machines and plants, the sending of engineers [and] technical experts, and the training of technical experts."[12]

In January 1943 Germany began shipment of its most effective combat aircraft, notably the Messerschmitt (ME) 109 and the Focke-Wulf (FW) 190 fighters, to Japan. In addition to those aircraft already shipped, the Japanese military attaché in Berlin, Gen. Otani Seigo, offered Tokyo his assessment of other German aircraft, including the experimental ME 309 fighter and the proposed ME 264 bomber.[13] Although the ME

309 remained in the prototype stage, Otani urged the Japanese army to "purchase one of the experimental models immediately, and from two to four samples during 1943 for the purpose of study."[14] Although Tokyo agreed with this recommendation, Otani was unable to complete the purchase of the aircraft, as the Germans ceased development of the aircraft in October 1943. However, the German Armaments Ministry informed Ambassador Oshima that Germany had no objection if the Japanese wished to "manufacture the ME 309 to meet [Japan's] needs." As a result, Tokyo directed Otani to arrange for the shipment of technical data and plans for both the ME 309 and the ME 264 to Japan "by the special means now available to the Navy, i.e., by submarine."[15] However, this plan would take two years to materialize.

Japan's attempts to acquire German aircraft abated somewhat until the spring of 1944, when Ambassador Oshima informed Hitler of Japan's "great concern on the matter of expanding her Air Force," a concern that Hitler promised Germany would "do its very best" to address.[16] One reason for Japan's renewed interest was the Messerschmitt Company's successful experiments with jet-propelled aircraft. In a March 1944 report to Japan's vice minister of war, Otani requested that Tokyo "dispatch technicians [to Germany] at once . . . to study this plane [the ME 262]."[17] Otani also informed the chief of the Imperial Army Air Force that "Japan would do well to purchase the manufacturing rights for the new ME 209 fighter."[18] In the fall of 1944 the Japanese formally contacted Messerschmitt director Graf Plum and requested the plans and patents for the ME 262 as well as the rocket-propelled ME 163 interceptor. Plum granted the request and proposed prompt shipment to Japan via U-boat as soon as the situation proved favorable.[19] However, the mere acquisition of these plans would not solve Japan's problem; Japanese industry still lacked the engineering and technical expertise required for jet aircraft production.

Acknowledging that profiting from Germany's success with fighter aircraft was "important if Japan is to have mastery of the air," Otani informed Tokyo that Germany had agreed to send an aircraft designer to Japan.[20] On 6 April 1944 the Japanese vice minister of war informed Otani that officials of the Imperial Navy had requested that "arrangements be made to bring some designing engineers of the Messerschmitt Company to Japan in one of our submarines."[21] However, no Japanese submarine was scheduled to arrive in Europe; given the depleted state of the Japanese submarine force and the success of the Allies in antisubmarine warfare, it was doubtful that a boat would survive the journey anyway. Nevertheless, plans to ship prototype aircraft and engineers to Japan in three concurrent missions continued.[22] The first submarine, *U-864* (Wolfram), was scheduled to deliver the ME 309, ME 209, and ME 264 and two Messerschmitt engineers named von Klingensperg and Schaurens to Japan; however, she was attacked and sunk off the coast of Bergen in March 1945.[23] The second, and as it proved final, mission was being ferried to Japan aboard *U-234* when Fehler surrendered.[24]

In early 1942 German leaders decided to prioritize the development and subsequent production of jet-propelled aircraft. Germany was a leader in the development of early jet-powered aircraft; the Heinkel 178, which first flew at Marienehe on 27 August 1939, was the world's first pure jet aircraft. Confident in the future of turbojet propulsion, the German Air Ministry awarded the Junkers Company a contract for a jet turbine engine, the Jumo 004; in 1940 designer Willi Messerschmitt completed his initial design for a jet-powered fighter, designated the 262. Ultimately, Messerschmitt's design was mated with Junker's Jumo 004, and in July 1942 the ME 262 made its first successful flight at the Messerschmitt testing center at Leipheim. In April 1944 the ME 262 became the world's first operational jet aircraft.[25]

As the ME 262 progressed toward operational status, Allied intelligence analysts began to monitor reports of the new German aircraft. In January 1944 the Office of Strategic Services received a report that German production of a new aircraft that could attain speeds upward of 1,000 kilometers per hour (621 miles per hour) had begun in December 1943. The new aircraft employed "increased motor power [which was] responsible for the high speed of this plane" and was outfitted with parts manufactured at the Junkers factory at Dessau.[26] Despite the use of Junkers parts and engines, the aircraft was assembled by Messerschmitt in factories located at Augsburg and Oschersleben, and it featured "no changes in armament" over existing Luftwaffe fighters.

Predictably, the Allied response to such assessments was one of incredulity, as exemplified by the comment of a Lieutenant Pearson, who upon reading the OSS report noted that "621 [miles per hour] is a pretty high speed! [There] may be some smoke in this report."[27] Continued information reported that the new aircraft used rockets to assist with takeoff, saving the fuel-intensive turbojets for combat. The ME 262 was fitted with a pressure frame to withstand atmospheric pressures within an altitude range of 15,000–17,000 meters (49,212–55,774 feet), at which the aircraft could reach level speeds of over 1,000 kilometers per hour. More ominously, however, the ME 262 appeared to address one of the greatest weaknesses of the Luftwaffe: the desperate shortage of pilots. A 5 August OSS report originating from Stockholm stated that the extremely maneuverable ME 262 was "generally very easy to fly. . . . Within a half-year a beginner can be trained into a full-fledged combat pilot." The potential of the aircraft itself had been exhibited over Germany in 1944, when a group of twelve ME 262s shot down an entire formation of thirty Allied bombers within a thirty-minute time span.[28]

By November 1944 Allied intelligence had begun to consider the threat of the ME 262 as it applied not only to Allied forces in Europe but also to American forces in the Pacific. Intercepted diplomatic messages revealed that the Japanese had been actively seeking German aircraft as early as March 1944;[29] in May 1944 the Japanese military attaché in Berlin had requested that Japanese technicians "be sent to Germany at once to study [the ME 262]."[30] In November the Naval Air Technical Intelligence Service received a report from Capt. S. B. Spangler of the Power Plant Design Branch that recommended a comparison between German and Japanese aircraft. Spangler recognized that "in the design of Japanese aircraft engines, it is common knowledge that the Japanese have heavily borrowed . . . from their Axis partner Germany." The Power Design Branch was not primarily concerned about German developments; however, they would have to be closely monitored to predict possible Japanese tendencies. Spangler further voiced the fears of Air Intelligence by noting, "It is inconceivable that [the Japanese] are not working on jet propulsion, closely following German work in this direction. . . . It therefore seems . . . logical that [Japanese] development will follow a similar pattern."[31] Whereas this pattern was evident in Japanese production of aircraft such as the ME 109, FW 190, and JU 87, the Japanese were delinquent in initiating production of the ME 262 and ME 163.[32] However, steps were being taken to intensify Japanese efforts at deploying these aircraft; the latest and arguably most vital began with the departure of *U-234* from Europe. Within her hull, *U-234* carried Messerschmitt engineer Dr. August Bringewald, procurement and manufacturing specialist Franz Ruf, plans and drawings for the ME 163, and, crated but nonetheless complete, an ME 262 turbojet aircraft.

The two-man Messerschmitt contingent was headed by engineer August Bringewald, often referred to as "Willi Messerschmitt's right-hand man," who in Germany had been in charge of production for the ME 262 as well as other combat aircraft. Bringewald was to direct production of the ME 262 in Japan and also prepare the way for production of the ME 163.[33] His companion was Franz Ruf, a specialist in the procurement of industrial machinery and its utilization for aircraft production. Ruf had previously supervised the construction of manufacturing facilities for German aircraft throughout Europe, particularly in Romania, and was now charged with developing facilities in Japan to build the ME 262 and ME 163.[34]

August Bringewald was born in 1901 in Hagen and completed his compulsory education in Dortmund, graduating in 1918. His ultimate goal was to become an engineer, and after graduation he gathered experience by volunteering to work in various factories as a machinist. After three years of volunteer work, Bringewald entered the Beuth Technical School in Berlin, matriculating in 1924. He soon began work for AEG and Bergman, continuing his education by attending night classes at a technical school for engineers. In 1927 Bringewald left AEG and entered the employ of Dr. Paul Meyer, a specialist in electrical engineering; however, Meyer soon went out of business, and from 1931 to 1933 Bringewald, like many Germans during the world depression, was unemployed. In 1933 he obtained a position as section chief of construction with Heinkel. In 1935 he left Heinkel for Henschel Aircraft and in 1938 left Henschel for Messerschmitt. At Messerschmitt, Bringewald worked as a construction engineer, simultaneously serving as the Augsburg plant's general manager. ONI investigators noted Bringewald's familiarity with German production difficulties brought about by Allied bombing, as well as with patent and production agreements between German and Japanese aircraft manufacturers. In addition, Bringewald could comment on the German air industry from the perspective of a civilian and offered the ONI "interesting information about the German attitude toward Japan."[35]

Bringewald recalled his personal experiences with Japanese aircraft officials in Germany and therefore was able to help the ONI ascertain the extent of Japan's contact with German civilian personnel. Bringewald had initially been introduced to Japanese personnel in early 1944, when he was informed of Japan's interest in the ME 262. After meeting in Berlin with Japanese military officials, including General Otani, Bringewald traveled to Leipheim and Ulm, where he presented a series of lectures on the "general construction and special features" of the ME 262 to an assembly of the Japanese liaison staff. After the conclusion of these lectures, Bringewald had no further personal contact with the Japanese until the fall of 1944, when he reported to Berlin and received administrative details and orders from Otani regarding his assignment in Japan.[36]

During the summer of 1944 Bringewald was notified by co-workers at Augsburg that Japanese engineers visiting the plant had repeatedly questioned Messerschmitt technicians about the ME 262, specifically regarding production problems that Japanese engineers had encountered with the aircraft. One area of great concern to the Japanese was the difficulty they had manufacturing the turbine engine. Bringewald reported that this came as no surprise to him, as German engineers themselves had experienced substantial problems with the Jumo 004 engine. However, if the Japanese had received additional information regarding the Jumo, it must have originated with Junkers, as Messerschmitt did not conduct any research or development on the engines themselves.

The ME 262 was not the only innovative German aircraft in which the Japanese expressed interest. Bringewald was notified that as part of his responsibilities in Japan he would supervise the construction of the ME 163 rocket-propelled interceptor. However, he was unable to leave his duties at Augsburg to familiarize himself sufficiently with the ME 163; consequently his knowledge of the aircraft was limited to what he learned during a three-day inspection of the ME 163's assembly plant. Bringewald was of the opinion that the Japanese never showed a serious interest in the ME 163; during their numerous tours of the Augsburg facility, Japanese engineers and officials never inquired about the aircraft. While it was possible that the Japanese had received sufficient data to initiate construction of the ME 163, Bringewald considered it improbable.[37] The engine had been under development for some time, and he had heard of no attempts to send plans, documents, or technicians to Japan.[38]

Although Japanese liaison with Messerschmitt was multifaceted, all endeavors between the two were directed by one individual. Bringewald pointed out that Dr. Graf Thun, chief of Messerschmitt's Foreign Department, was responsible for all matters concerning the Japanese; "through his hands and over his signature" passed all material that was given or licensed to the Japanese, including those aircraft and parts that were assembled at plants other than the Augsburg facility. In addition, Dr. Thun was rumored to possess information not only about Japanese jet aircraft manufacture but also about Japanese progress in rocket technology as well as information given to the Japanese by German aircraft manufacturers other than Messerschmitt.[39]

Under Thun, the practical liaison between Messerschmitt and Japan was effected by a Dr. Layritz. Layritz, who was on Thun's staff, supervised the transfer of licensed materials, such as blueprints and drawings, to the Japanese. In addition, he attended all conferences with the Japanese, where he worked with Commander Nagamori, Japan's agent for the receipt of licensed materials. Nagamori, a member of the Japanese naval attaché's staff, was responsible for the procurement of necessary materials and licenses specifically for the ME 262 and ME 163. Bringewald attended three conferences with Layritz and Nagamori in Jettingen during which the transfer of blueprints and drawings was discussed; three additional conferences were held in Berlin, although these were of an organizational rather than a practical nature. Bringewald recalled that at one of the meetings Nagamori surprised him by stating that the Japanese had been experimenting with their own turbine engine; however, they had experienced little success and consequently "were in urgent need of the ME 262."[40]

Bringewald pointed out that despite Japan's desperate need for German expertise, distrust between the Axis partners remained a substantial obstacle. Although Messerschmitt had agreed to supervise the construction of Germany's premier aircraft for Japanese use, the Japanese would not give the German engineers "even the most primitive information which would enable [them] to plan an organizational set-up of an aircraft factory in Japan." Ignoring German pleas for access to vital information, Japanese officials stated that they "were convinced [of] the abilities of German personnel being sent to Japan" and were confident that even without preliminary planning, German engineers would have little or no difficulty manufacturing the ME 262 and ME 163 once they arrived in Japan. The lead time required for plant construction, training of workers and technicians, and material procurement was of little concern to the Japanese—a powerful indication of the chasm that existed between Eastern and Western production styles.[41]

From Bringewald's testimony the ONI was able to substantiate suspicions concerning the Japanese military hierarchy's low regard for scientists and other nonmilitary specialists, particularly those of Western origin. Bringewald stated that his and Ruf's "relations with the Japs [sic] were not too good." As an example, in describing the final days of fellow *U-234* passengers Tomonaga and Shoji, he said that "when they distributed their personal belongings [to the crew], we were excluded. . . . . Whenever they passed by us, we turned [our backs]; they noticed that." As for contact with the two Japanese officers, Bringewald mentioned that "we talked with them the barest minimum, same with the Commander [Fehler], he only spoke with them when necessary."[42] The Japanese officers' very evident disregard for the two German civilians was insulting to an individual of Bringewald's stature; on at least one occasion, Bringewald said, he "felt like beating up one of them."[43] ONI investigators must have wondered how effective German engineers could have been in Japan if all of them shared Bringewald and Ruf's sense of alienation.

Franz Ruf did not possess a purely aeronautical background like his companion Bringewald. Born in Augsburg in 1907, Ruf completed his compulsory education and then spent eight additional years attending a graduate program for mechanics. In 1921 he began an apprenticeship program for Maschinenfabrik Augsburg-Nürnberg (MAN), completing the apprenticeship by 1925. His grades were excellent, and in an unusual gesture MAN retained him as a regular employee for an additional five years. During the latter years of his employment he traveled extensively in Holland and Germany, primarily setting up printing presses.

While working at MAN, Ruf continued to study, taking classes in shorthand, bookkeeping, iron production, and the fabrication of factory tools and machinery. In 1930 he joined Georg Fischer of Eisengiesserei in Schaffhausen, Switzerland, where for six months he rebuilt generators into diesel engines for submarines. In August of that year he returned to Augsburg and MAN, now working in the assembly division. In 1935 he passed his *Meister* (journeyman) examination and subsequently went to work for Bayerische Flugzeugwerke–Augsburg in the Operations Department. In 1937 Bayerische Flugzeugwerke was renamed Messerschmitt-A.G.-Augsburg, and Ruf was put in charge of all industrial machinery and equipment used in the manufacture of aircraft parts.

In 1939 Ruf became chief group leader and deputy departmental director for procurement of industrial machinery. In addition, he became a consultant for firms that produced industrial machinery and equipment for Messerschmitt. In 1943 he was awarded special supervision over production of all machinery and parts manufacturing in Italy. He held this position until September 1944, when he was summoned to Augsburg and informed of his assignment to supervise and offer counsel on the procurement and production of industrial machinery for the manufacture of the ME 262 in Japan.[44]

Ruf described his responsibilities in Japan as falling under four basic headings. First, he was to direct the production of the manufacturing tools and appliances with which the aircraft parts would actually be made. Next, he was to supervise the construction of patterns and forms that would be used as templates to ensure consistency in mass-production of the aircraft. Third, he was to coordinate the supply of applicable templates for use on the assembly lines and, fourth, he was to supervise the construction of the machinery for the assembly lines. Among Ruf's possessions aboard *U-234* were hundreds of pages of plans, drawings, prints, and color-coded charts for the construction of templates and tools, paint schemes, line installations, and parts lists. In addition, he carried patterns and forms for fuselage and wing fairings, wing assemblies, ailerons, landing flaps, wingtip caps, tail assemblies, stabilizers, elevators, tail fins, and rudder assemblies.[45] As a result, with the surrender of *U-234* came not only a complete ME 262 aircraft but, perhaps more important, the technical and manufacturing wherewithal to mass-produce the aircraft.

Unlike the other passengers aboard *U-234*, Bringewald and Ruf were civilians assigned by their corporate employer to work in Japan. The two engineers had signed contracts of special employment with the Messerschmitt Company, which determined the parameters for their mission to Japan. Typically the length of such a mission was one year, but in this case the company retained the right to recall the two at any time. In addition, Messerschmitt would provide funds for the engineers' living expenses in Tokyo as well as financial protection for their families, left behind in Germany. To provide their employees with a measure of security, Messerschmitt financed a pension and life insurance policy, effective in the case of disability or death, and guaranteed the protection of their personal property in Germany during their absence. As a final stipulation of their contract, they were reminded that they were representatives not only of the Reich but also of Messerschmitt, and were expected to conduct themselves accordingly.[46] Bringewald and Ruf lived up to this professional expectation, but it was not the Japanese who were impressed; rather, it was the ONI interrogators at Portsmouth.

Often interrogated together, Bringewald and Ruf provided insight into the workings of Germany's military-industrial complex, especially regarding Japan's role as a customer for German goods. The Messerschmitt missions to Japan were a joint venture between Germany's Reich Ministry of Industry (RIM), Japanese military attaché Otani, and the Messerschmitt Company. When first notified of the mission to Tokyo, both Bringewald and Ruf expressed reservations at being assigned a mission by the German military. Only when a director from the Messerschmitt main office in Augsburg ordered the pair to depart did they acquiesce, now regarding the trip, with its inherent risks, as part of their jobs.[47]

Thanks to the interception of diplomatic communications, Allied intelligence was aware of Japanese attempts to replicate German jet aircraft designs. However, the ONI did not know which branch of the Japanese military would supervise these attempts, nor exactly where the Japanese planned to produce such aircraft. Bringewald revealed that he and Ruf were to work under the auspices of the Japanese army, and that they had been given formal letters of introduction from Otani to the commander of the Japanese South Army and the commander of the army unit stationed at their destination. However, because the letters had been sealed prior to *U-234*'s departure and had been destroyed before arriving in Portsmouth, Bringewald and Ruf had no idea what that destination was to have been.[48]

The engineers were given no specific information concerning the fulfillment of their mission once they had arrived in Japan. For example, they were not informed whether they would be assigned to an existing factory or be expected to build a new factory or factories dedicated to the production of the ME 262 and ME 163. Given the emphasis on antibombardment protection, Bringewald was particularly surprised that information had not been provided to him or Ruf regarding whether the factory would be built above ground or below, or whether it would be a dispersed facility or a single complex. Furthermore, they had not been informed of the state or capabilities of Japanese aircraft facilities, nor had they even been given an estimate of their chances of success. The only information Bringewald received from his superiors was that the factory, whether existing or proposed, was supposedly located in central Japan; he would receive further instructions when the *U-234* reached Japan. In exasperation, Ruf described the entire undertaking as a "stab in the dark."[49]

From testimony by other personnel, the ONI was under the impression that Japan had not embarked on a program of jet-propelled aircraft production. This information, however, had come primarily from military sources such as Nieschling and Kessler, and not from civilians who might have had better access to Messerschmitt information regarding the state of Japan's jet research. Bringewald informed the ONI that two Japanese engineers in Berlin, a Captain Tautani and a Captain Nagomuri, had informed him that engineers in Japan were working on the development of a turbine engine, although they were experiencing "continuous difficulties."[50] Both Bringewald and Ruf indicated that they were not aware of progress in Japan on jet aircraft, but they did not believe that Japanese engineers were capable of building the ME 262 without "complete specifications and technical supervision from

German specialists."[51] The German engineers were both convinced that the Japanese did not have an operational jet fighter in service. They qualified this assessment by pointing out that the Japanese did not have sufficient data to build the jets, as no components "have ever been sent to Japan and at the present time [May 1945], there is no German specialist in Japan who could assist the Japanese in building these aircraft."[52]

Bringewald and Ruf provided the ONI with a comprehensive, albeit speculative, interpretation of their mission as they understood it. Although no production deadlines had been set by the Japanese, both engineers calculated that, barring interference from the Japanese military, it would take at least one and a half years for the first ME 262 to be completed. This estimate was offered under the unlikely assumption that all materials and labor, both skilled and common, would be readily available for the project. Ruf calculated that outfitting an existing factory for production of the German jets rather than building a new facility, a scenario that provided the quickest manufacturing start-up, would require around three million man-hours. This staggering estimate did not take into consideration the debugging and troubleshooting period that would inevitably accompany the initiation of production.

Bringewald and Ruf also provided the ONI with an estimate of conceivable production figures, using their experiences in Germany as points of reference. Assuming a workweek of seven eight-hour days, the Germans anticipated manufacturing five hundred ME 262 aircraft per month.[53] Obviously this capacity could be increased by the employment of additional shifts. Although this production estimate was calculated without regard for such likely problems as material and labor shortages or Allied bombing attacks, the engineers remained confident that, once operational, the German manufacturing facility or facilities could produce the ME 262 in sufficient numbers.

Curiously, whereas the ME 262 would be produced as a front-line operational aircraft, the ME 163 would not be produced initially in series, but rather would be put to experimental purposes only, despite having been operationally deployed in Germany since August 1944.[54] One possible explanation for this mystery involved the volatility of the ME 163's fuel. The jet provided 3,748 pounds of thrust while consuming large quantities of a hydrogen peroxide–phosphate mixture known as *T-Stoff,* which used as a catalyst a solution of hydrazine hydrate and methanol known as *C-Stoff.*[55] Inevitably, any explosion on board the aircraft would result in the total obliteration of both plane and pilot. If the Japanese were indeed concerned about this, it would have been a

curious paradox: pilot welfare suddenly becoming a policy consideration in a militaristic society that had been sending hundreds of untrained
kamikaze pilots to their deaths in wooden airplanes with alarming regularity. For their part, Bringewald and Ruf had no idea why the Japanese were reluctant to deploy the ME 163.

Bringewald and Ruf also provided information to the ONI on problems the Germans themselves had experienced in mass-producing the
ME 262. Ruf pointed out that in 1944, German aircraft manufacturers
had begun to encounter difficulties procuring the necessary industrial
machinery in general, and precision testing equipment in particular—
indications that, despite Reich Minister of Armaments Albert Speer's
optimistic assertions, the war had taken its toll on the German industrial juggernaut. Production also suffered because of the lack of raw
materials. For example, the shortage of the durable lightweight metal
Dural meant that the stress-bearing surfaces of the ME 262, such as the
nose and leading edges of the wings, had to be made of a heavier, more
brittle grade of steel plate, 0.6 to 0.8 centimeter thick, which carried a
substandard tensile strength of 120 kilograms per square centimeter.[56]

Finally, Bringewald pointed out two major obstacles to Germany's
development and production of jet aircraft. One was the increasing
scarcity of skilled labor; slave workers, while numerous, lacked the
technical knowledge and efficiency needed for turbojet production. The
second difficulty involved the growing disaffection with the jet program
that was evident in the German High Command, where support was
shifting toward the A-4 rocket, more commonly known as the V-2.[57]

American intelligence analysts had good reason to worry about Japanese possession of German rockets. A Strategic Bombing Survey review
of Army Air Corps photoreconnaissance conducted after the August
1943 Allied bombing raids on the German rocket complex at Peenemünde indicated that while the raids had significantly damaged the
launching and research facilities to the east, the main testing area at
Peenemünde West, unknown to Allied mission planners at the time,
had been virtually ignored.[58] The raids had not put a stop to German
rocket research, and therefore it is entirely conceivable that the Japanese continued to solicit German rocket technology beyond 1943 and
into 1945. In addition, American encounters with the Japanese Baka
flying bomb in the Pacific, as well as the aforementioned discovery of a
V-1 missile in Germany that had been configured to accommodate a
human pilot, contributed to ONI concerns that the Japanese might
already be producing operational rockets.

Bringewald and Ruf helped resolve the confusion concerning Japanese intentions regarding the German rockets. While General Kessler had previously expressed doubt that the Japanese had received information concerning these weapons, both Bringewald and Ruf, citing Japan's "great interest" in Germany's rocket program, were convinced that Japan did indeed possess technical information on the rockets. Ruf referred to a conversation he had overheard in Berlin between Military Attaché Otani and another Japanese officer, in which Otani was informed of German plans to send V-1 blueprints and documentation to Japan on one of the earlier submarine missions.[59] In view of the corroborating evidence from the two German engineers, the ONI reached the consensus that the Japanese probably did possess the weapons, although what intentions they harbored regarding their use remained a mystery.

Neither Bringewald nor Ruf ventured any opinion on Japanese intentions concerning the V-1 and V-2, but both doubted that the Japanese possessed enough technical information to produce the rockets without German help.[60] Their assumption presented ONI officials with a puzzling situation. If the Japanese were in fact incapable of producing the effective German V-1 or V-2, then the inconsistent Baka must be of purely Japanese origin. Both Bringewald and Ruf were pioneers, and subsequently experts, in German turbojet and rocket research and production; their claim that they were "completely unfamiliar" with any Japanese jet- or rocket-propelled aircraft, and also unaware of any German attempts to produce a V-1 rocket that could be modified to carry a pilot, compounded ONI concerns.

Consequently, the ONI reconsidered its assessment of the sophistication of Japanese rocket research; obviously some development had occurred, even if only rudimentary. Indeed, if the Baka represented the peak of Japanese rocket technology, further progress would definitely require the cooperation of the Germans. Although the crude Japanese rockets did not possess the deadly accuracy of Germany's V-weapons, they did nonetheless work, and in some cases even produced laudable results. American military planners could no longer discount the presence of rocket weaponry in the Japanese arsenal, whether it consisted of German vengeance weapons or the erratic Baka "cherry blossom." Allied pilots would now be forced to employ new defensive tactics designed to counter the threat of ground-to-air missiles.

The technological arsenal that constituted *U-234*'s cargo was understandably a cause of great concern to American military planners who contemplated the deployment of thousands of soldiers, sailors, and airmen to Japan. While the weaponry in and of itself was intimidating,

American concerns regarding its practical application by Japan were abated somewhat by the assumption that Japan possessed neither the technical expertise nor the manufacturing acumen to mass-produce the new weapons. The presence of August Bringewald and Franz Ruf on *U-234* provided the ONI with sufficient information to develop accurate assessments of Japanese capabilities in the fields of jet and rocket weapon technology, in place of calculated assumptions.

A poignant footnote to the contributions of these two individuals occurred in late May 1945, when amid much pomp and ceremony an operational German ME 262 was officially presented to American officials at Wright Field in Dayton, Ohio. The individual conducting the presentation had previously requested that the donation be of an official nature, as the aircraft represented the culmination of his life's work. The presenter was Dr. Willi Messerschmitt's "right-hand man," August Bringewald.[61]

On 14 August 1945 Bringewald and Ruf were ordered transferred to the "anti-Nazi" prisoner-of-war facility at Ruston, Louisiana.[62] However, both the navy and the army desired further exploitation of the pair, and so their transfer orders were canceled. Bringewald and Ruf remained at Fort Meade, working at the naval research facility at Patuxent River, Maryland.[63] On 17 December 1945, by order of the secretary of war, they were transferred to the custody of the Army Air Corps and assigned duty at Wright Field.[64] In April 1946 both Bringewald and Ruf were ordered transferred to New York for repatriation; however, the Provost Branch of Security and Intelligence delayed their departure until 15 June.[65] By 17 June, Bringewald and Ruf had once again been assigned transfer to New York as part of repatriation movement 9408, but once again they were delayed. They were removed from movement 9408 and the jurisdiction of the provost marshal general and placed in movement 405, which was coordinated by the ONI and army intelligence.[66] As a result, they were returned to Wright Field before eventually returning to Germany.

Bringewald and Ruf were repatriated on 6 August 1946. Upon arrival in Le Havre, France, they took a train to Augsburg, where their families resided. They did not remain in Germany long, for neither regarded the future of aviation in postwar Germany as promising, and subsequently they returned with their families to the United States to work as "Paperclip" personnel. However, their status as Paperclippers was brief; Bringewald later recalled that "certain groups [at Wright] did not welcome the Paperclip people. . . . Conditions and [the] war in Korea made strange bedfellows." As a result, many left the program for college or industry. Ruf remained in Dayton and continued working for the air force until his retirement;[67] however, his ultimate fate is unknown. Bringewald accepted a position at Republic Aviation in New York, retiring after twenty years as vice president for manufacturing. He returned to Dayton, where he remained until his death in 1993.[68]

Conclusion

On 19 November 1947 the submarine rescue vessel USS *Tringa* made way through the stormy waters off Cape Cod, escort to a doomed lady. The *Tringa* was completing her mission of hauling salvage hulks to a predesignated point, where they would be utilized as targets in torpedo trials for the U.S. Navy. On this morning she towed her final victim, a German Type XB U-boat. As the *Tringa* approached her destination 40 miles northeast of Provincetown, Massachusetts, the USS *Greenfish* (SS-351) lay waiting to send the U-boat to the ocean floor. The *Tringa*'s companion and the *Greenfish*'s prey were one and the same: *U-234*.

With her surrender in May 1945, *U-234*'s days as an operational warship had ended; however, she had not outlived her usefulness to the U.S. Navy. On 19 May the chief of naval operations issued instructions regarding the inspection and testing of captured U-boats, five of which were berthed on the United States' East Coast. The directive announced that dockside inspections of the submarines would be supervised by the commanding officer of the Portsmouth Navy Yard, while operational tests would be coordinated by the commander of submarines, Atlantic Fleet (COMSUBSLANT).[1] Investigators were instructed to enter preliminary assessments onto a "Submarine Condition Sheet," from which naval personnel could determine which boats might be of further use to the navy. The CNO further directed Portsmouth to furnish and train U.S. Navy personnel to man the submarines during operational testing, authorizing employment of the original German crews only when deemed necessary. In the case of *U-234*, cargo was subject to the direction of the Office of Naval Intelligence, and was therefore to be segregated and removed prior to any investigations or tests.[2]

The purpose of these tests of the German submarines was to determine their structural and operational integrity compared with that of American submarines. The Bureau of Ships (BuShips) subjected the U-boats to a battery of tests measuring standardized performance both on the surface and while submerged, deep-submergence integrity, *Schnorchel* operation (where applicable), sound and magnetic ranging, and sonar and radar efficiency. To ensure the safety of the crew, BuShips ordered the submarines dry-docked prior to deployment for strength tests to determine that they could safely be submerged to a depth of 250 feet.[3]

On 29 May, Lt. Cdr. H. G. Dyke of the CNO's office notified the Office of Scientific Research and Development (OSRD) that the "Navy is anxious for your organization . . . to inspect the boats."[4] Because *U-234* was a Type XB, and therefore had operational features not present on the other four boats, she was placed second in priority only to the Type IXD/2 *U-873*. On 2 June representatives of the OSRD and naval contractors arrived in Portsmouth for the initial inspection of *U-873* and *U-234*. Some of the more visible members of this contingent were Dr. Vannevar Bush, director of the OSRD; Dr. Karl Compton of the Office of Field Services and president of the Massachusetts Institute of Technology; Dr. James Conant of the Underwater Sound Laboratory and president of Harvard University; and representatives from the Woods Hole Oceanographic Laboratory, the Columbia University Special Studies Group, Bell Telephone Laboratories, the DuPont Corporation, and the American Telephone and Telegraph Company.[5] In addition, Dr. Julian K. Knipp of the Radiation Laboratory at MIT traveled to Washington to view *U-234*'s captured documents.[6]

By the end of 1945, the dockside investigations and inspections were complete. On 21 February 1946 the commander of the Special Submarine Force in New London, Connecticut, notified COMSUBSLANT that German submarines *U-234*, *U-858*, *U-873*, and *U-2513* were cleared for further operational tests, and he designated 26 February through 1 April as the testing period for *U-234*.[7] By March, naval engineers and system analysts had examined *U-234* extensively, both at sea and in dry dock, and published their findings in a six-hundred-page report, "Surrendered German Submarine Report, Type XB." In June, sonar technicians removed *U-234*'s underwater detection equipment and transferred it to an unspecified navy lab for examination[8]—the first in a succession of equipment removals that would ultimately render *U-234* little more than a hulk. In September 1947, navy ordnance officials authorized use of *U-234* as a target for torpedo exploder testing, and in November navy tugs towed her from Portsmouth Harbor to a meeting with the *Tringa*. Now, on 19 November, like a condemned man walking his last mile, *U-234* followed the *Tringa* to meet the executioner.

The USS *Greenfish*, a Guppy III–class patrol boat, was on her third simulated war patrol, and her first under new skipper Cdr. R. C. Giffen. The *Greenfish* was well armed, featuring six forward torpedo tubes, with an additional four astern.[9] Neither Giffen nor his crew expected to expend more than a single torpedo to accomplish their mission; their experience had shown them that one was enough to sink a U-boat. However, the outfitting crews aboard *U-234* took great pride in their work, and they had made her as "unsinkable" as possible, securing and double-checking each valve, petcock, hatch, and sea opening.[10] The next morning, Giffen closed on *U-234* and relayed the order to fire when ready. In fire control, gun boss Charles Priest signaled Firecontrolman Myron Prevatte, who sent the torpedo speeding toward *U-234*.[11] After the ensuing explosion, Giffen was surprised to spot *U-234* defiantly remaining afloat, and he ordered a second shot. Again Prevatte pressed the firing key, and this time there were no surprises. On 20 November 1947, at 43°37' N, 69°33' W, *U-234* took a last gasp, then embarked on her final voyage to a destination six hundred feet below.

What place does *U-234* occupy in the history of World War II? Given Japan's surrender following the August 1945 atomic-bombing of Hiroshima and Nagasaki, the entire episode might appear to be only a footnote. But had Germany and Japan exchanged advanced countermeasures and weapons systems earlier in the war, could Japanese industry have developed them to provide an effective deterrent to American efforts to bomb Japanese cities? Moreover, could Japan have developed self-sufficiency in the production and implementation of radio technology, rockets, and jet-powered weapons? After the capitulation of Japan, these questions admittedly became matters of conjecture, but they did merit the consideration of the eventual proprietors of German technology, particularly the United States.

The difficulties faced by Japan and Germany in formulating a successful exchange program reflected both cultural and economic differences. Having risen from the economic and social ruin of the post–World War I years, Germany entered the war an industrial colossus, armed with what was arguably the most powerful and modern military on Earth. In essence, Germany had had no other choice. Its potential enemies would be the victors of 1918, particularly Britain and France, both of which could muster substantial industrial and military might. Given the right circumstances, even the Soviet Union, though struggling under the devastation of Stalin's purges, could present a formidable foe. In a worst-case scenario Germany might eventually be forced to square off against the world's greatest industrial power, the United States. In any case, German military leaders knew that to wage and win this war, they would have to strike quickly with effective modern armaments, while at the same time remaining at the forefront of new weapons technology.

In 1936 Japan embarked on a war of Asian liberation against Western colonial powers that were preoccupied in Europe. Considering the success of their ruthless subjugation of China, Indochina, and Indonesia, the Japanese saw no reason to question their own military proficiency. Furthermore, the successful 7 December 1941 raid on Pearl Harbor provided Tokyo with additional assurance that Japan's military, particularly the Imperial Japanese Navy, was of sufficient mettle to deter and defeat its enemies, particularly the United States.

In addition, Japan's military was infused with the tradition of Bushido, the spiritual warrior code that stood in such marked contrast to the more secular and mechanized code of the Europeans. Once Emperor Hirohito proclaimed Japan's struggle a crusade worthy of its ancestors, defeat ceased to be an option. The "Greater East Asian War" was a holy war, to be prosecuted with a "youthful, patriotic zeal."[12] In the push to create an army of nationalistic zealots, Japan allowed its substantial technological apparatus to suffer; technologically, the Japanese lagged far behind the Allies, who were themselves struggling to keep up with the Germans. By the time Tokyo realized that the Shinto tradition alone was no match for America's military and industrial proficiency, it was too late; Japan was not prepared to undergo the metamorphosis from ideological to technological warfare required for survival.

Regarding the technical exchanges that took place between Germany and Japan, it is difficult to measure the benefits that Japan derived from its ally's prototypes and manufacturing data. From the interrogations of *U-234*'s passengers, it appears that the production in Japan of German weaponry presented greater difficulties than either country had anticipated. There are several possible explanations for this difficulty. First, Japanese engineers and manufacturing personnel were not skilled enough to grasp and master the sophisticated German technology; the level of technical education in Japan trailed that of the Western industrialized nations by years. Historian Saburo Ienaga regards this deficiency in technical education, along with the "emasculation of academic freedom, without which objective and scientific knowledge could not be acquired and diffused," as a major factor in Japan's lack of military preparedness.[15] Second, although Germany sent some of its finest engineers and scientists to instruct the Japanese, it would have taken two to three times that many experts to bring the Japanese to the desired level of proficiency, and the U-boats simply could not meet that demand for transport. Also, Japan was suffering acute labor and raw material shortages. Germany's jet aircraft and rockets required new lightweight metals and alloys to which Japan had little or no access; by the end of the war, Japanese pilots were flying aircraft made of wood.

Finally, the limited effect of Germany's technical aid to Japan can be viewed as a failure of timing. As early as 1940, difficulties in reaching a consensus on technical exchange agreements, many of which difficulties were based on mutual distrust, were already costing the Japanese valuable time. By the time these misunderstandings were settled, Germany could not deliver aid in shipments of sufficient size because its blockade-running merchant fleet had been decimated. By 1944, as German designs and equipment continued to arrive, the loss of valuable raw materials from the far reaches of its empire had disrupted Japan's industry to the point of inefficiency. By the spring of 1945, devastating American air raids had left Japanese manufacturing unable to put the German weapons into serial production. In summary, although Japan secured considerable technical and material assistance from its German ally, the level and amount of this aid were insufficient to meet Japan's burgeoning needs. Japan and Germany simply ran out of time.

The capture of *U-234* may have been irrelevant to the outcome of the war, but it demonstrated once again the value of Allied intelligence operations. ONI officials put a high priority on the capture of *U-234* because they possessed intelligence, in the form of MAGIC intercepts, regarding the individuals and materials the submarine might be carrying. On 22 April 1945 Japanese minister Kase in Switzerland had informed Tokyo that "Hitler and other high-ranking Nazi officials" would abandon Europe in the closing days of the war and flee to

Japan.[14] This information appeared to be verified by a 3 May 1945 intercept revealing that Gen. Ulrich Kessler was aboard *U-234* with a party that included "an expert in aerial defense, another in radio-controlled weapons, a specialist in radar and infra-red . . . two German civilian engineers who are experts in the mass production of the ME-262 . . . [and] two Japanese naval officers."[15] By the time *U-234*'s surrender was announced to the American press, there was rampant speculation as to the identity of the personnel on board, as evidenced by a banner headline in the 18 May 1945 *Boston Post:* "Big Hunt on for Hitler in U-Boat." However, as a result of the MAGIC signal intelligence, naval officials had formed a remarkably accurate assessment of exactly who was on board *U-234,* and subsequently positioned their Eastern Sea Frontier forces to accept her surrender.

U-234's personnel also served the U.S. government's Project Paperclip well. The areas of primary concern to the United States with regard to German technological advances—namely countermeasures, turbojet aircraft, radio technology, and rocketry—were all amply represented in *U-234*'s cargo holds. In addition, numerous blueprints, drawings, and documents accompanied the machines, and, in the persons of Heinz Schlicke, Erich Menzel, August Bringewald, and Franz Ruf, so did the scientific, engineering, and manufacturing expertise. Schlicke, Bringewald, and Ruf returned to America after repatriation to lend their considerable abilities to helping ensure America's standing as the postwar world's technological leader. Without a doubt, America's defense systems and weapons received a boost from the information and subsequent service obtained from *U-234*'s passengers.

It has been said that America never finishes a war but merely changes enemies. This axiom holds true for the post–World War II period, when the United States immediately shifted its focus from Germany and Japan to the Soviet Union. An immediate matter of concern was the fear that the Soviets would commandeer Germany's top scientists and create a dangerous technology gap between the Soviet Union and the United States. In 1945, German technical expertise was a valuable commodity, and the Soviets were acquiring it as rapidly as they could, dismantling German wartime manufacturing facilities and transferring them to the Soviet Union, commandeering the services of German technical personnel living in Soviet-occupied areas, and even making aggressive attempts to recruit Germans who were working for the Americans.

The United States countered these efforts with programs like Project Paperclip and the Alsos technical missions to Europe. In January

1946, as captured German personnel were being repatriated to Germany, Secretary of War James Forrestal pointed out to Secretary of State James F. Byrnes that such programs would "eliminate the potential threat of continued work by such scientists in Germany or elsewhere outside the United States."[16] Forrestal was right. Without programs like these, Schlicke, Menzel, and Bringewald—who all resided in areas of Germany that were under Soviet occupation—would undoubtedly have been commandeered for Soviet service. The Soviets did manage to collect enough German scientists and materials to claim early scientific victories, as evidenced by the development of a Soviet nuclear weapon in 1947 and the launching of Sputnik in 1957. However, among those German scientists who were afforded a choice of where to work, the best of them came to America, attracted by the lure of better living and working conditions. In the Cold War oscillations over whose Germans were the best, America ultimately emerged on top.

The United States would have defeated Japan regardless of Fehler's decision to surrender that May morning in 1945; *U-234*'s story, while intriguing, was of little consequence to the outcome of the war. However, the surrender of *U-234* did provide a measure of security to American servicemen by bringing to the attention of U.S. military intelligence the possibility of Japanese integration of German technology, in time for the United States to develop countermeasures should the need arise. Ironically, *U-234*'s biggest contribution was not in the continuance of the overt violence of total war but rather in the darkened battlefields of a war of deterrence; indeed, *U-234*'s passengers were among the first of the Cold Warriors. This is the niche in history that the men of *U-234* can rightfully claim. Failing in their initial mission, they succeeded in a much greater arena: fostering the safety and security of free nations in the postwar nuclear world.

Appendix

U-234's Uranium Oxide

UPON *U-234*'S ARRIVAL in Portsmouth, ONI and navy officials began the arduous task of processing the submarine's 162-ton cargo. On 21 May, Lt. (jg) John G. Faron, who directed one of the unloading crews, sent Capt. G. R. Phelan a preliminary inventory of *U-234*'s cargo. In addition to "computers for the *'Grossbatterie'* system . . . designs for ME 163 . . . igniters for bombs and torpedoes [and] designs and samples of Lorenz 7-H bombsight," Faron noted "a large quantity of uranium oxide."[1] Two days later *U-234*'s translated cargo manifest confirmed what would become her legacy: mine-shaft location 38, labeled ST 1270/1–10, contained ten cases, or 560 kilograms (1,235 pounds), of uranium oxide, designated for the Japanese army.[2]

Since Johann Fehler's surrender in 1945, *U-234*'s cargo of uranium oxide has been the subject of debate, prompting much speculation about its presence aboard the submarine as well as the use to which it would have been put had it reached Japan. It is difficult to account for the uranium cargo; many U.S. World War II–era nuclear-related documents remain classified under national security endorsement, and personal accounts often disagree. This examination will consider *U-234*'s uranium oxide cargo as it is represented in available documentary and primary-source evidence—documents that do not suffer lapses of memory and that reflect the disposition of the precise time at which they were produced.

Japan's interest in acquiring German uranium was fueled by necessity. Early efforts to locate deposits of uranium within the Greater East Asia Co-prosperity Sphere had revealed only marginal amounts of usable ore; the Japanese army's procurement director, Gen. Kawashima Tora-nosuke, recalled that upon witnessing the minuscule amount of uranium produced by the promising Kikune mine in Korea, he "wanted to cry."[3] Meanwhile, in Europe, Germany had acquired substantial stocks of uranium oxide through the seizure of over 1,000 tons of uranium oxide ore from the Union Minière warehouse in Belgium as well as rich ore deposits in Czechoslovakia. Japan's wartime industry needed uranium oxide for the extraction of radium, and Japanese physicists also required the ore for experimentation with isotope separation and uranium enrichment. Therefore, on 7 July 1943, Japanese Imperial Army headquarters in Tokyo requested that the Japanese attaché in Berlin, Oshima Hiroshi, approach the Germans concerning "the possibility of exporting to Japan pitchblende (uranium) from the Czechoslovakia region."[4]

In September, Oshima notified Tokyo that negotiations with the Germans into the matter were progressing, but he needed a statement "showing [uranium's] importance for purposes of study."[5] This was an alarming demand; Japanese officials were not used to revealing the exact reasons for their requests. Dr. Nishina Yoshio, Japan's director of nuclear research, confided to his assistant Kigoshi Kunihiko that he did not wish to disclose his plans for using the uranium to the Germans, who would not stand for Japanese competition in the field of nuclear research. Nishina was investigating isotope separation and uranium enrichment and, if successful, would require substantial amounts of uranium oxide. His need for uranium was critical, and he did not want to jeopardize one of the few sources from which he could obtain the precious ore; any scarcity of uranium would bottleneck his research. Kigoshi suggested that Nishina tell the Germans that the uranium would be used as a catalyst for chemical reactions, thus diverting suspicions that Japanese research rivaled that of Germany. Convinced that the Germans would believe this story, Nishina authorized the formal request and forwarded it to the Japanese War Ministry.[6]

Germany did indeed possess impressive quantities of uranium oxide, and a good deal of the ore was stored at Kiel. German naval munitions experts had discovered that the heavy atomic weight of the substance rendered uranium oxide ideal for the coating of large-caliber naval guns; later in the war the Luftwaffe followed suit and began using the ore in the manufacture of missile warheads. The clamor for uranium oxide for this use was so great that by 1943 the munitions industry's requests for the ore competed with those of Germany's atomic researchers in Berlin. Metallic uranium plates, vital for the construction of experimental atomic piles, became a rarity; German uranium suppliers such as Auer and Degussa often explained missed shipments by complaining that the military hoarded most of the readily available stocks of metallic uranium. While it is not difficult to imagine that Germany could have arranged uranium oxide shipments to Japan upon request, it is extremely doubtful that German military and armament officials would have parted with valuable metallic uranium. As a result, most experts agree with Dr. Helmut Rechenberg of the Max Planck Institute for Physics that, given the depleted capacity of German industry to produce metallic uranium during the late war years, it can be assumed "with great certainty that the uranium material [aboard *U-234*] was not metal but oxide."[7]

On 15 November, Japan's Vice Minister of War J. Tory directed Oshima to obtain 100 kilograms (221 pounds) of uranium oxide and forwarded Nishina's cover story that the ore would be used "as a catalyst in the manufacture of butanol."[8] Five days later Oshima reported that the Germans possessed substantial quantities from which they would able to supply the requested uranium and "its by-products at present." However, Oshima was confused as to how much was required; he informed Tokyo that although the latest messages had requested 100 kilograms, "this is an error of one ton compared with the quantity [previously] mentioned. Therefore, please be advised that we will order one ton."[9]

In Berlin, Oshima forwarded the request to Maj. Kigoshi Yasukazu— who, coincidentally, was the brother of Nishina's assistant Kigoshi Kunihiko[10]—and directed him to acquire the uranium from the Germans. However, Reich officials viewed the request with suspicion. They did not believe that the Japanese intended to use the uranium solely for chemical experiments or the manufacture of butanol, and therefore refused to ship the ore. This reluctance infuriated General Kawashima, who sent an angry memorandum to German officials revealing that Japan actually desired the uranium for atomic research. In a footnote to his cable Kawashima admonished the Germans for their lack of solidarity and compliance with the Tripartite Alliance, asking, "What is going on here that you don't want to cooperate?"[11]

Kawashima's indignation, and Oshima's considerable diplomatic talents, finally persuaded Berlin to acquiesce. In late 1943 Germany agreed to ship the uranium oxide to Japan via two Japanese submarines.[12] Kigoshi Yasukazu, who coordinated the uranium oxide acquisition, accompanied both consignments to Kiel and supervised the loading of both submarines. The initial shipment, which departed Kiel on 30 March 1944, was lost en route to the Far East when its conveyance submarine, Ro-501, was sunk.[13] However, what happened to the second shipment remains somewhat of a mystery. Kigoshi himself could not verify the fate of the submarine.[14] According to some reports, the boat never left Germany.[15] However, in a May 1945 Associated Press interview, Adm. Jonas Ingram, commander of the U.S. Navy's Atlantic Fleet, revealed that during the summer of 1944 two Japanese submarines were engaged by American forces off the coast of Iceland. One of these submarines was sunk; the other was only damaged and subsequently escaped.[16] Both submarines had been attempting to access the Atlantic via the Iceland-Faroes passage, the traditional route of U-boats deploying from the North Sea to the Atlantic; it is therefore likely that these two submarines were Ro-501 and her sister boat, both of which had sortied from Kiel. In addition, in a 1953 article in the Japanese journal Dai-horin, Japanese army major Yamamoto Yoichi claimed that in 1944 Japan did receive 500 kilograms (1,100 pounds) of uranium oxide from Germany by submarine.[17] On the basis of this evidence, it appears that the 1943 uranium oxide request was loaded on board Japanese submarines at Kiel, and at least part of the original one ton arrived in Japan in late 1944.[18]

Japan eventually developed reserves of uranium oxide throughout the various territories under its dominion.[19] However, increased requirements from the scientific and military communities soon put a strain on this inventory.[20] In 1944 the Japanese Army Air Technical Department (JAATD) initiated the extraction of 500 kilograms of uranium oxide from the Kikune mine in Korea; however, by the time serial mining began, the JAATD had already requested an additional 500 kilograms. In mid-1944 the Imperial Japanese Navy also asked the Ministry of Munitions for 500 kilograms of uranium oxide.[21] And at the Kyūrikagaku kenkyūjo (Physics and Chemistry Research Institute) in Tokyo, where Dr. Nishina and Kigoshi Kunihiko were attempting to enrich uranium,[22] the dearth of resources had prompted Nishina to request a consignment of uranium as well. Japan's inventory being of neither the quantity nor the quality to meet these requirements, Germany once again received a request for help from its Axis partner.[23]

In December 1944 Oshima received the request in Berlin and subsequently relayed it to officials of Germany's overseas-shipping authority, the Marinesonderdienst-Ausland (MSD). MSD officials worked with Kigoshi Yasukazu to coordinate the logistics of gathering the uranium and delivering it to Kiel for loading onto one of three submarines scheduled for departure to Japan in the spring of 1945. In addition, the Marine Sonderstabsweigstellebeinat (Special Naval Home Substation Branch) in Kiel dispatched the MSD's Commander Becker to various facilities throughout southern Germany to determine "what and how much was to be included in the cargo."[24] By February 1945 the procurement was complete, and Major Kigoshi met MSD officials in Kiel to organize and oversee the loading of 560 kilograms of uranium oxide onto the next submarine mission to Japan, Johann Heinrich Fehler's *U-234*.[25]

The loading of *U-234*'s uranium oxide is described in Wolfgang Hirschfeld's memoirs. Hirschfeld stated that each container, "possibly steel and lead, nine inches along on each side and enormously heavy," was inspected and labeled by the two Japanese passengers, Tomonaga and Shoji. The containers were then delivered to a loading party under the direction of Lt. (jg) Karl Pfaff and lowered into one of the (forward) vertical mine shafts. Hirschfeld also recalled that in addition to Pfaff, Tomonaga, and Shoji, Major Kigoshi was quayside at Kiel, directing the loading of "ten cases of uranium oxide" into the bowels of *U-234*.[26]

Much of the confusion surrounding *U-234*'s cargo of uranium oxide arises from conflicting accounts of how the ore was handled once it arrived in America. In Portsmouth most of *U-234*'s cargo was immediately unloaded, processed, and dispersed to various facilities for testing and evaluation; however, the uranium oxide remained aboard the submarine for a time while American authorities pondered exactly how to dispose of it.

Cdr. Alexander W. Moffat, the surface unit commander of the Eastern Sea Frontier's Northern Group, was present at *U-234*'s unloading. In his memoir Moffat stated that the uranium oxide was removed from the submarine the week following her arrival in Portsmouth. He claimed that "the first items to come ashore were the two saddle tanks [which had been] burned free of the deck by welders." Once the saddle tanks had been secured on the dock, "technicians removed a sample of the contents for laboratory analysis. . . . It seemed to be an odorless granular powder. . . . Word soon spread that the saddle tanks contained uranium."[27]

The account Hirschfeld gave in his own memoir is vastly different from Moffat's. Hirschfeld claimed that the uranium was not unloaded until July, when he witnessed six cargo containers lifted from the forward mine shafts and deposited on the dock. Once ashore, the tubes were examined by men "carrying small hand appliances," which, Hirschfeld was informed, were Geiger counters. Apparently the six containers "were contaminated to such an extent with radiation" that the exact location of the uranium could not be determined.[28] To aid in locating the uranium, Hirschfeld recalled, ONI officials decided to commandeer Karl Pfaff, who had directed *U-234*'s loading in Kiel.

The disparity between Moffat's and Hirschfeld's testimony cannot be easily explained away; in any case, it is certain that Pfaff played an important role in the navy's disposition of the uranium. Although originally interned in the holding facility at Fort George G. Meade in Maryland, Pfaff had been transferred to the army's interrogation facility at Fort Hunt in Alexandria, Virginia. On 27 May the Office of the Chief of Naval Operations alerted Portsmouth to information regarding *U-234*'s cargo that had come to light during Pfaff's interrogation at Fort Hunt. Pfaff had disclosed that he had been in charge of the cargo in Kiel, both preparing the manifest and personally supervising the loading of all mine tubes. Pfaff had further informed his captors that they should ensure, when unloading the submarine, that the "long containers [were] unpacked in horizontal position and short containers in vertical position," and he declared himself "available and willing" to aid in the unloading should the ONI desire his help.[29] A return 28 May memorandum from Portsmouth to the CNO reported that the containers had already been unloaded and that Portsmouth was awaiting a CNO directive whether to open the containers there or ship them to Washington for disposition. In reference to Pfaff's offer of help, the 28 May memorandum also specified that "Pfaff should be available where containers are opened."[30]

Pfaff had revealed that the uranium oxide was packed in "gold-lined cylinders [and] as long as cylinders not opened can be handled like crude TNT. . . . The containers should not be opened as substance will become sensitive and dangerous."[31] This assessment presented the navy with two problems. First, it raised the possibility that the containers had been wired with explosives to prevent the rare ore from falling into enemy hands. And even if the containers were not booby-trapped, navy officials still had little information about the safety issues involved in handling uranium oxide; in 1945 the handling of radioactive materials was not something with which most naval personnel were familiar. For this reason American intelligence officers approached Pfaff during his interrogation at Fort Hunt and asked the young German to accompany them and supervise the opening of the uranium containers.

In a 1995 interview, Pfaff recalled that he was escorted to "a large arena in Indian Head, a naval station on the Potomac River, where all the cargo was spread out." He concluded that this place was a depository for "a lot of secret stuff"; he did not realize at the time that Indian Head, Maryland, was home to the U.S. Navy's Ordnance Investigation Laboratory and the Naval Powder Factory, a logical venue for analysis of the uranium oxide.[32]

Prior to Pfaff's arrival, naval investigators had X-rayed the containers and had mistaken the internal handling devices, which were actually wooden poles, for booby traps.[33] As a result, when Pfaff arrived he encountered a rather nervous enlisted man who had been assigned to cut the containers open with an acetylene torch. Before cutting into the cylinder, the rating turned to Pfaff and lamented that he had a wife and kids; he didn't want to die. Pfaff reminded the man that if the cylinder was booby-trapped, he (Pfaff) would be blown to bits too. Besides, the cargo was intended for the Japanese; why would Germany seek to "blow them up"? His fears abated, the sailor proceeded to cut the containers open.[34] Other than a small fire caused by the torch igniting rags that had been used to pack the items inside the cylinders, the opening of the cargo containers proceeded without incident.[35]

Pfaff's chronology of his stay at Indian Head is supported by a 23 June 1945 memorandum from T. F. Darrah, commanding officer of the Indian Head facility, to the chief of the navy's Bureau of Ordnance (BuOrd) and a Lieutenant McQuade of the ONI. Darrah reported that on 23 June his activity shipped eleven items, which he identified as cargo containers from *U-234*, although he did not designate their destination.[36] However, the 2 July 1945 agenda for a meeting of a "Washington Group Trust" described item number 2 as "a report on captured material from German U-boat *U-234*" and identified the location of the material as a warehouse in Brooklyn, New York.[37] Whether this material was *U-234*'s uranium oxide is not clear; however, other items on the agenda were related to uranium matters, and given the alternative repositories for the ore, it is likely that the uranium oxide was shipped to the Brooklyn location pending further disposition.[38]

The destination of *U-234*'s uranium has also been the subject of conflicting accounts. In a 1995 interview Maj. John Lansdale, former head of security for the Manhattan Project, stated that *U-234*'s uranium went directly to the Manhattan District's processing facility at Oak Ridge, Tennessee. Proponents of this account postulate that once at Oak Ridge, the uranium was processed and used in one of the atomic bombs dropped on Hiroshima and Nagasaki. The notion that uranium originally intended for Japan eventually reached its destination, albeit not in the desired form, is attractively ironic; however, this scenario is unlikely. Lansdale admitted that he recalled no details as to what happened to the uranium after it was sent to Oak Ridge and therefore could offer no opinion as to whether it was used in either the Hiroshima or the Nagasaki bomb.[39] As Dr. Philip Morrison, a professor of physics at the Massachusetts Institute of Technology and a former Manhattan Project official, points out, "It is highly unlikely time would have allowed the uranium to make it into the Manhattan Project bombs."[40]

The accounts of Lansdale, Moffat, and Hirschfeld are sufficiently diverse to arouse curiosity; of such multiplicity are legends born. How do we separate legend from fact?

Given the ominous nature of the uranium oxide, it is unlikely that American intelligence personnel would have left the cargo aboard U-234 from mid-May until July, as Hirschfeld recalled. The expediency shown by Portsmouth, the ONI, and the CNO's office in unloading the containers and enlisting the aid of Karl Pfaff to open them supports this assumption. Commander Moffat's and Major Lansdale's accounts are similar to one another. Lansdale relegates the uranium oxide to Oak Ridge and so provides a convenient destination. Moffat's assertion that the saddle tanks, containing the uranium in powder form, were opened on the dock is inconsistent with all other accounts of the physical appearance and location of the uranium, and it could be regarded as an "official explanation." It must be remembered that both Moffat and Lansdale were dedicated career military officers operating in the sensitive operational environment of 1945. Their judgment concerning national security interests no doubt shaped their accounts.

Whatever the discrepancies between the accounts of the various individuals involved, the basic facts and sequence of events can be pieced together from the official documentation as follows. The 27 May memorandum from the CNO to Portsmouth reported Pfaff's ominous description of the cargo ("loaded in gold-lined cylinders . . . sensitive and dangerous") and his offer to help unload the ore. The 28 May memorandum from Portsmouth to the CNO stated that the containers in question were "off ship and ready for shipping. . . . Request decision whether cargo containers opened here or shipped to Washington. . . . Pfaff should be available where containers are opened." (Interestingly, both memoranda included the chief of the Bureau of Ordnance on their restricted distribution lists.) In a 1995 interview Pfaff stated that he was at some point taken from Fort Hunt to Indian Head; he did not recall the exact date, but from the 27 and 28 May CNO memoranda we can deduce that it must have been in early June 1945. Subsequently, in a 23 June memorandum the commanding officer at the Indian Head Ordnance Investigation Laboratory, T. F. Darrah, notified the chief of the Bureau of Ordnance that he was releasing eleven items from *U-234*, all of which bore identifying numeration consistent with that of other cargo containers unloaded from *U-234*. Finally, the 2 July 1945 agenda of the Washington Trust Group, which, according to other items on its agenda, was primarily concerned with matters relating to uranium, disclosed that the group was going to discuss "material from *U-234*," stored in a warehouse in Brooklyn. This is the most logical account of the handling of *U-234*'s uranium cargo, and the one most likely to be true. The trail of *U-234*'s uranium oxide ends in Brooklyn; no other official documentation or compelling personal testimony has yet revealed the ultimate destination of *U-234*'s cargo.

A farther-ranging controversy involves the physical nature of *U-234*'s uranium. Uranium oxide is a compound of low radioactivity and emits no harmful gamma radiation. The fissionable isotope uranium 235 must be removed from uranium oxide through the process of isotope separation; to achieve high levels of radiation, it must be processed in a reactor. During World War II the United States possessed the world's only known functional reactor, although Germany and Japan were working to develop their own. However, Hirschfeld said that in his opinion the uranium oxide loaded aboard *U-234* was "highly radioactive." In addition, he claimed that prior to loading, *U-234*'s Japanese passengers Shoji and Tomonaga wrote "U235" in black characters on the "brown paper wrapping [that was] gummed around each of a number of containers of uniform size," implying that the boxes contained radioactive uranium in metallic form.[41] Once at Portsmouth, Hirschfeld recalled American officials arriving with Geiger counters, which allegedly verified that the cargo was sufficiently radioactive to have contaminated the entire forward area of the submarine. Pfaff, meanwhile, had revealed that the cargo containers were lined with gold, an effective shield against radioactivity. Do these assertions indicate that *U-234* was carrying fissile material to Japan, which by proxy would prove the existence of a functional German nuclear reactor during the war years?

Once again, inconsistencies in personal testimony add to the confusion. Whereas Hirschfeld described Tomonaga and Shoji as actively participating in the loading of the ore, inspecting and labeling it, Pfaff claimed that "the Japanese passengers on board were not concerned with the uranium. . . . They were just passengers trying to get home to

Tokyo."[42] Moreover, according to British author Geoffrey Brooks, who translated Hirschfeld's memoirs and has interviewed him extensively, Hirschfeld "was not close to the loading operation" in Kiel and prior to 1992 did not know how many cases were involved in packaging the uranium. During the loading, Hirschfeld was on *U-234*'s conning tower; his closest proximity to the loading operation would have been about 70 feet. At that distance it would have been difficult to tell whether the containers were cylindrical or cubical, and to see exactly what the Japanese were writing on the packages.[43]

Furthermore, author Richard Rhodes points out that the label "U235" "can't possibly mean [that] the boxes contained U_{235}. . . . [The United States] labored mightily in vast separation plants to accumulate the sixty kilograms we used in Little Boy."[44] The presence of 560 kilograms of radioactive uranium 235 would indicate German uranium separation on such a massive scale that the whole world would have known of it. Rhodes concludes that "the likeliest content of [*U-234*'s] containers was refined ore for reactor development."[45] Dr. Michael Thorwart at the University of Augsburg's Institut für Physik confirms that Germany never possessed a critical reactor; while Werner Heisenberg's group had succeeded in improving neutron production in Haigerloch, substantial gains were not realized until April 1945. There is no conclusive evidence that Germany had developed an operational reactor by the end of the war, much less one that could operate on a scale sufficient to produce the amount of material aboard *U-234*. In Tailfingen Dr. E. Bagge developed a working isotope separation device; however, it also became operational too late to aid the German war effort, first achieving separation only on 24 April 1945.[46]

As for Pfaff's contention that the contents of the cylinders would become sensitive and dangerous upon opening, Rhodes explains that powdered uranium oxide is pyrophoric and ignites when exposed to air, a problem that American physicists faced during the early days of American reactor development. In addition, highly irradiated material is "physically extremely hot and radioactively highly penetrating. . . . I doubt if the gold lining [of the cylinders] would have been sufficient to contain [the radiation] had it been highly irradiated."[47]

Lt. Col. Richard Thurston, a former U.S. Army biologist and radiological warfare expert, proposes another explanation for *U-234*'s radioactivity. Thurston points out that the contents of the containers might have been radium or a radium compound, which would explain both the radioactivity of the cargo and the need for gold shielding. In addition, radon gas escaping from the radium could have permeated the submarine's cargo area, rendering it difficult to determine which mine shafts held the radioactive cargo.[48] In any event, according to Dr. Kigoshi Kunihiko, the wartime assistant to Japan's director of nuclear research, the entire episode is irrelevant: "If the uranium loaded on *U-234* was neutron irradiated, it seems very hard to suppose that Japanese scientists at that time [could] evaluate and . . . treat properly such processed uranium."[49]

The U.S. Army's Alsos mission also raised questions about the true nature of *U-234*'s ore. An 18 July 1945 Alsos intelligence report revealed the discovery of substantial quantities of various alloys in Germany. In this report H. S. Van Klooster, an Alsos expert consultant, described a 1943 German secret investigation into the characteristics of pyrophoric thorium and cadmium alloys with "copper, silver, and gold up to fifty per cent atomic weight." Van Klooster also observed that German metallurgists had experimented with powdered alloys that "caught fire spontaneously when kept in air. . . . The spontaneous combustion is most pronounced in the case of silver-thorium or gold-thorium alloys."[50] The volatility that Pfaff attributed to the contents of the containers—he contended that the material would become unstable when opened—would be consistent with one of these pyrophoric alloys. In addition, in a 1984 letter *U-234* passenger Kay Nieschling wrote that the cargo "concerned a cadmium alloy that [the Americans] were not yet familiar with over there."[51]

Although Germany and Japan were further advanced in their nuclear programs than first suspected, it is unlikely that the Axis partners had developed a critical-mass reactor or applicable bomb program by the spring of 1945. Stanford University professor Dr. David Holloway points out that in May 1945, when the NKVD's Gen. Avraamii Zaveniagin's Soviet scientific mission arrived in Germany to investigate the German atomic program, they found that German scientists "had not separated uranium-235, nor had they built a nuclear pile; nor had they progressed very far in their understanding of how to build an atomic bomb."[52] The devastation of war at home, the scarcity of essential raw materials, the lack of an extensive government-supported scientific infrastructure, and the absence of a substantial economic and industrial framework all combined to hinder progress. Germany simply could not compete with the United States.

Although the extent of Axis atomic research may not yet be fully understood, *U-234*'s consignment of uranium oxide was not indicative of any large-scale Axis program, nor did it provide American authorities with any substantial windfall of unique value. Richard Thurston correctly observes that "there is no reason to believe that [*U-234*'s cargo] contained any elements not readily available to the U.S. and British teams working at Los Alamos and other places."[55] In all probability, *U-234*'s cargo was examined, analyzed, and shipped to whichever department needed it; likely destinations might include reactor development, military use, or medical or research purposes. Or maybe, as Thurston offers, tongue in cheek, the cargo is "stored intact in the same cave in Kansas as the Ark of the Covenant."[54] In any event, *U-234*'s uranium oxide will continue to mystify and to spark debate. When the big Type XB slipped below the surface of the North Atlantic for the last time in 1947, she left an enduring legacy as one of the continuing controversies of World War II.

Notes

LIST OF ABBREVIATIONS

BMA   Bundesarchiv-Militärarchiv, Freiburg, Germany
MDS MAGIC   Diplomatic Summaries, National Archives, College Park, Md.
NA   National Archives, College Park, Md.
NANE   National Archives, Northeast Region, Waltham, Mass.
NANY   National Archives, Northeast Region, New York
NHC   Operational Archives, Naval Historical Center
PNS   Portsmouth Naval Shipyard Museum and Archives, Portsmouth Naval
              Shipyard, Kittery, Maine
UBA   U-Boot Archiv, Cuxhaven-Altenbruch, Germany
USSBS   United States Strategic Bombing Survey

PREFACE

1. Alan S. Milward, *War, Economy, and Society, 1939–1945* (Berkeley: University of California Press, 1977), 23.
2. Ibid., 26.
3. Paul Kennedy, *The Rise and Fall of British Naval Mastery* (London: Ashfield Press, 1976), 297.
4. Albert Speer, *Inside the Third Reich* (New York: Macmillan, 1970), 215.
5. Milward, *War, Economy, and Society,* 57.
6. Ibid.

7. Ibid., 58.
8. Richard Overy, *Why the Allies Won* (New York: W. W. Norton and Co., 1995), 201.
9. Milward, *War, Economy, and Society,* 35.
10. Ibid., 31.
11. Ibid., 30.
12. Ronald Spector, *Eagle against the Sun: The American War with Japan* (New York: Random House, 1985), 42.
13. Saburo Ienaga, *Taiheiyo Senso* [The Pacific War] (Tokyo: Iwanami Shoten, 1968), 135.
14. Milward, *War, Economy, and Society,* 139.
15. Ibid., 58.
16. Ibid.

CHAPTER 1. GENESIS

1. John W. M. Chapman, ed. *The Price of Admiralty: The War Diary of the German Naval Attaché in Japan, 1939–1943* (Ripe, East Sussex: Saltire Press, 1989), 1:205.
2. "Secret Supplementary Protocol, Item V," in ibid., 3:505.
3. "Three Powers Pact," in ibid., 504.
4. Amendment, German Embassy no. G. 1000, "Strictly Confidential," 27 September 1940, in ibid., 505.
5. Jyo-ni no. 134, "Secret Note No. 2," 27 September 1940, in ibid., 506. Japan was awarded mandate status over Germany's Pacific possessions as a result of the 1919 Treaty of Versailles.
6. "Secret Supplementary Protocol," 27 September 1940, in ibid., 507.
7. Report of interrogation, former Reich war minister Marshal von Blomberg, 13 September 1945, "Five Years of Nazi Germany, 1933–38," 90, box 721A, RG 165, NA. German irritation at the perceived lack of Japanese reciprocity was not new. German naval officials had been trying to facilitate technical agreements with the Japanese as far back as 1924, and subsequent missions by Adms. Wilhelm Canaris (1924), Karl Witzell (1937), and Erich Raeder (1941) returned to Berlin with the same fundamental conclusion that cooperation with the Japanese was basically a one-way street.
8. "Oberkommando der Kriegsmarine, 1. Skl. Ic No. 5359/41 Geh. 8," 11 February 1941, "Secret," in Chapman, ed. *Price of Admiralty,* 3:534–35.
9. Johanna Menzel Meskill, *Hitler and Japan: The Hollow Alliance* (New York: Atherton Press, 1966), 144–45. The Japanese list of demands has never been located, but it reportedly included substantial requests for artillery, radar, and submarine and aircraft technology.
10. John W. Masland, "Japanese-German Naval Collaboration in World War II," U.S. Naval Institute *Proceedings* 75 (February 1949): 180.
11. "Oberkommando der Wehrmacht, Wi-Ru-Amt/Wi VII No. 193/41 Gkdos, Secret Memorandum from General Keitel," 3 April 1941, in Chapman, ed., *Price of Admiralty,* 3:541.

12. Report of interrogation, von Blomberg.

13. Chapman, ed., *Price of Admiralty,* n. 16, 3:598; 4:1091.

14. Ibid., 3:550.

15. Ibid., 4:1091.

16. Ibid., 3:534.

17. Ibid., 4:1090–91.

18. Ibid., 948.

19. Memorandum, Field Marshal Wilhelm Keitel, chief of the High Command of the Armed Forces, subject "Japan," 3 April 1941, in ibid., 3:541–42.

20. SRS 549, 20 March 1942, 2, MDS; SRS 682, 13 August 1942, 11–12, MDS. Oshima noted that a German manufacturer who was contracted by the Mitsui Corporation to build "iron manufacturing machinery" had been forced to cease production because of the increase in German munitions demands.

21. "Text of German-Japanese Agreement and Supplementary Agreement Regarding Technical Cooperation," SRS 801, 9 December 1942, attachment E1, MDS.

22. SRS 705, 5 September 1942, MDS.

23. Meskill, *Hitler and Japan,* 151–52. The cartridge steel process was under a patent held by the Krupp Armament Company.

24. SRS 929, 8 April 1943, MDS.

25. SRS 847, 24 January 1943, MDS; SRS 887, 25 February 1943, MDS.

26. Memorandum, Col. Russell H. Sweet to Division of Naval Intelligence, attention Capt. John L. Riheldaffer, subject "Captured Documents and Interrogation of Personnel on German Submarine *U-234*," 26 May 1945, file "Miscellaneous," box 3, RG 38, NA.

27. Intercepted enemy communiqué, PPB79–80, 16 August 1944, file "*U-234*," UBA.

28. "Convention between the *Grossdeutschen Reich* and the Empire of Japan about War-Important Inventions," (date missing) 1944, frames 4708436–42, roll 74, microcopy T-179, NA.

29. Memorandum to Reichsführer SS, "Japanischer Plan, Deutsche Fachkraefte nach Japan einzufuehren," 24 August 1944, in "Japan-China, May 1944–December 1944," frames 0643984–85, roll 92, microcopy T-82, NA.

30. Draft of proposal, "Entwurf eines Abkommens zwischen dem Grossdeutschen Reich und dem Kaiserreich Japan uber Kriegswichtige Erfindungen," 16 November 1944, in "Japan-China May 1944–December 1944," frames 4708436–42, roll 74, microcopy T-179, NA; Masland, "Japanese-German Naval Cooperation," 185.

31. Memorandum, Dr. Karl Ritter, "Ritter Japan: Aufzeichnung St S Steengracht," 28 December 1944, in "Japan-China, May 1944–December 1944," frame 363352, roll 737, microcopy T-120, NA.

32. Memorandum to Reichsführer SS from (signature illegible), 24 August 1944, frames 0643984–85, roll 92, microcopy T-82, NA.

33. Intercepted memorandum, PPB16, 25 November 1944, file "*U-234*," UBA.

34. "Minutes of the Conference of the Commander in Chief, Navy, with the *Führer,*" 3 December 1944, item II.1, in *Führer Conferences on Naval Affairs, 1939–1945* (Annapolis, Md.: Naval Institute Press, 1990), 419.

35. Intercepted memorandum, PPB17, 15 January 1945, UBA.
36. Intercepted memorandum, PPB48, 23 January 1945, UBA.
37. Intercepted memorandum, PPB14, 15 December 1944, UBA; intercepted memorandum, PPB15, 18 December 1944, UBA.
38. "Captured German Documents," USSBS, 145, file 1a (11), roll 2, microcopy M-1655, RG 243, NA.
39. Interview, Dr. Peter Bringewald (Dallas, Texas) with author, 12 June 1998.
40. "Preliminary Report on Interrogation of General Ulrich Kessler," 30 May 1945, file "Kessler, Ulrich," box 495, RG 165, NA. Japan's greatest fear was that in retaliation for Japanese connivance with Germany, Russia would grant the United States air bases in Russia from which the Americans could strike at the home islands.
41. SRS 929, 8 April 1943, MDS.
42. Allison W. Saville, "German Submarines in the Far East," U.S. Naval Institute *Proceedings* 87 (August 1961): 85.
43. Geoffrey Brooks, "The Voyage of the German Submarine *U-234* during the Period March–May 1945 and Its Historical Implications," unpublished article included in letter from Wolfgang Hirschfeld (Plön, Germany) to author, 16 May 1996.
44. "Statement by Dr. Wilhelm Classen," 18 March 1946, 1–2, box 711, RG 165, NA.
45. SRS 1632, 9 April 1945, 5, MDS.
46. SRS 1664, 11 May 1945, 10, MDS.
47. Ronald Lewin, *The American Magic: Codes, Ciphers, and the Defeat of Japan* (New York: Farrar, Straus, and Giroux, 1982), 206. Lewin cites the Chief Customs Bureau of the Soviet Union as his source for the German tonnage figures.
48. Chapman, ed., *Price of Admiralty*, 3:566 n. 6. Japan, which had signed a nonaggression pact with the Soviet Union, toyed with the idea of sending crated aircraft parts from Berlin through Russia as part of the diplomatic bag and disguised as medical supplies. However, the large crates proved too conspicuous, and Moscow made it "abundantly clear" that it would not tolerate the export of arms through its territory, pointing out that such practices violated Soviet neutrality.
49. "Draft of a Military Agreement among Japan, Germany, and Italy," 11 December 1941, in ibid., 4:923.
50. F. H. Hinsley, *British Intelligence in the Second World War*, abridged ed. (Cambridge: Cambridge University Press, 1993), 138–39.
51. Ibid., 306.
52. Lewin, *American Magic*, 210.
53. "For the Chief of Special Staff of the *Oberkommando der Wehrmacht*," 5 January 1945, box 295, RG 226, NA.
54. Carl Boyd, *Hitler's Japanese Confidant: General Oshima Hiroshi and Magic Intelligence, 1941–1945* (Lawrence: University Press of Kansas, 1993), 212 n. 30.
55. SRS 929, 8 April 1943, 12, MDS.
56. SRS 967, 16 May 1943, 14, MDS.
57. SRS 848, 25 January 1943, MDS.
58. Chapman, ed., *Price of Admiralty*, 3:499.

59. Ibid., 4:1054–55 n. 29.
60. Saville, "German Submarines," 84.
61. Ibid.
62. "For the Chief of the Special Staff of the *Oberkommando der Wehrmacht*," 13 July 1945, box 295, RG 226, NA.
63. Ibid.
64. Ibid.
65. SRS 929, 8 April 1943, MDS.
66. Meskill, *Hitler and Japan*, 141.
67. "For the Chief of the Special Staff," 4.
68. Ibid., 2. The container idea was canceled because of the decrease of about half in total cruising range of the submarine, and Italy's defeat meant that Italian submarines would not be available.
69. Saville, "German Submarines," 84.
70. Ibid., 3.
71. "Report on the Conversion to Fuel and Ore Freight Carriers of Certain Types of German and Italian Submarines and Their Possible Use as Blockade Runners," 21 June 1942, box 1, RG 38, NA. German attempts to utilize the type XB were not lost on the Allies; in a 1942 OP-Z-16 report, the ONI reported that "a series of U-boats . . . originally built as minelayers [are] rumored to have been converted to fuel carriers."
72. SRS 967, 16 May 1943, MDS.
73. "For the Chief of the Special Staff," 3.
74. "Marineetappe Japan nach stehende Herren als Hilskrafte verpflichet worden," 10 February 1942, Admiral Canaris, OKW/Ausland IV, Bd. VI, p. 2362, RM 13/1, III M 190/1, BMA. In addition to these personnel moves, the OKM also assigned Hans-Dietrich Leonard to assist at the Japanese port of Yokohama.
75. "Kriegstagbuch der Etappenorganisation der Kriegsmarine (Marinesonderdienst)," 10 August 1942, OKW/Ausland IV, Bd. VI, p. 2725, RM 13/1, III M 190/1, BMA.
76. Japanese intelligence report, subject "Trade between Japan and Germany," 27 June 1945, box 295, RG 226, NA.
77. Saville, "German Submarines," 91.
78. SRS 1650, 27 April 1945, 2, MDS.
79. Ibid., 3, 4.

CHAPTER 2. THE LAST BOAT

1. V. E. Tarrant, *U-Boat Offensive, 1914–1945* (Annapolis, Md.: Naval Institute Press, 1989), 10, 7. R. H. Gibson and M. Pendergast state that an average of four U-boats at sea "had forced the most powerful battlefleet in history to abandon its base and retreat to a second . . . and third [base], each being progressively more remote from . . . the North Sea" (quoted by Tarrant, 11).
2. Winston S. Churchill, *The World Crisis, 1911–1918* (New York: Charles Scribner's Sons, 1923), 2:1238.

3. Anthony Preston, *Submarines* (New York: W. H. Smith, 1982), 75. Although the Germans pioneered the use of the submarine as a minelayer, they were not the first to build an operational system; the Russian *Krab*, built in 1908, holds the distinction of being the first minelayer.

4. Figures from Tarrant, *U-Boat Offensive*, 161, 68. In addition to the UC and UE boats, nine of the new Type UCIII submarines were completed after the signing of the Armistice, with fifty-four more scrapped in the shipyards.

5. Ibid., 77. The IvS was headed by the wartime chief designer of the Germania Werft in Kiel, Hans Techel, and employed a German naval representative in the person of Cdr. Ulrich Blum. Liaison between IvS and Germany was conducted through a dummy company in Berlin, the Mentor Bilantz, which included a technical department staffed by personnel from the Admiralty Construction Office.

6. Preston, *Submarines*, 93.

7. Karl Dönitz, *Zehn Jahre und zwanzig Tage* [Ten Years and Twenty Days] (Bonn: Athenäum–Verlag Junker and Dünnhaupt, 1958), 10. Germany was allowed to possess 45 percent of the British warship tonnage total, but an exception was allowed for the construction of submarines, the allotment of which could reach up to 100 percent.

8. Ibid., 43, 42. Hitler had assured his naval commanders that no war with England would break out in the foreseeable future and that "they had no cause to worry."

9. Ibid., 26.

10. Ibid., 42. In a 28 August 1939 memorandum to Commander-in-Chief Grand Admiral Erich Raeder, Dönitz wrote that in order to "operate successfully, we must have at least one hundred [U-boats] always operational [and] we should require a grand total of at least three hundred."

11. Eberhard Rössler, *The U-Boat: The Evolution and Technical History of German Submarines,* trans. Harold Erenberg (Annapolis, Md.: Naval Institute Press, 1981), 110.

12. Dönitz, *Zehn Jahre,* 64.

13. Ibid.

14. Ibid., 67.

15. Rössler cited in ibid., 67.

16. Rössler, *U-Boat,* 108–9.

17. Ibid., 110. The SMA was a larger anchor mine than its predecessors that also featured remote magnetic detonation. It measured 215 centimeters (84.7 inches) long by 133 centimeters (52.4 inches) in diameter and weighed 1,600 kilograms (3,528 pounds) but featured a reduced explosive charge of 350 kilograms (772 pounds).

18. Ibid., 111–12; Erich Gröner, *Die deutschen Kriegsschiffe, 1815–1945* [German Warships, 1815–1945] (Bonn: Bernard and Graefe Verlag, 1983), 77.

19. Gröner, *Deutschen Kriegsschiffe,* 77.

20. "Former German Submarine Type XB: Designs, Models, and Plans," July 1946, 2, report 2G-10B, S1-1 to S1-6, "Surrendered German Submarine Report, Type XB, Portsmouth Naval Shipyard, 1946," PNS.

21. Gröner, *Deutschen Kriegsschiffe*, 77. From 1943 onward, the 10.5-centimeter cannon was removed and the antiaircraft armament was reinforced by the addition of a 3.7-centimeter twenty-five-hundred-round gun and twin 2-centimeter eight-thousand-round guns.

22. "Hull Structure," March 1946, report 2G-10B-S8, "Surrendered German Submarine Report," 2.

23. Ibid., 4.

24. "Weight, Stability, and Integrity," March 1946, report 2G-10B-S29, "Surrendered German Submarine Report."

25. J. P. Mallmann Showell, *U-Boats under the Swastika* (New York: Arco, 1973), 107.

26. Gröner, *Deutschen Kriegsschiffe*, 77. *U-219* (Burghagen) was taken over by the Imperial Japanese Navy in May 1945 and became I-505. She was scrapped by the Allies in 1948.

27. Rössler, *U-Boat*, 249; "Report of the Interrogation of the Crew of the *U-234* Which Surrendered to the USS Sutton on 14 May, 1945," 27 June 1945, 1, NHC.

28. Wolfgang Hirschfeld, *Hirschfeld: The Story of a U-Boat NCO, 1940–1946*, as told to Geoffrey Brooks (Annapolis, Md.: Naval Institute Press, 1996), 191. To qualify for a mate's certificate, a youth had to complete fifty months at sea, at least twenty of which had to be served aboard sailing vessels.

29. Ibid.

30. Report of interrogation, Johann Fehler, 31 May 1945, 1, box 466, RG 165, NA.

31. Hirschfeld, *Hirschfeld*, 191.

32. Clay Blair, *Hitler's U-Boat War: The Hunters, 1939–1942* (New York: Random House, 1996), 406.

33. Edward P. Von der Porten, *The German Navy in World War II* (New York: Thomas Y. Crowell, 1969), 127. The 202 passengers included 140 Americans, 150 missionaries of various nationalities, and members of the British-American Ambulance Corps.

34. I. C. B. Dear and M. R. D. Foot, eds., *The Oxford Companion to World War II* (Oxford: Oxford University Press, 1995), 93. Although British authorities were aware of the loss of the documents, neither Brooke-Popham, the British public, nor Britain's allies were told of the loss. Public knowledge was made available only upon the declassification of the MAGIC decrypts in 1980.

35. Cajus Bekker, *Verdammte See* [Hitler's Naval War] (Hamburg: Gerhard Stalling Verlag, 1971), 213.

36. Hirschfeld, *Hirschfeld*, 192.

37. Von der Porten, *German Navy*, 134.

38. Johann Fehler and A. V. Sellwood, *Dynamite for Hire: The Story of Hein Fehler* (London: Werner Laurie, 1956), 124.

39. Report of interrogation, Fehler, 31 May 1945.

40. Fehler and Sellwood, *Dynamite*, 124–25.

41. Ibid.

42. Report of interrogation, Fehler, 31 May 1945. Fehler told his ONI interrogators that his mission in Kiel had been to "supervise" the building of *U-234*. However, Fehler had no experience in naval construction or engineering, and it

is more likely that, as a first-time skipper, he had been sent to Kiel to observe the boat's construction as a learning tool.

43. Letter, Jürgen Oesten (Hamburg) to author, 30 August 1998.

44. Dönitz, *Zehn Jahre*, 489.

45. Fehler and Sellwood, *Dynamite*, 128.

46. Hirschfeld, *Hirschfeld*, 192.

47. Interview no. 59, Grand Admiral Karl Dönitz, 28 June 1945, 12, box 723, RG 243, NA.

48. "Report of Interrogation of Crew," 3.

49. Hirschfeld, *Hirschfeld*, 193.

50. Ibid., 194.

51. Report of interrogation, Fehler, 31 May 1945, 1.

52. Letter, Johann Fehler (Hamburg) to Harry Cooper (Fox Lake, Ill.), 20 January 1985.

53. "Report of Interrogation of Crew," 4; Alexander W. Moffat, *A Navy Maverick Comes of Age* (Middletown, Conn.: Wesleyan University Press, 1978), 136.

54. Hirschfeld, *Hirschfeld*, 197. Hirschfeld stated that the vacuum was so great that Boatswain Peter Schölch's dental fillings fell out.

55. Fritz Von Sandrart, "The Last Trip to Japan of a German U-Boat," *Luftwaffen Review* (January/February 1971): 442–45.

56. Ronald Lewin, *The American Magic: Codes, Ciphers, and the Defeat of Japan* (New York: Farrar, Straus, and Giroux, 1982), 211. In a telling statistic, the total material transported by U-boats between Japan and Germany did not amount to more than what could have been delivered in a single load by a surface merchant vessel.

57. SRS 990, 8 June 1943, 4, MDS.

58. Fehler and Sellwood, *Dynamite*, 146.

59. Message, Fifteenth U-Flotilla to Comsubs Op, Com Adm U/B's, 16 April 1945, box 113, RG 38, NA.

60. "Report of Interrogation of Crew," 4.

61. Memorandum, Jack H. Alberti, Office of the Chief of Naval Operations, to Capt. John L. Riheldaffer, USN, subject "*U-234*," 22 May 1945, box 13, RG 38, NA.

62. "Manifest of Cargo for Tokio [*sic*] on Board *U-234*," inventory of individual cargo spaces, 26 June 1945, microfiche F-3160, NHC.

63. Ibid.

64. Hirschfeld, *Hirschfeld*, 199.

65. Hirschfeld's dismissive description of *U-235* as merely "a small training boat" is inaccurate. *U-235*, an operational submarine, was sunk in Kiel Harbor on 14 May 1943 in an Allied air raid. She was raised and recommissioned on 29 October 1943, only to be mistaken by the German torpedo boat T-17 for an Allied submarine and sunk on 14 April 1945 en route to Norway. Letter, Dr. Jürgen Rohwer (Stuttgart, Germany) to author, 22 February 1999.

66. Hirschfeld, *Hirschfeld*, 199.

67. Fehler and Sellwood, *Dynamite*, 148.

68. Von Sandrart, "Last Trip to Japan," 442.

69. Fehler and Sellwood, *Dynamite,* 156.
70. Hirschfeld, *Hirschfeld,* 193.
71. "Report of Interrogation of Crew," 5.
72. Hirschfeld, *Hirschfeld,* 204.
73. Message, Fehler to Fifth Flotilla, 25 March 1945, box 113, RG 38, NA.
74. Message, Fehler to Fifth Flotilla, 26 March 1945, box 113, RG 38, NA.
75. Message, Fifteenth U-Flotilla to Comsubs Op, 6 April 1945, box 113, RG 38, NA.
76. Message, Fehler to Comsubs Op, ComAdm U/B's, Sea Defense Commandant, Oslo Fjord, Port Captain, Kristiansand, 5 April 1945, box 113, RG 38, NA.
77. Message, Comsubs Op to Fehler, 12 April 1945, box 113, RG 38, NA; message, Berlin to Fehler, 13 April 1945, box 113, RG 38, NA.
78. Message, Fifth Flotilla to Comsubs Op, Com Adm U/B's, 16 April 1945, box 113, RG 38, NA.
79. Telephone interview, Dr. Peter Bringewald (Dallas, Texas) with author, 20 June 1998.
80. Message, Tokyo to Berlin, 19 April 1945, box 113, RG 38, NA.
81. Message, chief inspector in Germany #165 to chief, Military Preparations, 15 April 1945, box 113, RG 38, NA.
82. Von Sandrart, "Last Trip to Japan," 442.
83. Ibid.
84. Hirschfeld, *Hirschfeld,* 204.
85. Von Sandrart, "Last Trip to Japan," 443.
86. Ibid.
87. Hirschfeld, *Hirschfeld,* 205–6.
88. Ibid., 205.
89. Von Sandrart, "Last Trip to Japan," 444.
90. Hirschfeld, *Hirschfeld,* 206.
91. Letter, Wolfgang Hirschfeld (Plön, Germany) to Dr. Dean Allard (Washington, D.C.), 28 February 1992.
92. Letter, Jürgen Oesten (Hamburg) to author, 30 August 1998.
93. Letter, Wolfgang Hirschfeld (Plön, Germany) to author, 4 February 1996.
94. "Following Order Issued by the Grand Admiral," 7 May 1945, box 113, RG 38, NA.
95. Ibid.
96. Hirschfeld, *Hirschfeld,* 208.

CHAPTER 3. THE PROBLEM OF SURRENDER

1. Letter, Heinrich Fehler (Hamburg) to Harry Cooper (Fox Lake, Ill.), 21 February 1988.
2. "Report of the Interrogation of the Crew, of the *U-234* Which Surrendered to the USS Sutton on 14 May, 1945," 27 June 1945, 5, NHC.
3. Wolfgang Hirschfeld, *Hirschfeld: The Story of a U-Boat NCO, 1940–1946,* as told to Geoffrey Brooks (Annapolis, Md.: Naval Institute Press, 1996), 210.
4. Independent room conversation, Fehler, 29 May 1945, 1230 hours, 3, box 466, RG 165, NA.

5. Independent room conversation, Kessler, 21–22 June 1945, 2330–0010 hours, 2.
6. Johann Fehler and A. V. Sellwood, *Dynamite for Hire: The Story of Hein Fehler* (London: Werner Laurie, 1956), 177.
7. Independent room conversation, Fehler, 27 May 1945, 3–4.
8. Ibid., 2, 3, 6.
9. Ibid., 6.
10. Letter, Fehler to Cooper, 21 February 1988; Fehler and Sellwood, *Dynamite,* 180. Kessler favored surrendering to the United States.
11. Report of interrogation, Richard Bulla, 24 May 1945, 2, box 456, RG 165, NA.
12. Nagamori Yoshio, "Memories of Two Japanese Officers Who Died the Hero's Death in the Atlantic," 4, file II, UBA.
13. Message, Vice Admiral Abe, Stockholm, Sweden, to navy minister and chief of staff, Tokyo, 28 May 1945, box 113, RG 38, NA.
14. Nemot was reportedly aboard *U-501* and Arima reportedly aboard *U-134*. However, Dr. Jürgen Rohwer disputes these assertions.
15. Nagamori, "Memories," 4.
16. Ibid., 2.
17. Ibid.
18. Message, Abe to navy minister, 28 May 1945.
19. Ibid.
20. Nagamori, "Memories," 2.
21. Independent room conversation, Fehler, 29 May 1945, 2.
22. Hirschfeld, *Hirschfeld,* 208.
23. Letter, Fehler to Cooper, 21 February 1988.
24. Fehler and Sellwood, *Dynamite,* 174.
25. Von Sandrart, "Last Trip to Japan," 444.
26. Interroom conversation, Fehler, 29 May 1945, 2.
27. Hirschfeld, *Hirschfeld,* 211. *U-234*'s doctor, Dr. Franz Walter, later confirmed that at the moment of their discovery, both Japanese passengers were still alive, though in a terminal condition. Dr. Walter pointed out that the amount of Luminal ingested would have killed a European more quickly, but the Japanese constitution was stronger.
28. Letter, Fehler to Cooper, 21 February 1988.
29. Memorandum, Cdr. B. F. Roeder, USN, to Captain Phelan, USN, "Suicide Note Taken from *U-234*," 7 June 1945, box 3, RG 38, NA.
30. Ibid.
31. Fehler and Sellwood, *Dynamite,* 183.
32. Independent room conversation, Fehler, 29 May 1945, 1230 hours, 3.
33. Ibid., 2.
34. Nagamori, "Memories," 1.
35. Ibid.
36. Fehler and Sellwood, *Dynamite,* 152.
37. SRS 1546, 13 January 1945, 1–4, MDS.
38. SRS 1557, 25 January 1945, 4–5, MDS.
39. SRS 1568, 4 February 1945, 4, MDS.

40. Message, chief inspector in Germany to chief of military preparedness, 26 February 1945, box 113, RG 38, NA.

41. Message, Comsubs Berlin to Tokyo, 8 March 1945, box 113, RG 38, NA.

42. SRS 1656, 3 May 1945, 1–2, MDS.

43. Memorandum, COMINCG and CNO to NAVOP 7, subject "Points of Surrender," 27 April 1945, box 531, RG 181, NANE.

44. Letter, Fehler to Cooper, 21 February 1988.

45. Hirschfeld, *Hirschfeld*, 210.

46. Letter, Wolfgang Hirschfeld (Plön, Germany) to author, 4 February 1996.

47. Wolfgang Hirschfeld, *Feindfahrten: Das Logbuch eines U-Bootfunkers* [Enemy Voyage: The Logbook of a U-Boat Radioman] (Berlin: Neuer Kaiser Verlag, 1991), 366.

48. Letter, Hirschfeld to author, 4 February 1996.

49. Hirschfeld, *Hirschfeld*, 212.

50. Ibid.

51. *Dictionary of American Naval Fighting Ships* (Washington, D.C.: Naval History Division, Department of the Navy, 1976), 6:689.

52. V. E. Tarrant, *The U-Boat Offensive, 1914–1945* (Annapolis, Md.: Naval Institute Press, 1989), 138–40. Most of the U-boat action was at sea. However, several boats were sunk in closer proximity to the American coast: *U-857* (Premauer) was sunk on 7 April just off Cape Cod, *U-548* (Krempl) on 30 April off Cape Hatteras, and *U-853* (Frömsdorf) on 6 May south of Long Island.

53. Confidential memorandum from Headquarters, First Naval District, Boston, to DIO, subject "Surrendered U-Boats," 11 May 1945, box 56/C/R45, NHC.

54. Secret memorandum for the assistant commandant, operations, subject "U-Boat Situation," 11 May 1945, box 56/C/R45, NHC.

55. Memorandum, T. W. Nazro to commander-in-chief, U.S. Fleet, subject "Capture of *U-234*, Events Leading To," 9–17 May 1945, 1–2, box 56/C/R45, NHC.

56. Memorandum, commanding officer, USS *Sutton*, to commander-in-chief, U.S. Fleet, "Capture of *U-234*, Events Leading To," 29 May 1945, 2, box 56/C/R45, NHC.

57. Memorandum, commanding officer, USS *Sutton*, to commander-in-chief, U.S. Fleet, 12 May 1945, box 56/C/R45, NHC.

58. Memorandum, First Naval District to assistant commandant, operations, subject "U-Boat Situation," 12 May 1945, box 56/C/R45, NHC.

59. Secret war diary, Northern Group, May 1945, 11, box 56/C/R45, NHC.

60. Hirschfeld, *Feindfahrten*, 366.

61. Franklin M. Gates, "Officer of Prize Crew Narrates Events in Surrender of *U-234* One Year Later," *Portsmouth (N.H.) Herald*, May 1946, Scrapbook, vol. 28, 88–89, Portsmouth Public Library.

62. Deck log, USS *Sutton*, 14 May 1945, 1200–1600 hours, 283, box 56/C/R45, NHC.

63. Memorandum, "Capture of *U-234*," 9–17 May 1945, 3.

64. Gates, "Officer of Prize Crew," 88. See also memorandum, CINCLANT to COMSUBLANT, subject "Prize Crews," 3 May 1945, box 531, RG 181, NANE. In anticipation of the surrender of U-boats in American waters, CINCLANT ordered the submarine commands at New London, Connecticut, and

Portsmouth, New Hampshire, to train and equip at least one prize crew each and have the crew available on twelve hours' notice.

65. Letter, Wolfgang Hirschfeld (Plön, Germany) to author, 13 May 1996; Hirschfeld, *Feindfahrten*, 367; Hirschfeld, *Hirschfeld*, 213. Hirschfeld later commented that his personal copy of the *KTB* was hidden in a closet but was gone when he was released from prison. Regarding the disposal of the microfilm, Schlicke was reported to have said, "And there goes the rocket that could fly the Atlantic."

66. Letter, Fehler to Cooper, 20 January 1985.

67. "Report of Interrogation of Crew," 1.

68. Gates, "Officer of Prize Crew," 89.

69. Deck log, USS *Sutton*, 15 May 1945, 284.

70. Ibid., 14 May 1945, 284; Bulla quoted in Gates, "Officer of Prize Crew," 88.

71. Memorandum, CINCLANT to USS *Sutton*, subject "Delivery of *U-234*," 16 May 1945, box 531, RG 181, NANE. The *Sutton, Muir,* and *Carter* proceeded to New York, where they underwent upkeep while awaiting further orders.

72. Memorandum, First Naval District, Boston, Massachusetts, to watch officers, subject "U-Boat Surrenders in Northern Group Waters," 3 May 1945, box 531, RG 181, NANE.

73. Letter, Capt. V. D. Herbster, USN, to Lt. Charles E. Winslow, commanding officer, USCG *Argo*, "Personal and Confidential," 12 May 1945, box 531, RG 181, NANE.

74. Secret war diary, Northern Group, May 1945, "*U-234*," 12, box 56/C/R45, NHC.

CHAPTER 4. PORTSMOUTH

1. Memorandum, Capt. V. D. Herbster, assistant commandant (operations), Eastern Sea Frontier, to commandant, First Naval District, subject "Surrender of German Submarines," 5 May 1945, secret war diary, Northern Group, May 1945, box 56/C/R45, NHC.

2. "Operational Order 3-34: Press Task Unit," 5 May 1945, secret war diary, Northern Group, May 1945.

3. Western Union cable, commander, Eastern Sea Frontier, to commander, Northern Group, 11 May 1945, box 531, RG 181, NANE.

4. Operational order PRO-2/0555, commandant, First Naval District, to commandant, Portsmouth Navy Yard, subject "Surrendered German Submarines, Cooperation with Working Press and Radio in Covering," 11 May 1945, box 531, RG 181, NANE.

5. Confidential wire, commander, Northern Group, Eastern Sea Frontier, to *Argo*, subject "Delivery of Enemy Subs," 11 May 1945, box 531, RG 181, NANE.

6. *Portsmouth Periscope*, 9 June 1945, 3.

7. Memorandum, commander, Northern Group, to *Argo*, subject "Surrender Stories," 11 May 1945, box 531, RG 181, NANE.

8. Memorandum, commandant to commanding officer, naval air bases, subject "Photos of Enemy Subs," 12 May 1945, box 531, RG 181, NANE.

9. Robert G. Kennedy, "Nazis Won't Talk to Newsmen; Two More Subs Due," *Portsmouth (N.H.) Herald*, 16 May 1945, 1(A).

10. Memorandum, commander, Eastern Sea Frontier, to commander, Task Group 2.1, subject "Interviewing of Prisoners," 13 May 1945, box 531, RG 181, NANE.

11. Memorandum, *Sutton* to COMINCH, CINCLANT, subject "Info on *U-234*," 15 May 1945, box 531, RG 181, NANE.

12. Memorandum, COMINCH to CESF, subject "Disposition of 234 Prisoners," 15 May 1945, box 531, RG 181, NANE.

13. Sidney M. Shalett, "Huge Nazi Sub Seized in Flight to Japan; Three Luftwaffe Chiefs, Two Dead Japs Aboard," *Boston Herald,* 17 May 1945, 1–2(A).

14. T. W. Nazro, "War Diary Entry," 14 May 1945, box 56/C/R54, NHC.

15. Carlyle Holt, "Big U-Boat Taken by US; Two Jap Suicides Aboard," unnamed newspaper, 17 May 1945, file "*U-234* and General," PNS.

16. SRS 1645, 22 April 1945, MDS. Kase was cautious about supporting the supposed flight of German leaders to Japan, stating that, in view of the "ferocious atrocity campaign" that the Allies were waging against Germany, "identity with the Nazis to the bitter end should be avoided so far as possible."

17. Lester Allen, "Find Three Nazi Chiefs in U-Boat," *Boston Post,* 17 May 1945, 1(A).

18. "Hint Tops of Nazi Biggies Bound Here on Seized Sub," *Boston Daily Record,* 19 May 1945, 3(A).

19. "Fourth U-Boat Due Today," *Boston Herald,* 19 May 1945, 1.

20. Lester Allen, "Big Hunt on for Hitler in U-Boat," *Boston Post,* 18 May 1945, 1(A).

21. "Log of Public Relations—Restricted," 17 May 1945, box 531, RG 181, NANE. Cdr. N. R. Collier, district public-relations officer in Boston, opined that the high-ranking official was a Captain Smedburg of COMINCH Ingram's office.

22. Ibid.

23. Memorandum, Cdr. N. R. Collier, First Naval District, to Captain Herbster, deputy commander, Northern Group, subject "Publicity on Surrender of *U-234*," 18 May 1945, box 531, RG 181, NANE.

24. Telephone conversation, Capt. V. D. Herbster and Commodore Kurtz, 18 May 1945, box 531, RG 181, NANE.

25. Letter, Hirschfeld to author, 4 February 1996.

26. Johann Fehler and A. V. Sellwood, *Dynamite for Hire: The Story of Hein Fehler* (London: Werner Laurie, 1956), 200. Fehler relates an instance in which, upon refusing to smile for a Coast Guard sentry, he was struck in the jaw with the butt of the sentry's machine gun.

27. *Portsmouth (N.H.) Herald,* 21 May 1945.

28. Wolfgang Hirschfeld, *Hirschfeld: The Story of a U-Boat NCO, 1940–1946,* as told to Geoffrey Brooks (Annapolis, Md.: Naval Institute Press, 1996), 216.

29. Memorandum, Lt. (jg) M. T. Brunner, USNR, to commander, naval intelligence, 15 May 1945, box 13, RG 38, NA.

30. Enciphered memorandum, authenticated by Brunner, to United States Coast Guard vessel *Argo,* 16 May 1945, box 13, RG 38, NA.

31. Memorandum, Admiral Winters, commandant, Portsmouth Navy Yard, to OTC Surrender Unit, Northern Group, Eastern Sea Frontier, subject "Receipt of Prisoners," 19 May 1945, box 531, RG 181, NANE.
32. Hirschfeld, *Hirschfeld*, 216.
33. Ibid.
34. Memorandum, OP-16-Z to OP-16, subject "Souvenirs from Enemy U-boats," 1 June 1945, box 1, RG 38, NA.
35. Memorandum, Jack H. Alberti, Office of the Chief of Naval Operations, to Capt. John L. Riheldaffer, subject "Report on Events at Portsmouth Navy Yard in Connection with the Surrender of German Submarines *U-234, U-805, U-873* and *U-1228*," 22 May 1945, box 13, RG 38, NA.
36. Ibid.
37. Ibid. Although guards who returned captured articles were afforded leniency, this policy did not extend to the many dockworkers who worked aboard *U-234*. On 21 May a member of the working party was found to have a deck of German playing cards in his possession; he was arrested and court-martialed by Admiral Winters.
38. Telephone conversation, Herbster and Kurtz, 18 May 1945.
39. Memorandum, Herbster to Admiral Winters, 18 May 1945, box 531, RG 181, NANE; memorandum, Lt. (jg) F. H. Hanbury, USNR, to Lt. Cdr. T. Hatton, 17 May 1945, box 13, RG 38, NA.
40. Edward Lundquist, "What If the Germans Had Listened to U-Boat Skipper?" *The Dolphin*, 30 September 1983, 18–19. Fritz Steinhoff's brother was Dr. Ernst Steinhoff, who, like his brother, was a leading proponent of undersea projectile launching. After the war Dr. Steinhoff worked with the U.S. Navy's Polaris missile program.
41. Letter, Johann Fehler (Hamburg) to Wolfgang Hirschfeld (Plön, Germany), 3 February 1981, UBA.
42. Quoted from Louis M. Lyons, "Nazi Prisoners to Stay Here Awhile," *Providence (R.I.) Sunday Journal*, 13 May 1945, 4(A).
43. Joseph M. Scalia, "History, Archaeology, and the German Prisoner of War Experience in Rural Louisiana: The Ruston Alien Internment Facility, 1943–1945." *Louisiana History: The Journal of the Louisiana Historical Association* 38 (summer 1997): 314.
44. List of suspected political affiliations of *U-234* crew, box 13, RG 38, NA. Peter Wiesmayer was considered the leader of *U-234*'s National Socialist contingent; initial ONI evaluations labeled him a "somewhat psychopathic case, possible fanatic type [who is] overly anxious to please."
45. Interroom conversation, Menzel and Schlicke, 26 May 1945, 1930–1950 hours, box 515, RG 165, NA.
46. Telephone conversation, Herbster and Kurtz, 18 May 1945, box 531, RG 181, NANE.
47. See Hirschfeld, *Hirschfeld*, 218.
48. Memorandum, Jack H. Alberti to Capt. John L. Riheldaffer, subject "*U-234*," 24 May 1945, 1, box 4, RG 38, NA.

49. Memorandum, chief of naval operations and commander-in-chief, Atlantic Fleet, to commander, First Naval District, subject "*U-234* Cargo, Disposition Of," 23 May 1945, box 531, RG 181, NANE.

50. Memorandum, chief of naval operations to commander, Portsmouth Navy Yard, subject "Mine Tubes, Unloading Of," 27 May 1945, box 531, RG 181, NANE.

51. Geoffrey Brooks, "The Voyage of the German Submarine *U-234* during the Period March–May 1945 and Its Historical Implications," unpublished article included in letter from Wolfgang Hirschfeld (Plön, Germany) to author, 16 May 1996. Boatswain Peter Schlöch, who was supervising the unloading, was aware of the location of the uranium but did not impart this knowledge to his captors.

52. Letter, Hirschfeld to author, 16 May 1996. Pfaff's cooperation with the ONI did not remain secret. Upon his release from Fort Meade he was therefore sent to an "anti-Nazi" internment facility in Louisiana for protective custody. After his repatriation to Germany, Pfaff soon returned to the United States; his immigration proceeded easily and swiftly, in evident recognition of his previous cooperation.

53. Ibid.

54. Memorandum, "Mine Tubes, Unloading Of"; memorandum, CNO to commander, Portsmouth Navy Yard, subject "Cargo *U-234*, Information On," 28 May 1945, box 531, RG 181, NANE.

55. Alexander W. Moffat, *A Navy Maverick Comes of Age* (Middletown, Conn.: Wesleyan University Press, 1978), 136.

56. "Manifest of Cargo for Tokio [*sic*] on Board *U-234*," 26 June 1945, microfiche F-3160, NHC.

57. Richard E. Winslow, *Portsmouth-Built: Submarines of the Portsmouth Naval Shipyard* (Portsmouth, N.H.: Peter E. Randall, 1983), 93; memorandum to OP-20-3-G1-A, "Cargo Unloading List for *U-234* at Portsmouth, New Hampshire, on and from 23 May 1945," 23 May 1945, box 13, RG 38, NA.

58. Anthony Pritchard, *Messerschmitt* (New York: G. P. Putnam's Sons, 1975), 46–47. The ME 209 holds the speed record for a low-altitude flight by a piston-engine aircraft, which it set on 26 April 1939 with Fritz Wendel at the controls.

59. "Material Sent to Wright Field," no date, "Records of *U-234;* Aircraft Drawings and Drawing Lists," box 3, RG 38, NA.

60. "ONI Routing Slips," file "AAF: Final to Wright Field," box 7, RG 38, NA.

61. Memorandum, Col. Russell H. Sweet to Division of Naval Intelligence, attention Capt. John L. Riheldaffer, subject "Captured Documents and Interrogation of Personnel on German Submarine *U-234*," 26 May 1945, file "Miscellaneous," box 3, RG 38, NA.

62. Memorandum, Captain Phelan to Commander Watson and Lieutenant Noble, subject "Disposition of Material from *U-234*," 4 August 1945, box 5, RG 38, NA.

63. Memorandum, Alberti to Riheldaffer, 24 May 1945, 2, 6, box 5, RG 38, NA.

64. Memorandum, chief of naval operations to commander, Portsmouth Navy Yard, subject "POW and Fuses from *U-234*," 25 May 1945, box 531, RG 181, NANE.

65. Memorandum, Alberti to Riheldaffer, subject "Report on Events at Portsmouth," 22 May 1945, box 56/C/R45, NHC. Erich Menzel confirmed Alberti's report, lamenting in his cell that he had not been allowed to remove any Hennessy from the boat.
66. Ibid.
67. Ibid.
68. Memorandum, production officer to planning officer, subject "Stability of U-234," 28 May 1945, box 531, RG 181, NANE.
69. Memorandum, chief of naval operations to commander, First Naval District, 26 June 1945, box 531, RG 181, NANE.
70. Lee A. White, cited in Robert K. Wilcox, *Japan's Secret War: Japan's Race against Time to Build Its Own Atomic Bomb* (New York: Marlowe and Co., 1995), 160.
71. Memorandum, commandant to Commander Phelan, subject "Captured Enemy Equipment," 5 July 1945, box 531, RG 181, NANE.
72. Memorandum, commandant to Bureau of Ships, 8 August 1945, box 531, RG 181, NANE.

CHAPTER 5. THE GENERAL

1. Report of interrogation, Ulrich Kessler, 22 May 1945, 3, box 495, RG 165, NA.
2. SRS 1650, 27 April 1945, 3, MDS; SRS 1646, 23 April 1945, 9, MDS. In a footnote to the 23 April summary, the intelligence monitor acknowledged that while the 20 April message implied that Kessler was already en route to Japan via submarine, there was no other evidence to suggest that he had actually embarked on his mission or, if he had, aboard which submarine he was traveling.
3. "Preliminary Report on Interrogation of General Ulrich Kessler," 30 May 1945, file "Kessler, Ulrich," box 495, RG 165, NA.
4. Ibid., 3. Kessler claimed that his first article was frequently quoted by American experts when addressing organizational matters. His second article dealt with Winston Churchill and defended the future British prime minister against criticism for his role in the Gallipoli defeat.
5. Johann Fehler and A. V. Sellwood, *Dynamite for Hire: The Story of Hein Fehler* (London: Werner Laurie, 1956), 180.
6. "Preliminary Report on Interrogation of General Ulrich Kessler," 3.
7. Ibid., 4.
8. Ibid.
9. Report of interrogation, Kessler, 22 May 1945. In addition to information regarding military matters and German-Japanese military cooperation, Kessler revealed that he was cognizant of political subjects such as the Japanese-Russian exchange of information in Turkey, the execution of German agents in Japan, German-Russian peace proposals dating back to 1943–44, and details of the conspiracy surrounding the 20 July attempt on Hitler's life.
10. The most recent source of this information was Nieschling; see independent room conversation, Kay Nieschling, 29 May 1945, 1930–2300 hours, box 522,

RG 165, NA. Upon hearing reports that Germany's experimental launching of a submerged rocket had been sabotaged in Austria, Nieschling lamented, "German victory lies at the bottom of an Austrian lake."

11. Report of interrogation, Kessler, 1 June 1945.
12. *The Dolphin,* 30 September 1983, 18–19. Actually, Germany had launched missiles from a submarine. During the summer of 1942, *U-511,* under the command of Lt. Cdr. Fritz Steinhoff, successfully fired a V-2 missile from a depth of 75 feet near Peenemünde. However, because of the awkward launching apparatus and Hitler's lack of interest, the project was scrapped.
13. Report of interrogation, Kessler, 1 June 1945.
14. Ibid., 4 June 1945.
15. Clay Blair, *Hitler's U-Boat War: The Hunters, 1939–1942* (New York: Random House, 1996), 764–67. During 1942, 142 Allied ships, comprising 1.07 million gross tons, were sunk along the Atlantic and Gulf coasts of the United States.
16. Report of interrogation, Kessler, 4 June 1945, 1.
17. SRS 1637, 14 April 1945, 3, MDS. As early as 24 March 1945, the German naval attaché in Tokyo, Paul Wennecker, petitioned Berlin to request that the Japanese grant German personnel in Japan "formal recognition of extraterritoriality" in anticipation of an American invasion.
18. Jerome B. Cohen, *Japan's Economy in War and Reconstruction* (Minneapolis: University of Minnesota Press, 1949), 199.
19. Report of interrogation, Kessler, 7 June 1945, 1–2.
20. Ibid., 28 May 1945, 4.
21. Ibid., 3, 1. The plans for the ME 262 had initially been sent to Japan on a submarine in December 1944, but the U-boat had been lost at sea. Kessler admitted that the Japanese test flights had been discovered by Berlin "quite unexpected[ly] and quite by accident."
22. Ibid., 7 June 1945, 4. The implications of a powered test flight pointed to Japanese advances in turbo-jet power plants rather than the aeronautical integrity results provided by a glider flight.
23. Ibid. Until the declassification of Kessler's interrogation records by the National Archives and Records Administration, most scholars agreed with Cohen (*Japan's Economy,* 217) that Japan never attempted a test flight of the ME 163 until July 1945.
24. Report of interrogation, Kessler, 7 June 1945, 2.
25. Ibid., 9 June 1945, 2. It was Kessler's opinion that the Luftwaffe's effectiveness had been broken during the 1940 Battle of Britain and that it had never recovered.
26. Ibid., 1, 2. The De Havilland Mosquito XVI had a service ceiling of 11,887 meters (39,000 feet) and a top speed of 668 kilometers per hour (415 miles per hour); the ME 163 had a top speed of 949 kph (590 mph); the ME 262 maxed out at 869 kph (540 mph).
27. Ibid., 1. This plan of attack was to be especially effective when executed by the smaller, more agile ME 163.
28. Ibid., 25 June 1945, 7.
29. Ibid., 28 May 1945, 8.

30. John Prados, *Combined Fleet Decoded: The Secret History of American Intelligence and the Japanese Navy in World War II* (New York: Random House, 1995), 716. The Ohka, or "cherry blossom," was assigned to the Japanese 721st Air Group and made its first appearance during the Okinawa campaign in April 1945.

31. Report of interrogation, Kessler, 28 May 1945, 4. The Mistel consisted of a radio-controlled ME 109 ferried into battle by a Junkers 188 bomber. The body of the ME 109 was actually a bomb designed to disintegrate into liquid steel upon contact. Baka was the code name given to the Ohka by U.S. naval intelligence. It is a Japanese word meaning "fool." Cohen, *Japan's Economy*, 217.

32. Report of interrogation, Kessler, 28 May 1945, 5.

33. Ibid., 8.

34. Ibid., 1 June 1945, 1.

35. Ibid.

36. Ibid.

37. Ibid.

38. Ibid., 20 September 1945, 1, 2.

39. Ibid.

40. Ibid., 1.

41. William L. Shirer, *The Rise and Fall of the Third Reich: A History of Nazi Germany*, 4th ed. (New York: Touchstone Books, 1988), 372–75.

42. Ibid., 907, 1018.

43. Ibid., 1019. German bombs of the type designated for the destruction of Hitler's aircraft made a telltale hissing sound before detonation, which could expose the device. The British device made no such sound and was considered safe from detection.

44. Report of interrogation, Kessler, 28 May 1945, subject "Information re Political Alibi of General der Flieger Kessler," 2.

45. Ibid., 3.

46. Ibid., 3–4, 7.

47. Nagamori Yoshio, "Memories of Two Japanese Officers Who Died the Hero's Death in the Atlantic," 5, file II, UBA.

48. Letter, Louise W. Boothe (Lenox, Mass.) to Admiral Train, director of the Office of Naval Intelligence, 21 May 1945, box 495, RG 165, NA.

CHAPTER 6. THE PROBLEM OF AIR DEFENSE

1. Memorandum, OP-16-Z to OP-16-PT, subject "Passengers on *U-234*, Now Prisoners of War, Available for Interrogation," 29 May 1945, 1–3, box 13, RG 38, NA.

2. SRS 1054, 12 August 1945, 9, MDS. Oshima described the bombings as "utterly inhuman . . . [The British] used liquid fire composed of benzol, benzine, rubber, and phosphorus. It was practically the same as if they had used poison gas."

3. Saburo Ienaga, *Taiheiyo Senso* [The Pacific War] (Tokyo: Iwanami Shoten, 1968), 140–41. Ienaga notes that in the 29 September 1939 issue of *Asahi Gurafu*, the threat of Allied incendiary bombing was addressed with pictures of Japanese civilians dousing fires with wooden buckets. In the 14 April 1943

issue a similar article carried a photograph of an incendiary raid, accompanied by the caption "Don't be afraid of this bomb"; aerial defense against the threat of firebombing would be handled by neighborhood defense associations armed with buckets and hoses.

4. Quoted in John Toland, *The Rising Sun: The Decline and Fall of the Japanese Empire, 1936–1945* (New York: Random House, 1970), 745.

5. SRS 1063, 21 August 1943, 5, MDS.

6. Kenneth P. Werrell, *Blankets of Fire: U.S. Bombers over Japan during World War II* (Washington, D.C.: Smithsonian Institution Press, 1996), 25.

7. Peter Calvocoressi and Ben Wint, *Total War: The Causes and Courses of the Second World War* (London: Penguin Press, 1972), 469. One example of British radar proficiency was the H2S airborne system, which allowed the pilot to "see" his target regardless of visibility or the excessive heights to which he might be forced by antiaircraft fire.

8. Werrell, *Blankets of Fire*, 26.

9. Calvocoressi and Wint, *Total War*, 470–71.

10. Horst Boog, *Die deutsche Luftwaffenführung, 1943–1945: Führungsprobleme, Spitzengliederung, Generalstabsausbildung* [Leadership of the German Luftwaffe, 1943–1945: Leadership Problems, Order of Hierarchy, and General Staff Training] (Stuttgart: Deutsche Verlags-Anstalt, 1982), 204–14.

11. Calvocoressi and Wint, *Total War*, 471. Britain's Bomber Command suffered more casualties than any other branch during the war.

12. Alan S. Milward, *War, Economy, and Society, 1939–1945* (Berkeley: University of California Press, 1977), 299.

13. Werrell, *Blankets of Fire*, 29.

14. Jeffrey Ethell, *Mustang: A Documentary History of the P-51* (London: Jane's, 1981), 114–15.

15. John Costello, *The Pacific War, 1941–1945* (New York: Quill, 1981), 526.

16. John Keegan, *The Second World War* (New York: Penguin Books, 1989), 576–77; Michael S. Sherry, *The Rise of American Air Power: The Creation of Armageddon* (New Haven: Yale University Press, 1987), 277 n. 76. The exact death toll continues to be the subject of debate; the United States Strategic Bombing Survey put the figure at between seventy-nine thousand and eighty-four thousand, but modern estimates claim in excess of one hundred thousand dead.

17. Saburo, *Taiheiyo Senso*, 148.

18. Agawa Hiroyuki, *The Reluctant Admiral: Yamamoto and the Imperial Navy* (Tokyo: Kodansha International, 1979), 127. A notable exception to the refusal of Japanese leaders to recognize the vulnerability of Japan's cities was Adm. Yamamoto Isoraku. As early as 1939 Yamamoto had warned that Japanese cities, constructed largely of paper and wood, would "burn very easily . . . [and] if there were large-scale air raids, there's no telling what would happen."

19. Toland, *Rising Sun*, 745.

20. Keith Wheeler, *Bombers over Japan* (Chicago: Time-Life Books, 1982), 143.

21. Lester Brooks, *Behind Japan's Surrender: The Secret Struggle that Ended an Empire* (Stamford: De Gustibus Press, 1968), 81.

22. Werrell, *Blankets of Fire*, 276 n. 124, 237.
23. SRS 1656, 3 May 1945, 2, MDS.
24. Report of interrogation, Erich Menzel, 21 May 1945, 1, box 13, RG 38, NA.
25. Ibid.
26. Ibid., 2.
27. Ibid.
28. Ibid., 23 May 1945.
29. Ibid., 29 May 1945, 1.
30. Ibid., 26 June 1945.
31. Ibid., 23 June 1945.
32. Ibid., 26 June 1945.
33. Ibid., 15 June 1945.
34. Ibid., 26 June 1945. Menzel was also to address the matter of Japanese fighter cover and was directed to cooperate with a First Lieutenant Stepp.
35. Ibid., 15 June 1945. Menzel listed the following types of German aircraft used for reconnaissance: the Focke-Wulf 200 Kondor; the Blohm and Voss 222 and 138; the Heinkel 111; the Junkers 88, 188, 290 (planned but never utilized), and 388 (trials completed but never utilized); and the Messerschmitt 264 (it is probable that this entry should have read "ME 262," since about forty of the jet aircraft were utilized for reconnaissance). Alfred Price, *The Luftwaffe Data Book* (London: Greenhill Books, 1997), 193.
36. Report of interrogation, Menzel, 15 June 1945.
37. Ibid., 26 June 1945, 1–2.
38. Ibid., 2.
39. Ibid., 15 June 1945, 2.
40. Ibid., 3.
41. Ibid; ibid., 13 May 1945.
42. Ibid., 7 June 1945, 2.
43. Ibid., 5 June 1945, 1.
44. Ibid., 2.
45. Ibid., 1–2.
46. Ibid.
47. Ibid., 29 May 1945, 2.
48. I. C. B. Dear and M. R. D. Foot, eds., *The Oxford Companion to World War II* (Oxford: Oxford University Press, 1995), 516.
49. Report of interrogation, Menzel, 7 June 1945, 1.
50. Ibid.
51. Price, *Luftwaffe Data Book*, 185.
52. Dear and Foot, eds., *Oxford Companion*, 516.
53. Report of interrogation, Menzel, 7 June 1945, 1.
54. Ibid.
55. Ibid.
56. Ibid.
57. SRS 1016, 5 July 1943, 3, MDS. In April 1943 Tokyo informed Berlin that "all reports that we have been able to obtain in Japan about [Allied] radar equip-

ment are being turned over to the German Military Attache in Tokyo." This information was subsequently passed on to German specialists for evaluation.

58. Report of interrogation, Menzel, 29 May 1945, 1–2.

59. SRS 1047, 5 August 1943, 4, MDS. An example of this phase of cooperation was the Luftwaffe's 9 June 1943 shipment of technical drawings of its newest radar device, the Würzburg D-type wireless, to Japan.

60. Memorandum, Lt. (jg) John G. Faron, USNR, to Capt. G. R. Phelan, USN, subject "Cargo aboard 1600 Ton German Submarine at Portsmouth, New Hampshire, Partial List Of," 29 May 1945, box 4, RG 38, NA.

61. Report of interrogation, Menzel, 29 May 1945, 1.

62. Memorandum, "Passengers on *U-234*," 1–2.

63. Basic personnel record (alien enemy or prisoner of war), Fritz von Sandrart, no. 3WG-1268, box 535, RG 165, NA.

64. Report of interrogation, Ulrich Kessler, 9 June 1945, 3, box 495, RG 165, NA. Kessler stated that von Sandrart "was meant to help the Japanese with their AAA [because] he was more versed in tactical than technical knowledge."

65. Report on the interrogation of Fritz von Sandrart by Captain Halle, "Answers to Preliminary List of Questions Submitted by Flak Analysis Section, Tactical and Technical Branch, Analysis Division, AC/AS, Intelligence, A.A.F.," 1 June 1945, 1, box 535, RG 165, NA.

66. Memorandum to Captain Phelan, 21 May 1945, 1, box 5, RG 38, NA.

67. Ibid., 6.

68. Report of interrogation, Kessler, 9 June 1945, 1.

69. SRS 1047, 5 August 1943, MDS; intercepted report, item no. 9, "German Aid," 13 December 1944, USSBS, roll 2, microcopy M-1655, RG 243, NA.

70. Intercepted report, "German Aid," 13 December 1944, 3, 2. These items were probably delivered to Japan aboard the Japanese submarine I-30, which departed Lorient on 23 August 1942 and arrived in Singapore on 11 October.

71. Report of interrogation, Fritz von Sandrart, 28 May 1945, 5, 7, 4, box 13, RG 38, NA.

72. Ibid., 29 May 1945, 1.

73. "Essay by Colonel von Sandrart of the Luftwaffe on the Tactical Use of the *Grossbatterie* in German A/A Defenses," no date, 4, box 13, RG 38, NA.

74. Report of interrogation, von Sandrart, 29 May 1945, 1.

75. Ibid., 2.

76. Werrell, *Blankets of Fire*, 181.

77. Report no. M-522, subject "Internal Situation, Japan," 1 February 1945, OSS, box 89, RG 226, NA.

78. Report of interrogation, von Sandrart, 25 May 1945, 1.

79. USSBS interview no. 59, Karl Dönitz, 7 July 1945, published reports and supporting records, box 723, RG 243, NA.

80. "Essay by Colonel von Sandrart," no date.

81. Ibid., 9 June 1945. General Kessler reported that there were at least two anti-aircraft officers from the Imperial Army and one from the Imperial Navy present in Berlin.

82. Report of interrogation, von Sandrart, 29 May 1945, "Information on the General Reorganization of the Entire Air Raid Warning Net," 1.
83. Ibid., 1–2.
84. Ibid.
85. Ibid., 4.
86. Speed and ceiling figures from Dear and Foot, eds., *Oxford Companion*, 145.
87. Price, *Luftwaffe Data Book*, 232. The Mosquito's maximum ceiling of 11,887 meters (39,000 feet) placed it easily out of the reach of Germany's biggest antiaircraft gun, the 12.8-centimeter Flak 40, which had a maximum engagement altitude of 10,668 meters (35,000 feet).
88. Report of interrogation, von Sandrart, 29 May 1945, "Information on Reorganization," 4.
89. "Essay by Colonel von Sandrart of the Luftwaffe on the Tactical Use of the *Grossbatterie.*"
90. Ibid. The original design for the *Grossbatterie* system called for eight 8.8-caliber and six 10.5-caliber guns; however, because of the shortage of guns, this scale was achieved only in high-priority areas such as Berlin.
91. Ibid.
92. Ibid., 1–5.
93. Memorandum, "Cargo aboard 1600 Ton German Submarine," 1–2.
94. Interroom conversation, von Sandrart, 15 June 1945, 1145–1700 hours, box 535, RG 165, NA.
95. Ibid., 15 July 1945, 1930–2230 hours.

Chapter 7. Dönitz's Naval Mission

1. "Minutes of the Conference of the Commander in Chief, Navy, with the *Führer*," 3 December 1944, in *Führer Conferences on Naval Affairs, 1939–1945* (Annapolis, Md.: Naval Institute Press, 1990), 420.
2. Report of interrogation, Gerhard Falcke, 24 May 1945, box 466, RG 165, NA.
3. "Prisoner of War Report, Gerhard Falcke," 21 May 1945, box 466, RG 165, NA; report of interrogation, Falcke, 24 May 1945. ONI interrogators related that Falcke did not attempt to "hide his Nazi leanings" from them. Falcke insisted that Hitler was "an inspiring leader" but had surrounded himself with incompetents, and therein lay the failure of German National Socialism.
4. Report of interrogation, Falcke, 24 May 1945.
5. Ibid.
6. Ibid. The powers that sent technical representatives to Berlin were Russia, Spain, Italy, Bulgaria, Romania, and Japan.
7. Ibid.
8. Essay, Gerhard Falcke, "Zusammenarbeit der deutsch und japanischen Kriegsmarine" [Agreement between the German and Japanese Navies], no date, box 466, RG 165, NA.
9. "Prisoner of War Report, Gerhard Falcke," 24 May 1945. Falcke claimed that he was one of the few German naval officers proficient in technical matters, and it was for this reason that he had been selected for the mission to Japan.

10. Report of interrogation, Falcke, 22 May 1945, 1.
11. Ibid.
12. Ibid., 5.
13. Report of interrogation, Kay Nieschling, 24 May 1945, box 522, RG 165, NA.
14. "Zusammenarbeit der deutsch und japanischen Kriegsmarine," 2.
15. Ibid., 4.
16. Ibid.
17. Ibid.
18. Letter, Nomura Naokuni to Gerhard Falcke, 31 July 1941, box 466, RG 165, NA.
19. "Zusammenarbeit der deutsch und japanischen Kriegsmarine," 3, 2.
20. Report of interrogation, Falcke, 24 May 1945.
21. "Zusammenarbeit der deutsch und japanischen Kriegsmarine," 3.
22. Ibid. 4. Two such sensitive items that were not revealed to the Japanese were "those methods employed in conquering the Belgian Fort Eben-Emael and the actual depth to which German submarines could dive."
23. Ibid., 3.
24. "Prisoner of War Report, Gerhard Falcke," 21 May 1945, 2.
25. Report, "Captured German Documents, Accession List," 5 July 1945, box 4, RG 38, NA. The documents assigned to Falcke were labeled as property of the OKM and were of sufficient intelligence value that the ONI classified them as priority "A."
26. Report of interrogation, Falcke, 24 May 1945, 5.
27. Report, "Captured German Documents, Accession List," 4. Included in the list of patents going to Japanese industry were those from German industrial giants such as Krupp, Zeiss, E. Müller, I. G. Farben, Electroacustic, Junkers, and Lorenz.
28. "Arbeitsverhältnisse im Referat A V f," 22 November 1939, box 466, RG 165, NA.
29. Memoranda, 18 November 1941 and 23 March 1942, box 466, RG 165, NA.
30. "Arbeitsverhältnisse im Referat A V f."
31. Letter, Hermann Lange to Falcke, 28 September 1943, box 466, RG 165, NA.
32. Letter, Lange to Falcke, 14 April 1944, box 466, RG 165, NA. Falcke listed understaffing and a "bad secretary" as the primary reasons for his office's inefficiency.
33. Report of interrogation, Falcke, 18 June 1945.
34. Memorandum, Lt. Col. Earl L. Edwards, Provost Marshal General's Office, to commanding general, First Service Command, subject "Transfer of German Navy Prisoners of War," 18 May 1945, box 1376, RG 389, NA. Upon their arrival in Portsmouth, *U-234*'s crew were all sent to the navy's holding enclosure at Fort Meade, pending final disposition to various POW camps.
35. Memorandum, Col. A. F. Tollefson to commanding general, Eighth Service Command, 27 August 1945, box 1376, RG 389, NA.
36. Memorandum, Lt. Col. Detlow M. Marthinson, Eighth Service Command, to commanding general, Army Service Forces, 14 December 1945, box 1376, RG 389, NA. The Ruston facility was resigned to surplus status on 31 January 1946.

37. Robert S. Allen, "Post-war U-Boat Yielded Top Scientists on Hot Errand," *New York Post*, 25 November 1949, 41.
38. Report of interrogation, Richard Bulla, 24 May 1945, 1, box 456, RG 165, NA.
39. Ibid.
40. Edwin P. Hoyt, *Raider 16* (New York: World, 1970), 72.
41. Ibid., 108.
42. Edward P. Von der Porten, *The German Navy in World War II* (New York: Thomas Y. Crowell, 1969), 134.
43. Report of interrogation, Bulla, 24 May 1945, 1.
44. Ibid., 2.
45. United States Naval Intelligence, *German Naval Vessels of World War II* (Annapolis, Md.: Naval Institute Press, 1993), 204.
46. Clark G. Reynolds, "Hitler's Flattop: The End of the Beginning," U.S. Naval Institute *Proceedings* 113 (January 1967): 48.
47. Report of interrogation, Bulla, 24 May 1945, 2. Commenting on his being the first German officer sent to Japan, Bulla informed ONI interrogators that the Japanese "had always been very secretive about their naval air force."
48. During his interrogations, Nieschling even identified the weapons that the Nazis were developing. Report of interrogation, Nieschling, 23 May 1945, 2.
49. Report of interrogation, Bulla, 15 May 1945.
50. Ibid.; Robert C. Mikesh, *Japanese Aircraft: Code Names and Designations* (Atglen, Pa.: Schiffer Aviation and Military History, 1993), 156–58. Japan had already produced copies of the ME 262 and 163. The Japanese variant of the ME 262, the navy's Nakajima Kikka, flew only one successful flight during the war; its ME 163 counterpart, the J8M1 Mitsubishi Shushui, flew only in glider prototypes.
51. Interroom conversation, Bulla and Hellendorn, 25 May 1945, 0740–1145 hours, box 456, RG 165, NA.
52. Ibid., 6 June 1945, 1930–2300 hours.
53. Ibid., 5 June 1945, 1145–1700 hours.
54. Report of interrogation, Heinrich Hellendorn, 22 May 1945, 2, 1, file "Hellendorn, Heinrich," box 482, RG 165, NA.
55. Ibid., 1.
56. Ibid.
57. Interroom conversation, Bulla and Hellendorn, 27 May 1945, 1205 hours.
58. Ibid., 28 June 1945, 1930–2300 hours.
59. Ibid., 24 May 1945, 1145–1700 hours.
60. Ibid. 0730–1200 hours.
61. Report of interrogation, Bulla, 24 May 1945, 2.
62. Interroom conversation, Bulla and Hellendorn, 5 June 1945, 1900 hours.
63. Ibid., 24 May 1945, 0730–1200 hours.
64. Report of interrogation, Nieschling, 21 May 1945.
65. Ibid., 23 May 1945, 1.
66. Ibid., 21 May 1945, 2; ibid., 23 May 1945, 1. From March to August 1940 Nieschling served in Norway as a member of the staff of an Admiral Schenk.

67. Ibid., 23 May 1945, 1.
68. Memorandum, OP-16-Z to OP-16-PT, subject "Passengers on *U-234*, Now Prisoners of War, Available for Interrogation," 29 May 1945, 2, box 13, RG 38, NA.
69. Gordon W. Prange, *Target Tokyo: The Story of the Sorge Spy Ring* (New York: McGraw-Hill Books, 1984), xiii.
70. Sorge quoted in Andrew Christopher and Oleg Gordievsky, *KGB: The Inside Story of Its Foreign Operations from Lenin to Gorbachev* (New York: Harper Collins, 1990), 176.
71. Independent room conversation, Nieschling, 31 May 1945, 1930–2245 hours, 1, 2. One of Nieschling's contacts in the OKM was Grand Admiral Karl Dönitz. After the failed 20 July 1944 attempt on Hitler's life, Dönitz summoned Nieschling to discuss the extent of the OKM's involvement in the putsch.
72. Memorandum, "Passengers on *U-234*," 2.
73. Independent room conversation, Nieschling and von Humman, 20 June 1945, 0730–1200 hours, 1, box 522, RG 165, NA; ibid., 12 June 1945, 2115–2130 hours. Nieschling stated that *Mein Kampf* "was the book of the times," answering every question in a "most clear and explicit manner."
74. Ibid., 20 June 1945, 0730–1200 hours.
75. Ibid., 12 June 1945, 1900 hours; ibid., 31 May 1945, 1600–1700 hours. "Were-wolf" refers to postwar Nazi resistance in occupied Germany. Never a force of much consequence, Werewolf members engaged in small-scale terrorism and assassination. The Nazi presence in some U.S. POW camps was infamous for its summary justice; those considered unfaithful to Hitler were often murdered by their fellow prisoners.
76. Ibid., 20 June 1045, 0730–1200 hours.
77. Report of interrogation, Nieschling, 11 June 1945. Von Baumbach became a political embarrassment and a liability because of his friendship with Graf von Schulenberg, who was suspected of disloyalty and later implicated in the 20 July 1944 attempt on Hitler's life. As a result, von Baumbach was relieved of his position on 15 July 1944.
78. Ibid.
79. Independent room conversation, Nieschling, 31 May 1945, 1930–2245 hours.
80. Report of interrogation, Nieschling, 25 May 1945.
81. Ibid.
82. Independent room conversation, Nieschling, 31 May 1945, 1600–1700 hours; report of interrogation, Nieschling, 25 May 1945.
83. Report of interrogation, Nieschling, 25 May 1945.
84. Ibid., 8 June 1945, 1.
85. SRS 1623, 31 March 1945, 2, MDS. Nieschling's statements regarding German foodstuffs and munitions are questionable; a Vice President Puhl of the Reichsbank commented to Kojiro Kitamura of the Yokohama Specie Bank that the German people "realize that there is a shortage of food, ammunition, etc. . . . and [know] what fate is in store."
86. Report of interrogation, Nieschling, 25 May 1945.

87. SRS 1640, 17 April 1945, 4, MDS. German foreign minister Joachim von Ribbentrop informed Oshima Hiroshi that Germany would "get out of her present crisis by considerably increasing submarine warfare, and by the use of the new fighter planes."
88. Ibid.
89. Ibid., 3.
90. Report of interrogation, Nieschling, 8 June 1945, 3.
91. Ribbentrop informed Oshima that recent interrogations of captured American and British officers indicated a "rather deep-rooted antipathy toward Russia. . . . There are not a few who say that after forcing the collapse of Germany, they intend to beat up Russia." SRS 1624, 3 April 1945, A-2, MDS.
92. Report of interrogation, Nieschling, 8 June 1945, 3.
93. Ibid.
94. Ibid. Ribbentrop again told Oshima that the antipathy of the United States and England toward Russia was growing, and that they might turn on Russia after defeating Germany. SRS 1626, 3 April 1945, 1–2, MDS.
95. Report of interrogation, Nieschling, 8 June 1945, 6.
96. Independent room conversation, Nieschling, 20 June 1945, 0730–1200 hours.
97. Report of interrogation, Nieschling, 8 June 1945, 4.
98. Independent room conversation, Nieschling, 20 June 1945, 0730–1200 hours.
99. Report of interrogation, Nieschling, 8 June 1945, 4.
100. Ibid., 3.
101. Independent room conversation, Nieschling, 20 June 1945, 0730–1200 hours.
102. Report of interrogation, Nieschling, 8 June 1945, 5.
103. Ibid., 6.
104. Ibid., 5.

CHAPTER 8. THE SCIENTIST

1. Karl T. Compton, "Mission to Tokyo," *Technology Review* 4 (December 1945): 114–15. Because of its failure to investigate the advantages of modern technological warfare, Japan's military hierarchy made little use of civilian scientists, and then only under suffocating restrictions of secrecy and suspicion.
2. SRS 990, 8 June 1943, 1–2, MDS.
3. Ibid., 4.
4. Ronald Lewin, *The American Magic: Codes, Ciphers, and the Defeat of Japan* (New York: Farrar, Straus, and Giroux, 1982), 210–11.
5. Memorandum, "To Naval Attache, German Embassy, Tokyo," manifest of captured correspondence, box 3, RG 38, NA. Tokyo's population included a substantial German technical presence, as evidenced by the volume of correspondence found in *U-234*'s captured mailbags to and from various engineers and engineering firms.
6. SRS 1546, 13 January 1945, 4, MDS.
7. SRS 1656, 3 May 1945, 2, MDS.

8. Memorandum, Lt. Cdr. J. H. Marchant to Rear Adm. Luis de Flores, subject "German Scientific Personnel, Russian Exploitation Of," 2 January 1945, box 1, RG 181, NANY.
9. Memorandum, Marchant to de Flores, 14 December 1945, box 1, RG 181, NANY.
10. Memorandum, H. Struve Hensel to Robert P. Patterson, 2 January 1946, box 1, RG 181, NANY.
11. Michel Bar-Zohar, *La Chasse aux savants allemands* [The Hunt for German Scientists] (Paris: Librairie Arthème Fayard, 1965), 120.
12. Naval message, Headquarters G-2, Communications Zone, ETO, Paris, to WAR 36356, 21 July 1945, box 6, RG 181, NANY.
13. Bar-Zohar, *La Chasse*, 121.
14. Compton, "Mission," 118.
15. Memorandum, OP-16-Z to OP-16-PT, subject "Passengers on *U-234*, Now Prisoners of War, Available for Interrogation," 29 May 1945, 2, box 13, RG 38, NA.
16. Letter, Heinz Schlicke (Milwaukee, Wisc.) to author, 22 October 1996. Schlicke, who now resides in the United States, recalled being fed by American Quaker relief workers in Germany after the war; he "walked several miles twice a week for a mug of hot chocolate and two fresh rolls."
17. Memorandum, "Passengers on *U-234*," 2.
18. Letter, Schlicke to author, 22 October 1996.
19. Report of interrogation, Heinz Schlicke, 22 May 1945, 1, box 540, RG 165, NA.
20. Letter, Schlicke to author, 22 October 1996. Widely considered the best authority on communications technique, Kuepfmueller was the director of the research division of the Siemens Central Laboratories.
21. Report of interrogation, Schlicke, 8 June 1945.
22. Ibid.
23. "Liste der Japaner, mit denen Dr. Ing. Schlicke in Beruehrung gekommen ist bzw. kommen sollte," 31 August 1945, box 540, RG 165, NA.
24. Report of interrogation, Schlicke, 22 May 1945. After his assignment to Wennecker's staff, Schlicke was alerted "numerous times" throughout November and December of his impending departure; however, because of the changing nature of *U-234*'s mission, he did not leave Europe until April 1945.
25. Ibid.
26. Report, "Captured German Documents, Accession List," 5 July 1945, 4, box 4, RG 38, NA.
27. "Preliminary Report on Interrogation of General Ulrich Kessler," 30 May 1945, 11, file "Kessler, Ulrich," box 495, RG 165, NA.
28. Memorandum, chief of naval operations to distribution list, "Plans for Extended Exploitation of German Scientists," 21 February 1946, box 56/C/R54, NHC. In anticipation of the arrival of German scientists, the chief of naval intelligence devised a rating system to segregate scientists on the basis of their value. Category I consisted of those scientists "who have demonstrated scientific talents . . . of unique value to the Navy Department."

29. Letter, Schlicke to author, 16 December 1996.
30. Heinz Schlicke, "A Short Report on Training, Knowledge, and Preparation for Special Duties in Japan," appendix 3, "My Duties in Japan," no date, box 540, RG 165, NA.
31. Report of interrogation, Schlicke, 8 June 1945, 2.
32. Schlicke, "Short Report."
33. Ibid.
34. Memorandum, "Passengers on *U-234*," 3.
35. Schlicke, "Short Report."
36. F. H. Hinsley, *British Intelligence in the Second World War,* abridged ed. (Cambridge: Cambridge University Press, 1993), 602.
37. Memorandum, Lt. (jg) John G. Faron, USNR, to Capt. G. R. Phelan, USN, subject "Cargo aboard 1600 Ton German Submarine at Portsmouth, New Hampshire, Partial List Of," 29 May 1945, box 4, RG 38, NA.
38. Schlicke, "Short Report," appendix 2, no. 1. The Goliath was Germany's longest-wave transmitter, with an estimated 500 kilowatts of radiated power.
39. Letter, Heinz Schlicke to Harry Cooper (Fox Lake, Ill.), 11 March 1993.
40. Minutes of meeting, Schlicke and ONI, no date, box 6, RG 38, NA.
41. Report of interrogation, Schlicke, 4 June 1945.
42. Transcript, "First Lecture Given by Dr. Schlicke at the Navy Department," 19 July 1945, RG 38, box 13, NA.
43. Report of interrogation, Schlicke, 8 June 1945.
44. Ibid.
45. Letter, Schlicke to Cooper, 11 March 1993.
46. Letter, Schlicke to author, 16 December 1996. Schlicke repeatedly referred to Barkhausen as "the famous Dr. Barkhausen"; he was also known as the "Electron Jesus." It was Barkhausen who initially informed Schlicke of the Japanese ferrite research.
47. Ibid. This early research into the potential masking value of ferritic material initiated further investigations, the cumulative results of which led to today's stealth technology.
48. Schlicke, "Short Report," appendix 9, no. 15.
49. Report, "Japan-Unterrichtung über TV und Erprobungen," 19 September 1944, box 6, RG 38, NA.
50. "Report to the Japanese Concerning Absorption Material against Supersonics by Dr. Kneser," no date, 15, "Lectures on the Present Conditions of the *Fernlenk Technik*," fall 1943 through spring 1944, box 711, RG 165, NA.
51. ASDIC is an acronym for Allied Submarine Detection Investigation Committee, which in 1917 began to investigate the use of sound waves for locating submerged submarines. In 1943 the U.S. Navy developed a similar system, which it called Sonar.
52. "Report to the Japanese."
53. "Report by Dr. Kuepfmueller: Geometric Shapes for the Prevention of Detection by Radar or Supersonic Radiation," no date, 13, box 6, RG 181, NANY.
54. Ibid.

55. Report of interrogation, Schlicke, 8 June 1945.
56. Ibid., 4 June 1945.
57. Ibid., subject "Evaporograph," 15 August 1945.
58. Schlicke, "Short Report," appendix 2, no. 31.
59. Report of interrogation, Schlicke, 4 June 1945, 4–5.
60. Ibid., "Flamingo I," 19 August 1945.
61. Ibid., "Flamingo II," 21 August 1945.
62. Ibid., "Flamingo III."
63. Ibid., 4 June 1945, 3.
64. Ibid., 4.
65. Letter, Schlicke to author, 16 December 1996.
66. Memorandum, OP-16-Z to OP-16-PT, subject "Lectures to Be Given by Dr. Schlicke," 11 July 1945, box 540, RG 165, NA.
67. Bar-Zohar, *La Chasse*, 140.
68. "Negatives of Sketches 8–11 of Schlicke's Lecture," box 13, RG 38, NA.
69. JOIA report, "Heinz Schlicke," 26 March 1947, file "Status of Aliens 1947–1950," box 1, RG 181, NANY.
70. Bar-Zohar, *La Chasse*, 129. The initial number of German scientists to be extradited to the United States was three hundred. However, the number that was reported to the American public was substantially smaller to counter the lingering effects of wartime propaganda, particularly fears about "bringing German militarism to the United States."
71. Report by Lt. Cdr. J. H. Marchant, USNR, "Part IV—Guided Missiles," no date, exploitation lists 1945–51, box 6, RG 181, NANY.
72. Letter, Massachusetts Institute of Technology to Cdr. H. G. Dyke, 18 August 1945, box 6, RG 181, NANY; F. H. Hinsley, *British Intelligence in the Second World War: Its Influence on Strategy and Operations* (London: Her Majesty's Stationary Office, 1979–88), vol. 3, pt. 1, 516n. The Allies, of course, were not ignorant of the uses of infrared technology. The most effective Allied application was in the detection of U-boats, whose Metox receivers emitted detectable radiation. In 1943, upon learning of this, Dönitz ordered the removal of all Metox receivers, and priority was given to the development of the Hagenuk, a nonradiating receiver.
73. Letter, chief, Bureau of Aeronautics, to Lt. Cdr. W. H. van Benschoten, Special Devices, Office of Research and Inventions, subject "Request for Establishment of TED ORI-3105: Theoretical Investigation of the Possibilities of Radar Camouflage for Pilotless Aircraft," 24 October 1945, box 5, RG 181, NANY.
74. Memorandum, Lt. C. V. S. Roosevelt, USNR, to Lt. Cdr. W. H. van Benschoten, subject "Additional Personnel for Project 77," 26 September 1945, box 6, RG 181, NANY.
75. Memorandum, Lt. Cdr. W. H. van Benschoten to chief of naval operations, attention OP-23-PT, subject "Alien Personnel for Project 77, Request For," 31 October 1945, box 6, RG 181, NANY.
76. Memorandum, Rear Adm. H. G. Bowen to the provost marshal general of the army, War Department, 1 November 1945, box 6, RG 181, NANY.

77. Memorandum, Lt. Kermit Lansner, USNR, to officer in charge, Special Devices Division, Sands Point, New York, subject "Project 77, Developments Affecting," 30 April 1946, box 1, RG 181, NANY. The project was called Paperclip after the paperclips that were attached to personnel files to identify an alien as acceptable.

78. Memorandum, "Plans for Extended Exploitation," 1.

79. Clarence G. Lasby, *Project Paperclip: German Scientists and the Cold War* (New York: Atheneum, 1971), 184; memorandum, chief of naval operations to distribution list, "Exchange of Technical Intelligence," 4 October 1945, 1, box 56/C/R45, NHC. With the influx of German scientists and their inventions, American military intelligence officers weighed the wisdom of sharing the most sensitive items with their Soviet allies, who were likewise collecting German scientists. As a result, German technical intelligence was divided into two categories: information that could be revealed to the Soviets and that to which Soviet access would be denied. An 11 October memorandum from Gen. Dwight D. Eisenhower to the chief of naval intelligence reiterated the importance of denying the Soviets access to German technology.

80. JOIA report, "Heinz Schlicke." Schlicke's primary work centered on the "Theoretical Investigation of Radar Camouflage of Air Missiles by the Absorption Method" and "Investigation of Intercept Antenna Techniques over the Electro-magnetic Radiation Range from Forty Megacycles through the Infrared Spectrum."

81. Memorandum, R. W. Weber, CO, Operations and Personnel Division, 23 August 1950, box 1, RG 181, NANY.

82. Letter, Schlicke to author, 22 October 1996.

Chapter 9. The Men from Messerschmitt

1. Jerome B. Cohen, *Japan's Economy in War and Reconstruction* (Minneapolis: University of Minnesota Press, 1949), 244, 215, 216.

2. "Captured German Documents: Synopsis, Japanese Aircraft Industry," USSBS, 97, file 1a (11), roll 2, microcopy M-1655, RG 243, NA.

3. Ibid.

4. Ibid., 99, 100.

5. Ibid., 97. Because of the infancy of its aircraft industry, Japan's manufacturing capability was limited to production capacity since it did not enjoy the extensive production procedures of contemporaries such as Germany, England, and the United States.

6. Alan S. Milward, *War, Economy, and Society, 1939–1945* (Berkeley: University of California Press, 1977), 34. Milward points out that with the possible exception of the Soviet Union, Japan had the highest share of its population devoted to agriculture, a full 50 percent at the beginning of the war.

7. "Captured German Documents," USSBS, 99.

8. Ibid., 101, 97.

9. Ibid., 97.

10. Ibid., 143, 145.

11. SRS 612, 27 May 1942, 2, MDS, reel 1. It is probable that this reference concerns the highly effective Focke-Wulf, rather than the Fokker, 190.
12. SRS 801, 9 December 1942, supplement E1, MDS, reel 3.
13. SRS 847, 24 January 1943, 1–2, MDS, box 1. In a footnote to the MAGIC encrypt, the British Air Ministry noted that it had no intelligence regarding either the ME 309 or the ME 264.
14. SRS 950, 29 April 1943, 2, MDS, box 2.
15. SRS 1141, 7 December 1943, 6, MDS, box 6.
16. SRS 1254, 28 March 1944, 11, MDS, box 7.
17. SRS 1288, 1 May 1944, 1, MDS, box 7.
18. SRS 1254, 28 March 1944, 12, MDS, box 7.
19. Interview, Willi Messerschmitt, "Aircraft Plans Given to Japan," 28 June 1945, 1, file "Japanese-German Cooperation, Consolidated Interrogation Report," box 721A, RG 165, NA.
20. SRS 1254, 28 March 1944, 11, MDS, box 7. Otani claimed to have a clandestine source within the Messerschmitt Company. He also asserted that the Japanese military attaché in Berlin was "on excellent terms with Dr. Messerschmitt's right-hand man."
21. SRS 1288, 1 May 1944, 2, in MDS, reel 9.
22. Memorandum, Col. Russell H. Sweet to Division of Naval Intelligence, attention Capt. John L. Riheldaffer, subject "Captured Documents and Interrogation of Personnel on German Submarine *U-234*," 1, file "Miscellaneous," box 3, RG 38, NA.
23. Report of interrogation, August Bringewald and Franz Ruf, 25 May 1945, 1, file "*U-234:* Interrogations 1944–45," box 13, RG 38, NA.
24. Memorandum, "Captured Documents and Interrogation," 1. The third submarine, *U-876* (Bahn), was scheduled to deliver the ME 410 and ME 323 and other Messerschmitt engineers; however, Germany surrendered before *U-876* could depart Kiel.
25. F. H. Hinsley, *British Intelligence in the Second World War: Its Influence on Strategy and Operations* (London: Her Majesty's Stationary Office, 1979–88), vol. 3, pt. 2, p. 332.
26. Office of Strategic Services intelligence report RB-8022, subject "New Airplane," 13 January 1944, file "Confidential Correspondence, 1922–1944," box 428, RG 72, NA.
27. Ibid., notation handwritten on back of report.
28. OSS intelligence report T2192, 5 August 1944, file "Confidential Correspondence, 1922–1944," box 428, RG 72, NA.
29. SRS 1254, 28 March 1944, MDS.
30. SRS 1288, 1 May 1944, MDS.
31. Report, Capt. S. B. Spangler, Power Plant Design Branch, to Air Technical Intelligence (OP-16-VT), subject "Comparison between German and Japanese Aircraft, Recommendations For," 27 November 1944, file "Confidential Correspondence, 1922–1944," box 428, RG 72, NA. Spangler went on to suggest a comparison of various German and Japanese aircraft to "determine whether such a trend is not already visible."

32. Memorandum, Naval Bureau of Aeronautics, subject "Information on Japanese Instruments," 24 July 1945, file EF37, RDO, ConCor, box 93, RG 72, NA. Allied suspicions as to the extent of Japanese incorporation of German avionics were evidenced by the listing of "performance data, jet propulsion or pulse jet units, [or] propulsion for rocket bombs or missiles" at the Yokosuka Air Technical Training School on a July 1945 target summary.

33. Memorandum, OP-16-Z to OP-16-PT, subject "Passengers on *U-234*, Now Prisoners of War, Available for Interrogation," 29 May 1945, 3, box 13, RG 38, NA.

34. Report of interrogation, Bringewald and Ruf, 25 May 1945, 1.

35. Report of interrogation, August Bringewald, 22 May 1945, file "Bringewald, August," box 454, RG 165, NA.

36. Ibid., 5 July 1945.

37. Ibid.

38. Ibid., 22 May 1945. Although Bringewald was unaware of Japan's intentions concerning the ME 163, the Japanese received plans for the aircraft in 1943 and had actually test-flown their own prototype in December 1944.

39. Ibid., 3.

40. Ibid., 14 July 1945, 3.

41. Ibid.

42. Interroom conversation, Bringewald, 28 May 1945, 1145–1715 hours, 1, box 454, RG 165, NA.

43. Ibid., 2.

44. Report of interrogation, Franz Ruf, 5 June 1945, file "Ruf, Franz," box 534, RG 165, NA.

45. Ibid.

46. Memorandum, Cdr. B. R. Roeder to OP-20-3-GI-A, attention Captain Phelan, "Contract between Messerschmitt and Mr. Franz Ruf," 1 December 1945, translated 26 May 1945, file "Memo Series," box 5, RG 38, NA.

47. Report of interrogation, Bringewald and Ruf, 25 May 1945, 1–2.

48. Ibid., 2.

49. Ibid.

50. Ibid.

51. Hugh Morgan, *ME 262: Stormbird Rising* (London: Reed Consumer Books, 1994), 207. Actually, the Japanese were farther advanced in jet aircraft research than previously believed. On 6 August 1945 the Nakajima J9Y1, or Kikka, a smaller variation of the ME 262, made its initial test flight. The Kikka may have been a version of the ME 262, but in the words of the Army Air Corps' Gen. Harold Watson, it "wasn't a very good one."

52. Report of interrogation, Bringewald and Ruf, 25 May 1945, 3, 4. Bringewald and Ruf could state their assumptions with relative certainty; the Japanese had signed contracts with the Messerschmitt and Junkers aircraft companies only.

53. Ibid., 2.

54. Elizabeth-Anne Wheal, Stephen Pope, and James Taylor, eds., *Encyclopedia of the Second World War* (Edison, N.J.: Castle Books, 1989), 302. The ME 163, or Komet, initially flew in 1941 as an experimental aircraft. After extensive

avionic and armament revisions that rendered the ME 163 combat-capable, it was deployed to equip German home defense units in 1944 and made its debut on 14 August by attacking American B-17 bombers.

55. Eric Brown, *Wings of the Luftwaffe: Flying German Aircraft of the Second World War* (London: MacDonald and Jane's, 1977), 168.

56. Report of interrogation, Bringewald and Ruf, 25 May 1945, 3.

57. Ibid.; Dennis Piszkiewicz, *The Nazi Rocketeers: Dreams of Space and Crimes of War* (Westport, Conn.: Praeger, 1995), 73. Hitler's insistence that the ME 262 be used as a low-altitude bomber, rather than in the fighter-interceptor role for which it was intended, seriously hampered the aircraft's efficiency. In addition, by March 1944 Hitler had become convinced that the V- (vengeance-) weapons, particularly the new V-2 missile, would turn the tide of the war in Germany's favor, and he therefore placed V-2 production ahead of the ME 262 as the top armaments priority. On 13 June 1942 armaments minister Albert Speer witnessed both the successful initial flights of the ME 163 and the unsuccessful first launch of the V-2. The High Command's belief that the V-weapons, rather than jet aircraft, would ultimately save Germany is reflected in Speer's memoirs, in which he repeatedly refers to the V-2 while neglecting to mention the ME 163 test flights. Albert Speer, *Inside the Third Reich* (New York: Macmillan, 1970), 368.

58. Piszkiewicz, *Nazi Rocketeers*, 120.

59. Report of interrogation, Bringewald and Ruf, 25 May 1945, 4. Bringewald's and Ruf's opinions were corroborated by Kay Nieschling, who stated that the Japanese had possessed rocket information "for a long time." Report of interrogation, Kay Nieschling, 24 May 1945, box 522, RG 165, NA.

60. Report of interrogation, Bringewald and Ruf, 25 May 1945, 4. See also report of interrogation, Ulrich Kessler, 7 June 1945, 4, box 495, RG 165, NA. Kessler recalled a conversation with naval attaché Koshima in Berlin in which Koshima revealed Japanese fears that the Americans, who supposedly had seventy-five thousand rockets under construction, planned to use them against the home islands. The Japanese, on the other hand, planned to use the V-1/V-2s to drive the Americans from Japan's vast Southwest Pacific possessions, particularly the Philippines.

61. Letter, Wolfgang Hirschfeld (Plön, Germany) to author, 4 February 1996. Whether the ME 262 that Bringewald presented was the same one that had been on board the *U-234* is unknown. However, because of the timeliness of the presentation, the general assumption is that it was the same one, and that Bringewald had directed the assembly of it.

62. Memorandum, Col. A. F. Tollefson to commanding general, Eighth Service Command, Dallas, Texas, subject "Transfer of German Prisoners of War," 14 August 1945, box 1376, RG 389, NA.

63. Letter, August Bringewald (Dayton, Ohio) to Wolfgang Hirschfeld (Plön, Germany), 15 April 1988, UBA.

64. Directive, Office of the Secretary of War to Office of the Provost Marshal General, 17 December 1945, box 1376, RG 389, NA.

65. Memorandum, Tollefson to commanding officer, Fifth Service Command, Columbus, Ohio, 9 April 1946, box 1376, RG 389, NA.
66. Memorandum, Tollefson to commanding general, First Army Area, 17 June 1946, box 1376, RG 389, NA.
67. Letter, Bringewald to Hirschfeld, 15 April 1988.
68. Interview, Dr. Peter Bringewald (Dallas, Texas) with author, 29 April 1998.

CONCLUSION

1. Directive, CNO to CINCLANT, COMSUBSLANT, COMEASTSEAFRON, 19 May 1945, box 20, RG 298, NA.
2. Directive, CNO to naval districts and departments, subject "Inspections and Tests of Surrendered German Submarines," 28 May 1945, box 20, RG 298, NA.
3. Ibid.
4. Letter, Lt. Cdr. H. G. Dyke to Dr. Irwin Stewart, 29 May 1945, box 20, RG 298, NA.
5. Memorandum, BuShips to CNO, subject "Recommendations for Trials and Tests of Surrendered German Submarines," 23 June 1945, box 20, RG 298, NA.
6. Letter, Dr. Julian K. Knipp to Lt. Cdr. H. G. Dyke, 29 June 1945, box 20, RG 298, NA.
7. Memorandum, commander, Special Submarine Group, New London, Connecticut, to commander, U.S. Atlantic Fleet, 21 February 1946, box 20, RG 298, NA. To ensure that *U-858*, *U-873*, and *U-234* would remain operational for the entirety of the tests, the CNO granted permission to "cannibalize" *U-805* and *U-1228* for spare parts; see memorandum, CNO to naval districts and departments, subject "Trials and Tests of Surrendered German Submarines," 30 June 1945, box 20, RG 298, NA. The Type IXC *U-858* was sunk in 1947 during U.S. Navy torpedo trials; the Type IXD/2 *U-873* was towed to New York City in 1948, where she was sold for scrap; and the Type XXI *U-2513* sailed to the Dry Tortugas, where she was destroyed during rocket firing tests in 1951. The fifth submarine was the Type IXC U-505, which, after a War Bond fundraising tour, was bought by the Museum of Science and Industry in Chicago. Dedicated in September 1955, she remains on display at the museum to this day.
8. Memorandum, commander, Special Submarine Group, New London, Connecticut, to commander, U.S. Atlantic Fleet, 10 June 1946, box 20, RG 298, NA.
9. John E. Moore, ed., *Jane's Pocket Book of Major Warships* (New York: Macmillan, 1973), 44.
10. Letter, Lt. Paul C. Stroup (Pensacola, Fla.) to author, 23 March 1998.
11. Letter, Myron R. Prevatte (Whigham, Ga.) to author, 17 February 1998.
12. Saburo Ienaga, *Taiheiyo Senso* [The Pacific War] (Tokyo: Iwanami Shoten, 1968), 107, 109.
13. Ibid., 138.
14. SRS 1645, 22 April 1945, MDS.
15. SRS 1656, 3 May 1945, MDS.
16. Secretary of War James Forrestal to Secretary of State James F. Byrnes, 29 January 1946, box 1, RG 181, NANY. See also, for example, memorandum, Lt. Cdr.

J. H. Marchant to Rear Adm. Luis de Flores, subject "German Scientific Personnel, Russian Exploitation Of," 2 January 1945, box 1, RG 181, NANY; and memorandum, unnamed to Dr. Vannevar Bush, January 1946, box 1, RG 181, NANY.

APPENDIX

1. Memorandum, Lt. (jg) John G. Faron, USNR, to Capt. G. R. Phelan, subject "Cargo aboard 1600-Ton German Submarine at Portsmouth, New Hampshire, Partial List Of," 29 May 1945, box 4, RG 38, NA.

2. "Manifest of Cargo for Tokio [*sic*] on Board *U-234*," translated 23 May 1945, NHC, microfiche.

3. Kawashima Toranosuke quoted in Robert K. Wilcox, *Japan's Secret War: Japan's Race against Time to Build Its Own Atomic Bomb* (New York: Marlowe and Co., 1995), 101.

4. Japanese army attaché message translation, SRA 1576, 7 July 1943, box 2, RG 457, NA. The Japanese required radium for its medicinal value, for its phosphorescent qualities, and for the manufacture of butanol, an industrial alcohol.

5. Japanese army attaché message, SRA 4221, 1 September 1943, box 2, RG 457, NA.

6. Letter, Dr. Kigoshi Kunihiko (Tokyo) to author, 7 August 1998.

7. Letter, Dr. Helmet Rechenberg (Munich) to author, 25 February 1999.

8. Japanese army attaché message, SRA 6420, 15 November 1943, box 2, RG 457, NA. Although the translated document reads 1 kilogram (2.2 pounds), subsequent messages reveal this to be a typographical error. The actual request was for 100 kilograms (221 pounds).

9. Japanese army attaché message, SRA 5501, 20 November 1943, box 2, RG 457, NA.

10. Letter, Kigoshi Kunihiko to author, 7 August 1998. Because of strict security, as well as the lingering mistrust between the two Axis partners, neither brother knew of the other's involvement in the uranium transfer until after the war.

11. Gen. Kawashima Toranosuke quoted in Wilcox, *Japan's Secret War*, 104.

12. Ibid. In his 1980 interview with Robert Wilcox, Kawashima declared that the Germans agreed to supply the Japanese with 2 tons of uranium oxide. However, the 20 November wire from Oshima was the only documented mention of a quantity, and because of the division of the cargo aboard two submarines in 500-kilogram (1,100-pound) loads, it appears more likely that the shipped quantity was actually 1 ton (900 kilograms).

13. Carl Boyd and Yoshida Akihiko, *The Japanese Submarine Force and World War II* (Annapolis, Md.: Naval Institute Press, 1995), 132. Ro-501 was in her second incarnation; she had previously been *U-1224* and was transferred to the Japanese at Kiel on 28 February 1944. Her Japanese crew had arrived in Germany the year before aboard I-8. General Kawashima, Maj. Kigoshi Yasukazu, and Kigoshi Kunihiko later confirmed that Ro-501 was sunk in the Atlantic in May 1944.

14. Letter, Kigoshi Kunihiko to author, 7 August 1998.

15. John W. Dower, *Japan in War and Peace: Selected Essays* (New York: New Press, 1993), 80.

16. "Reveal Jap Subs in Atlantic," *Manchester (N.H.) Union,* 17 May 1945, 1(A).

17. Yamamoto Yoichi quoted in Deborah Shapely, "Nuclear Weapons History: Japan's Wartime Bomb Projects Revealed," *Science* 199 (January 1978): 155. Yamamoto reiterated his acknowledgment of the uranium's arrival in Japan in a 1980 interview with author Robert Wilcox. Wilcox, *Japan's Secret War,* 104.

18. According to Dr. Jürgen Rohwer, two Japanese submarines were indeed sunk in the Atlantic by U.S. naval forces during the summer of 1944. Ro-501 was sunk on 3 May at 18°08' N, 33°13' W, by the uss *Francis M. Robinson,* and I-52 was sunk at 15°16' N, 39°55' W, by the uss *Bogue.* However, I-52 was sunk in the *South* Atlantic, thus adding mystery to the identity of the second submarine that allegedly sortied from Kiel after Ro-501.

19. Letter, Kigoshi Kunihiko to author, 7 August 1998. According to Kigoshi Kunihiko, Dr. K. Kimura of the University of Kyoto succeeded in separating uranium from rare-earth minerals; by the end of the war Kimura had separated "hundreds of kilograms [of uranium] from ore."

20. Report by the Departments of State, War, and Navy Coordinating Subcommittee for the Far East, "Disposition of Uranium Oxide Impounded by SCAP," March 1946, 47, box 1, RG 331, NA. According to a postwar inventory, Allied investigators recovered approximately 125 kilograms (275 pounds) of uranium oxide in unopened bottles, an amount deemed "of negligible importance for military purposes." A 12 April 1948 investigation (SCAP memo, 12 April 1948, box 1, RG 331, NA) further revealed the "presence of radioactive stockpiles in seventy-eight industrial concerns."

21. Letter, Capt. Kitazawa Noritaka, National Institute for Defense Studies (Tokyo), to author, 13 July 1998. Captain Kitazawa points out that the Imperial Navy intended to use the uranium oxide as a catalyst for the synthesized production of methanol, used for aircraft fuel.

22. Letter, Dr. Jürgen Rowher (Stuttgart, Germany), to author, 17 February 1998.

23. Letter, Capt. Hans-Joachim Krug (Wolfrathausen, Germany), to author, 7 August 1998. Krug, the former first watch officer aboard *U-219,* was with the German naval and defense mission in Tokyo from August 1944 until the end of the war. He returned to Germany late in 1946.

24. Interrogation of Kay Nieschling, 27 July 1945, Command File, World War II, NHC.

25. Wolfgang Hirschfeld, *Hirschfeld: The Story of a U-Boat NCO, 1940–1946,* as told to Geoffrey Brooks (Annapolis, Md.: Naval Institute Press, 1996), 199.

26. Ibid., 198–99.

27. Alexander W. Moffat, *A Navy Maverick Comes of Age* (Middletown, Conn.: Wesleyan University Press, 1978), 138.

28. Hirschfeld, *Hirschfeld,* 218.

29. Memorandum, chief of naval operations to commanding officer, Portsmouth Navy Yard, subject "Mine Tubes, Unloading Of," 27 May 1945, box 531, RG 181, NANE.

30. Memorandum, commanding officer, Portsmouth Navy Yard, to CNO, subject "Cargo *U-234,* Information On," 28 May 1945, box 531, RG 181, NANE.

31. Memorandum, "Mine Tubes, Unloading Of."

32. Interview, Karl Pfaff (Bellingham, Wash.) with Robert Wilcox, 24 February 1995.

33. Ibid.

34. Bob Norling, "Ex-U-Boat Officer Here for Visit; First Saw Portsmouth as POW," *Portsmouth (N.H.) Herald,* 9 July 1954, 1(A). Pfaff recalled that although he breathed a sigh of relief once the cylinder had been cut, he shuddered as he discovered an antiaircraft shell within inches of where the torch had cut.

35. Interview, Pfaff with Wilcox, 24 February 1995. Pfaff recalled that once the welders opened the cylinders, he noticed "a tall civilian . . . with a large hat" examining the boxes. Because the stranger was rather conspicuous, Pfaff inquired as to his identity and was told that he was "Oppenheimer." Only later, as a prisoner of war in Louisiana, did he realize that the man with the large hat might have been J. Robert Oppenheimer, director of the Manhattan Project. While it cannot be confirmed that the man Pfaff saw was Oppenheimer, the physicist was in the vicinity during late May and early June 1945. He was in Washington to attend a meeting with Henry Stimson, James F. Byrnes, and Gen. Leslie Groves and the Interim Committee; that he would travel to southern Maryland to examine a captured German stock of uranium oxide is not out of the realm of possibility.

36. Memorandum, T. F. Darrah, Ordnance Investigation Laboratory, to chief, Bureau of Ordnance, cc: Lieutenant McQuade, ONI, subject "Manifest of Cargo for Tokyo on Board *U-234,* Forwarding Of," 23 June 1945, Command File, World War II, NHC.

37. "Agenda for Washington Group Meeting," 2 July 1945, box number unknown, Manhattan Project files, RG 326, NA. The Washington Group Trust was affiliated with the army's Manhattan District, with copies of the agenda forwarded to Gen. Leslie Groves, military director of the Manhattan Project. The group's British counterpart, with which Washington maintained liaison, was known as the London Group; Groves instructed that four days prior to meetings of the Washington Group, the agenda "should be exchanged with the British."

38. Ibid. Item number 4-B concerned the possibility of securing samples of uranium oxide from Turkey; item 4-C examined German geological explorations in Sweden; item 4-D addressed a Dr. Bain's questions concerning the isotopic content of uranium; item 8 considered the "usefulness of reconnaissance photographs . . . of certain areas where uranium and thorium" might be found; item 10-B arranged a meeting between Dr. Bain and Groves; and item 10-C discussed the Belgian Union Minière mines, the future of which would determine "efficient Trust Intelligence operations."

39. John Lansdale quoted in William J. Broad, "Captured Cargo, Captivating Mystery," *New York Times,* 31 December 1995, 22(A).

40. Dr. Philip Morrison quoted in David Arnold, "The Uranium Vanishes: A Mystery of World War II," *Boston Globe,* 27 July 1993, 1(A).

41. Hirschfeld, *Hirschfeld,* 198–99. Hirschfeld states that when he asked for an explanation for the label, the Japanese replied that the cargo was originally intended to be shipped on the submarine *U-235,* which was no longer going to

Japan. Hirschfeld later discovered that *U-235* was a "small Type VII training U-Boat which had never been earmarked for operations outside the Baltic."

42. Interview, Pfaff with Wilcox, 24 February 1995.

43. Letter, Geoffrey Brooks (Torremolinos, Spain) to L. Sidney Trevethan (Anchorage, Alaska), 16 January 1999.

44. Letter, Richard Rhodes (Madison, Conn.) to author, 14 January 1999.

45. Letter, Rhodes to author, 14 January 1999.

46. Letter, Dr. Michael Thorwart (Augsburg, Germany) to author, 18 February 1999.

47. Letter, Rhodes to author, 14 January 1999.

48. Letter, Richard Thurston (Spanaway, Wash.) to L. Sidney Trevethan (Anchorage, Alaska), 31 December 1998.

49. Letter, Kigoshi Kunihiko to author, 7 August 1998.

50. Alsos mission intelligence report, H. S. Van Klooster, subject "Pyrophoric Thorium Alloys," 13 July 1945, box 92, RG 72, NA.

51. Letter, Kay Nieschling (Bonn, Germany) to Wolfgang Hirschfeld (Plön, Germany), 5 July 1984.

52. David Holloway, *Stalin and the Bomb: The Soviet Union and Atomic Energy, 1939–1956* (New Haven: Yale University Press, 1994), 110.

53. Letter, Thurston to Trevethan, 3 February 1999.

54. Letter, Thurston to author, 4 February 1999.

Bibliography

<small>PRIMARY SOURCES</small>

Archival Holdings

Bundesarchiv-Militärarchiv, Freiburg, Germany
    RM 13/1, PG 32883, Case GE 894: OKW/Ausland IV KTB Bd. II
    RM 13/3, PG 32886, Case GE 896: OKW/Ausland IV Bd. VI
Portsmouth Athenaeum, Portsmouth, N.H.
    File *"U-234"*
Portsmouth Naval Shipyard Museum and Archives, Portsmouth Naval Shipyard, Kittery, Maine
    Records of *U-234*
U-Boot Archiv, Cuxhaven-Altenbruch, Germany
    File *"U-234"*
United States National Archives, Textual Branch, College Park, Md.
    Microfilm collection:
        Microcopy M-1655: United States Strategic Bombing Survey
        Microcopy T-82, roll 92: Records of National Socialist Cultural and Research Institutions
        Microcopy T-120: Foreign Office–State Department Documents, Unit Berlin
        Microcopy T-179, roll 74: Records of German and Japanese Embassies and Consulates, 1890–1945
        Microcopy T-1022: Records of the German Navy, 1850–1945

Textual collection:
Record Group 38: Records of the Chief of Naval Operations
Record Group 72: Bureau of Aeronautics
Record Group 74: Records of the Bureau of Ordnance
Record Group 77: Records of the Manhattan Engineering District, 1942–48
Record Group 80: General Records of the Department of the Navy, 1798–1947
Record Group 165: Records of the War Department General Staff
Record Group 226: Records of the Office of Strategic Services
Record Group 243: United States Strategic Bombing Survey
Record Group 319: Records of the Army General Staff
Record Group 331: Records of the Allied Operational and Occupation Headquarters, World War II
Record Group 373: Records of the Defense Intelligence Agency
Record Group 389: Records of the Provost Marshal General
Record Group 457: MAGIC Diplomatic Summaries
United States National Archives, Northeast Region, Waltham, Mass.
Record Group 19: Records of the Bureau of Ships
Record Group 181: Records of Naval Districts and Shore Establishments (First Naval District, Portsmouth Naval Shipyard)
United States National Archives, Northeast Region, New York
Record Group 181: Records of Naval Districts and Shore Establishments (Naval Training Device Center)
United States Navy Operational Archives, Naval Historical Center, Washington Navy Yard, Washington, D.C.
Command File, World War II: Records of the Commander in Chief, Atlantic Fleet

Books

Chapman, John W. M., ed. *The Price of Admiralty: The War Diary of the German Naval Attaché in Japan, 1939–1943.* Vols. 1–4. Ripe, East Sussex: Saltire Press, 1989.

Compton, Karl T. "Mission to Tokyo." *Technology Review* 4 (December 1945): 99–120.

Dönitz, Karl. *Zehn Jahre und zwanzig Tage* [Ten Years and Twenty Days]. Bonn: Athenäum–Verlag Junker and Dünnhaupt, 1958.

Fehler, Johann, and A. V. Sellwood. *Dynamite for Hire: The Story of Hein Fehler.* London: Werner Laurie, 1956.

Führer Conferences on Naval Affairs, 1939–1945. Annapolis, Md.: Naval Institute Press, 1990.

Giese, Otto, and James F. Wise. *Shooting the War: Memoirs of a World War II U-Boat Officer.* Annapolis, Md.: Naval Institute Press, 1994.

Groves, Leslie R. *Now It Can Be Told: The Story of the Manhattan Project.* New York: Harper and Brothers, 1962.

Hirschfeld, Wolfgang. *Feindfahrten: Das Logbuch eines U-Bootfunkers* [Enemy Voyage: The Logbook of a U-Boat Radioman]. Berlin: Neuer Kaiser Verlag, 1991.

———. *Hirschfeld: The Story of a U-Boat NCO*, 1940–1946. As told to Geoffrey Brooks. Annapolis, Md.: Naval Institute Press, 1996.

———. *Das Letzte Boot: Atlantic Farewell.* Rosenheim, Germany: Deutsche Verlagsgesellschaft, 1995.

The Magic Documents: Summaries and Transcripts of the Top Secret Diplomatic Communications of Japan, 1938–1945. Washington, D.C.: University Publications of America, 1980. Microfilm.

Moffat, Alexander W. *A Navy Maverick Comes of Age.* Middletown, Conn.: Wesleyan University Press, 1978.

Naito, Hatsuho. *Ohka hijo no tokko heiki* [Thunder Gods: The Kamikaze Pilots Tell Their Story]. Tokyo: Bungei Shunju, 1982.

Speer, Albert. *Infiltration.* New York: Macmillan, 1981.

———. *Inside the Third Reich.* New York: Macmillan, 1970.

U-Boat Commander's Handbook. Gettysburg: Thomas Publications, 1989.

United States War Department. *Handbook on Japanese Military Forces.* Baton Rouge: Louisiana State University Press, 1991.

———. *Handbook on German Military Forces.* Baton Rouge: Louisiana State University Press, 1990.

Articles

Allen, Lester. "Big Hunt on for Hitler in U-Boat." *Boston Post,* 18 May 1945, 1(A).

———. "Find Three Nazi Chiefs in U-Boat." *Boston Post,* 17 May 1945, 1(A).

Allen, Robert S. "Post-war U-Boat Yielded Top Scientists on Hot Errand." *New York Post,* 25 November 1949.

Compton, Karl T. "Mission to Tokyo." *Technology Review* 4 (December 1945): 99–120.

"Fourth U-Boat Due Today." *Boston Herald,* 19 May 1945, 1(A).

Gates, Franklin M. "Officer of Prize Crew Narrates Events in Surrender of *U-234* One Year Later." *Portsmouth (N.H.) Herald,* May 1946.

"Hint Tops of Nazi Biggies Bound Here on Seized Sub." *Boston Daily Record,* 19 May 1945, 3(A).

Holt, Carlyle. "Big U-Boat Taken by US; Two Jap Suicides Aboard." Unnamed newspaper, 17 May 1945, file "*U-234* and General," Portsmouth Naval Shipyard Museum.

Kennedy, Robert G. "Nazis Won't Talk to Newsmen; Two More Subs Due." *Portsmouth (N.H.) Herald,* 16 May 1945, 1(A).

Lyons, Louis M. "Nazi Prisoners to Stay Here Awhile." *Providence (R.I.) Sunday Journal,* 13 May 1945, 4(A).

"Navy Announces Officers' Names, Not Technicians." *Portsmouth (N.H.) Herald,* 21 May 1945, 1–2.

Nishina, Yoshio. "A Japanese Scientist Describes the Destruction of His Cyclotrons." *Bulletin of the Atomic Scientists* 6 (June 1947): 145, 167.

Norling, Bob. "Ex-U-Boat Officer Here for Visit; First Saw Portsmouth as POW." *Portsmouth (N.H.) Herald*, 9 July 1954, 1(A).

"Reveal Jap Subs in Atlantic." *Manchester (N.H.) Union*, 17 May 1945, 1(A).

Shalett, Sidney M. "Huge Nazi Sub Seized in Flight to Japan; Three Luftwaffe Chiefs, Two Dead Japs Aboard." *Boston Herald*, 17 May 1945, 1–2(A).

Von Sandrart, Fritz. "The Last Trip to Japan of a German U-Boat." *Luftwaffen Review* (January/February 1971): 442–50.

SECONDARY SOURCES

Books

Andrew, Christopher, and Oleg Gordievsky. *KGB: The Inside Story of Its Foreign Operations from Lenin to Gorbachev*. New York: Harper Collins, 1990.

Bar-Zohar, Michel. *La Chasse aux savants allemands* [The Hunt for German Scientists]. Paris: Librairie Arthème Fayard, 1965.

Bekker, Cajus. *Verdammte See* [Hitler's Naval War]. Hamburg: Gerhard Stalling Verlag, 1971.

Bernstein, Jeremy. *Hitler's Uranium Club: The Secret Recordings at Farm Hall*. Woodbury, N.Y.: American Institute of Physics, 1996.

Blair, Clay. *Hitler's U-Boat War: The Hunters, 1939–1942*. New York: Random House, 1996.

Boog, Horst. *Die deutsche Luftwaffenführung, 1943–1945: Führungsprobleme, Spitzengliederung, Generalstabsausbildung* [Leadership of the German Luftwaffe, 1943–1945: Leadership Problems, Order of Hierarchy, and General Staff Training]. Stuttgart: Deutsche Verlags-Anstalt, 1982.

Boyd, Carl. *Hitler's Japanese Confidant: General Oshima Hiroshi and Magic Intelligence, 1941–1945*. Lawrence: University Press of Kansas, 1993.

Boyd, Carl, and Yoshida Akihiko. *The Japanese Submarine Force and World War II*. Annapolis, Md.: Naval Institute Press, 1995.

Brice, Martin. *Axis Blockade Runners of World War II*. Annapolis, Md.: Naval Institute Press, 1981.

Brooks, Lester. *Behind Japan's Surrender: The Secret Struggle that Ended an Empire*. Stamford: De Gustibus Press, 1968.

Brown, Eric. *Wings of the Luftwaffe: Flying German Aircraft of the Second World War*. London: Macdonald and Jane's, 1977.

Calvocoressi, Peter, and Ben Wint. *Total War: The Causes and Courses of the Second World War*. London: Penguin Press, 1972.

Chant, Christopher, ed. *Warfare and the Third Reich: The Rise and Fall of Hitler's Armed Forces*. London: Salamander Books, 1996.

Churchill, Winston S. *The World Crisis, 1911–1918*. Vol 2. New York: Charles Scribner's Sons, 1923.

Cohen, Jerome B. *Japan's Economy in War and Reconstruction*. Minneapolis: University of Minnesota Press, 1949.

Costello, John. *The Pacific War, 1941–1945*. New York: Quill, 1981.

Cumings, Bruce. *The Origins of the Korean War*. Vol. 2, *The Roaring of the Cataracts, 1947–1950*. Princeton: Princeton University Press, 1992.

Dear, I. C. B., and M. R. D. Foot, eds. *The Oxford Companion to World War II*. Oxford: Oxford University Press, 1995.

Dictionary of American Fighting Ships. Vol. 6, R–S. Washington, D.C.: Naval History Division, Department of the Navy, 1976.

Dipple, John V. H. *Two against Hitler: Stealing the Nazi's Best-Kept Secrets*. New York: Praeger, 1980.

Dower, John W. *Japan in War and Peace: Selected Essays*. New York: New Press, 1993.

Dunnigan, James F., and Albert A. Nofi. *Victory at Sea: World War II in the Pacific*. New York: William Morrow and Co., 1995.

Eisenhower, David. *Eisenhower at War, 1943–1945*. New York: Random House, 1986.

Ethell, Jeffrey. *Mustang: A Documentary History of the P-51*. London: Jane's, 1981.

Ford, Brian. *German Secret Weapons*. New York: Ballantine Books, 1969.

Gallagher, Thomas. *Assault in Norway: Sabotaging the Nazi Nuclear Bomb*. New York: Harcourt Brace Jovanovich, 1981.

Gilbert, Martin. *The Second World War: A Complete History*. New York: Henry Holt and Co., 1989.

Green, William. *Rocket Fighter*. New York: Ballantine Books, 1971.

———. *The Warplanes of the Third Reich*. New York: Gallahad Books, 1970.

Gröner, Erich. *Die deutschen Kriegsschiffe, 1815–1945* [German Warships, 1815–1945]. Bonn: Bernard and Graefe Verlag, 1983.

Hadley, Michael L. *U-Boats against Canada: German Submarines in Canadian Waters*. Montreal: McGill–Queen's Press, 1985.

Henshall, Philip. *Vengeance: Hitler's Nuclear Weapon, Fact or Fiction?* Gloucestershire: Alan Sutton, 1995.

Herzog, Bodo. *60 Jahre Deutsche UBoote, 1906–1966* [Sixty Years of German Submarines, 1906–1966] Munich: Welsermühl Verlag, 1976.

Hinsley, F. H. *British Intelligence in the Second World War*. Abridged ed. Cambridge: Cambridge University Press, 1993.

———. *British Intelligence in the Second World War: Its Influence on Strategy and Operations*. London: Her Majesty's Stationary Office, 1979–88.

Hiroyuki, Agawa. *The Reluctant Admiral: Yamamoto and the Imperial Navy*. Tokyo: Kodansha International, 1979.

Holborn, Hajo. *A History of Modern Germany, 1840–1945*. Princeton: Princeton University Press, 1969.

Holloway, David. *Stalin and the Bomb: The Soviet Union and Atomic Energy, 1939–1956*. New Haven: Yale University Press, 1994.

Hoyt, Edwin P. *Raider 16*. New York: World, 1970.

Ienaga, Saburo. *Taiheiyo Senso* [The Pacific War]. Tokyo: Iwanami Shoten, 1968.

Irving, David. *The German Atomic Bomb: The History of Nuclear Research in Nazi Germany*. New York: Simon and Schuster, 1967.

Jane's Fighting Ships of World War II. London: Jane's, 1946.

Jungk, Robert. *Brighter Than a Thousand Suns: A Personal History of the Atomic Scientists*. New York: Harcourt Brace Jovanovich, 1970.

Keegan, John. *The Face of Battle*. New York: Penguin Books, 1976.

————. *The Second World War*. New York: Penguin Books, 1989.

Kennedy, Paul. *The Rise and Fall of British Naval Mastery*. London: Ashfield Press, 1976.

Kuroski, Franz. *Krieg unter Wasser, 1939–1945* [War under Water, 1939–1945]. Düsseldorf: Econ Verlag, 1997.

Lasby, Clarence G. *Project Paperclip: German Scientists and the Cold War*. New York: Atheneum, 1971.

Lenton, H. T. *German Warships of the Second World War*. New York: Arco, 1979.

Lewin, Ronald. *The American Magic: Codes, Ciphers, and the Defeat of Japan*. New York: Farrar, Strauss and Giroux, 1982.

Manchester, William. *American Caesar: Douglas MacArthur, 1880–1964*. Boston: Little, Brown and Co., 1978.

Meskill, Johanna Menzel. *Hitler and Japan: The Hollow Alliance*. New York: Atherton Press, 1966.

Mikesh, Robert C. *Japanese Aircraft: Code Names and Designations*. Atglen, Pa.: Schiffer Aviation and Military History, 1993.

Millot, Bernard. *Divine Thunder: The Life and Death of the Kamikazes*. New York: McCall, 1971.

Milward, Alan S. *War, Economy, and Society, 1939–1945*. Berkeley: University of California Press, 1977.

Moore, John E., ed. *Jane's Pocket Book of Major Warships*. New York: Macmillan, 1973.

Morgan, Hugh. *ME 262: Stormbird Rising*. London: Reed Consumer Books, 1994.

Müller-Hillebrand, Burkhart. *Germany and Its Allies in World War II: A Record of Arms Collaboration Problems*. Frederick, Md.: University Publishing of America, 1980.

Neufeld, Michael J. *The Rocket and the Reich: Peenemünde and the Coming of the Ballistic Missile Era*. Cambridge: Harvard University Press, 1995.

Overy, Richard. *Why the Allies Won*. New York: W. W. Norton and Co., 1995.

Padfield, Peter. *War beneath the Sea: Submarine Conflict during World War II*. New York: John Wiley and Sons, 1995.

Petrova, Ada, and Peter Watson. *The Death of Hitler: The Full Story with New Evidence from Secret Russian Archives*. New York: W. W. Norton and Co., 1995.

Piszkiewicz, Dennis. *The Nazi Rocketeers: Dreams of Space and Crimes of War*. Westport, Conn.: Praeger, 1995.

Powers, Thomas. *Heisenberg's War: The Secret History of the German Bomb*. New York: Little, Brown and Co., 1993.

Prados, John. *Combined Fleet Decoded: The Secret History of American Intelligence and the Japanese Navy in World War II*. New York: Random House, 1995.

Prange, Gordon W. *Target Tokyo: The Story of the Sorge Spy Ring*. New York: McGraw-Hill Books, 1984.

Preston, Anthony. *Submarines*. New York: W. H. Smith, 1982.

Price, Alfred. *The Last Year of the Luftwaffe, May 1944 to May 1945.* London: Arms and Armour, 1991.

———. *The Luftwaffe Data Book.* London: Greenhill Books, 1997.

Pritchard, Anthony. *Messerschmitt.* New York: G. P. Putnam's Sons, 1975.

Radzinsky, Edvard. *Stalin.* New York: Doubleday, 1996.

Rhodes, Richard. *Dark Sun: The Making of the Hydrogen Bomb.* New York: Simon and Schuster, 1995.

———. *The Making of the Atomic Bomb.* New York: Simon and Schuster, 1986.

Rössler, Eberhard. *The U-Boat: The Evolution and Technical History of German Submarines.* Trans. Harold Erenberg. Annapolis, Md.: Naval Institute Press, 1981.

Rowher, Jürgen. *Axis Submarine Successes, 1939–1945.* Annapolis, Md.: Naval Institute Press, 1983.

Scalia, Joseph M. "The Failed Voyage of *U-234:* The Intelligence Value of Germany's Final Technical and Diplomatic Mission to Japan, 1945." Master's thesis, Louisiana Tech. University, 1997.

Sherry, Michael S. *The Rise of American Air Power: The Creation of Armageddon.* New Haven: Yale University Press, 1987.

Shirer, William L. *The Rise and Fall of the Third Reich: A History of Nazi Germany.* 4th ed. New York: Touchstone Books, 1988.

Showell, J. P. Mallmann. *U-Boats under the Swastika.* New York: Arco, 1973.

Spector, Ronald H. *Eagle against the Sun: The American War with Japan.* New York: Random House, 1985.

Tarrant, V. E. *The U-Boat Offensive, 1914–1945.* Annapolis, Md.: Naval Institute Press, 1989.

Toland, John. *The Rising Sun: The Decline and Fall of the Japanese Empire, 1936–1945.* New York: Random House, 1970.

Trevethan, L. Sidney. "The Controversial Cargo of *U-234.*" Unpublished essay, 1999.

United States Naval Intelligence. *German Naval Vessels of World War II.* Annapolis, Md.: Naval Institute Press, 1993.

Van der Vat, Dan. *Stealth at Sea: The History of the Submarine.* Boston: Houghton Mifflin, 1994.

Volkogonov, Dmitri. *Stalin: Triumph and Tragedy.* Rocklin, Calif.: Prima, 1996.

Von der Porten, Edward P. *The German Navy in World War II.* New York: Thomas Y. Crowell, 1969.

Weintraub, Stanley. *The Last Great Victory: The End of World War II, July/August 1945.* New York: Truman Talley Books, 1995.

Werrell, Kenneth P. *Blankets of Fire: U.S. Bombers over Japan during World War II.* Washington, D.C.: Smithsonian Institution Press, 1996.

Wheal, Elizabeth-Anne; Stephen Pope; and James Taylor, eds. *Encyclopedia of the Second World War.* Edison, N.J.: Castle Books, 1989.

Wheeler, Keith. *Bombers over Japan.* Chicago: Time-Life Books, 1982.

Wilcox, Robert K. *Japan's Secret War: Japan's Race against Time to Build Its Own Atomic Bomb.* New York: Marlowe and Co., 1995.

Winslow, Richard E. *Portsmouth-Built: Submarines of the Portsmouth Naval Shipyard.* Portsmouth, N.H.: Peter E. Randall, 1985.

Wynn, Kenneth. *U-Boat Operations of the Second World War.* Vol. 1, *Career Histories, U1–U510.* Annapolis, Md.: Naval Institute Press, 1998.

Articles

Arnold, David. "The Uranium Vanishes: A Mystery of World War II." *Boston Globe,* 27 July 1993, 1(A).

Beach, E. L. "Radar and Submarines in World War II." *Defense Electronics,* October 1979, 48–56.

Broad, William J. "Captured Cargo, Captivating Mystery." *New York Times,* 31 December 1995, 22(A).

"Heiße Ladung." *Der Spiegel,* February 1996, 148–49.

Krause, Roland E. "The German Navy under Joint Command in World War II." U.S. Naval Institute *Proceedings* 73 (September 1947): 1029–43.

Langdon, Robert M. "And Your Task, Dear Partner." U.S. Naval Institute *Proceedings* 77 (April 1951): 365–69.

Langford, John D. "Japan and Germany—Why Seapower Failed." *United States Naval War College Review,* May 1964, 1–13.

Lundquist, Edward. "What If the Germans Had Listened to U-Boat Skipper?" *The Dolphin,* 30 September 1983, 18–19.

Masland, John W. "Japanese-German Collaboration in World War II." U.S. Naval Institute *Proceedings* 75 (February 1949): 179–87.

Michaux, Theodore. "Rohstoffe aus Ostasien: Die Fahrten der Blockadebrecher." *Wehrwissenschaftliche Rundschau* 11 (5 January 1955).

Reynolds, Clark G. "Hitler's Flattop: The End of the Beginning." U.S. Naval Institute *Proceedings* 113 (January 1967): 40–49.

Saville, Allison W. "German Submarines in the Far East." U.S. Naval Institute *Proceedings* 87 (August 1961): 80–92.

Scalia, Joseph M. "History, Archaeology, and the German Prisoner of War Experience in Rural Louisiana: The Ruston Alien Internment Facility, 1943–1945." *Louisiana History: The Journal of the Louisiana Historical Association* 38 (summer 1997): 309–27.

Shapely, Deborah. "Nuclear Weapons History: Japan's Wartime Bomb Projects Revealed." *Science* 199 (January 1978): 152–57.

Index

About the Author

Joseph M. Scalia, 42, attended Louisiana Tech University, where he graduated cum laude in 1995 with a bachelor's degree in history and received his master's degree in 1997. His research into the legend of *U-234* began in 1994 and subsequently became the topic of his master's thesis. Scalia has authored several articles; his latest, an examination of the naval engagement at Lake Borgne, Louisiana, during the War of 1812, was published in the *Journal of Mississippi History.*

Scalia's interest in the sea was fostered early in life by his grandfather, Pasquale Joseph Scalia, who served as CPO aboard a U.S. submarine during World War II. His grandfather's reminiscences, in addition to Scalia's observations during his own Navy service, instilled in him an appreciation of naval warfare's human element. As a result, readers will notice that Scalia does not merely examine a particular battle or ship, but also the human drama which unfolds during service at sea.

Scalia, a Louisiana native, has lived on Kent Island, Maryland, where he indulged his passion for sailing and kayaking on Chesapeake Bay. An author, lecturer, musician, and archaeologist, he now resides in Virginia, where he spends his time wandering the Blue Ridge Mountains, pondering what to do next.

The **Naval Institute Press** is the book-publishing arm of the U.S. Naval Institute, a private, nonprofit, membership society for sea service professionals and others who share an interest in naval and maritime affairs. Established in 1873 at the U.S. Naval Academy in Annapolis, Maryland, where its offices remain today, the Naval Institute has members worldwide.

Members of the Naval Institute support the education programs of the society and receive the influential monthly magazine *Proceedings* and discounts on fine nautical prints and on ship and aircraft photos. They also have access to the transcripts of the Institute's Oral History Program and get discounted admission to any of the Institute-sponsored seminars offered around the country.

The Naval Institute also publishes *Naval History* magazine. This colorful bimonthly is filled with entertaining and thought-provoking articles, first-person reminiscences, and dramatic art and photography. Members receive a discount on *Naval History* subscriptions.

The Naval Institute's book-publishing program, begun in 1898 with basic guides to naval practices, has broadened its scope in recent years to include books of more general interest. Now the Naval Institute Press publishes about one hundred titles each year, ranging from how-to books on boating and navigation to battle histories, biographies, ship and aircraft guides, and novels. Institute members receive discounts of 20 to 50 percent on the Press's more than eight hundred books in print.

Full-time students are eligible for special half-price membership rates. Life memberships are also available.

For a free catalog describing Naval Institute Press books currently available, and for further information about subscribing to *Naval History* magazine or about joining the U.S. Naval Institute, please write to:

Membership Department
U.S. Naval Institute
291 Wood Road
Annapolis, MD 21402-5034
Telephone: (800) 233-8764
Fax: (410) 269-7940
Web address: www.usni.org